SURVIVAL FOR WHAT?

Survival for What?

by

Zvi Kolitz

Philosophical Library

New York

296
到54

To my mother
In the Holy City of Jerusalem
With love.

And Jacob was left alone, and there wrestled a man with him until the breaking of the day. . . . And when he saw that he prevailed not against him, he touched the hollow of his thigh, and the hollow of Jacob's thigh was out of joint as he wrestled with him. . . . And he said: let me go for the day breaketh, and he said: I will not let thee go except thou bless me. . . . And he said unto him: what is thy name? And he said: Jacob. And he said: thy name shall be called no more Jacob, but Israel; for thou hast wrestled with God and with man and thou hast prevailed.

—Genesis 32:24

I call heaven and earth to witness that whether it be Jew or Heathen, man or woman, free or bondsman—only according to their *acts* does the Divine Spirit rest upon them.

—Tana Debe Eliyahu

Any thought which disregards the social state of the world and its political systems and is satisfied to float in a purely spiritual air, should be classed as a lie that has nothing to lean on.

—Rabbi Yitzhak Hacohen Kook

CONTENTS

INTRODUCTION

The young Jew, a Columbia graduate in Humanities, looked more pained than dismayed when he stood up, following my lecture on "the Spiritual Crisis in Jewry", and spoke:

"I would like to put to you some very frank questions. . . . I am bothered, and I am not the only one. . . . What makes Jews out of us now? . . . I mean, since we are no more the carriers of Jewishness in our private lives, since we don't observe anything that was regarded by our forefathers as the basis of Jewishness—what makes Jews out of us? . . . Are we Jews just because we are born Jews? Because our parents were Jews? Our parents—I don't know about our grandparents—with all due respect—knew as little about their Jewishness as we do, but were less bothered by it. . . ."

"Why are *you* bothered?" I asked.

"Because," he answered, "everything that has happened and is happening in our time adds to our confusion, even the things that were supposed to add to our satisfaction. Take freedom, for example. To our parents freedom meant security. To us, alas, it helps us only realize how dreadfully insecure we are, living, as we do, in the shadow of the bomb and of the growing realization, which dawned upon us after the last war, that man can no longer be trusted to handle his destiny. Or take Israel, as another example: Israel was supposed, so we were told, to renew the covenant of old so as to give new spiritual life to itself and to Jews wherever they live. But, instead, the young Sabrah students I used to meet laughed at my spiritual nostalgia, or whatever you may call it, saying that in Israel Hebrew Nationalism has made religion superfluous. I am not a religious Jew, mind you. I am, if anything, a searcher and I admit that I don't know the answers. All I can hope to do is pose the right questions, and one of the questions that bothers me most is this: what will bind me, not to say my children, to Israel once the religious and spiritual bond will be extinct, and Israeli nationalism, devoid of any relevant link to its prophetic grandeur, will be to me, an American who loves his country, like any other sterile nationalism I abhor? Am I to think that an Israeli without Jewishness is any better than a non-Israeli Jew without it? Is there more glory in Levantinization than in assimilation? And isn't Levantinization a less esthetic form of assimilation? And if Jewishness in a grand manner is, as some claim, the antidote both to assimilation *and* Levantinization, what is this Jewishness all about? I use this term, Jewishness, very often, but frankly I am annoyed by my using it without my knowing what it really means. I feel almost instinctively that it means infinitely more than I know about it, but nobody really bothers to tell me what it is, what it may mean for me *today*. If Judaism is something relevant, vital, universal, and unique, why do we know so little about it? Why do our rabbis, our theologians, our spiritual leaders fail to convey to us its message in a manner that would really make sense *existentially*? If, on the other hand, Jewishness is nothing but a relic—be it a memorable relic—of a great but dead past, what on earth do we need it for?

"And not only why do we need a relic-Judaism, but why do we need a Jewish people in general? Why not let its problem be solved through total assimilation? Why raise an outcry against the suppression of Jewish culture, Jewish religion, Jewish traditions in Russia at a time when this suppression may be the only way to get rid of something which has proven to be an affliction of so many for so long? Don't misunderstand me, please. I am not an assimilationist. Very far from it. I come from a good Jewish home and my father was a Zionist. But this Zionism turned out to be a one generation proposition. Zionism means nothing to me now. I am glad that there is an Israel in the world, of course, but that's about it. I'll help Israel with whatever I can, but isn't that all they expect from me beside my possibly going to settle there, which I will never do? Israel has done one thing to me, I admit, as to thousands of other Jews: it has flattered my Jewish ego, and this is no mean thing after Auschwitz! But this flattery was a psychological phenomenon of a temporary nature. After Auschwitz, Jewry craved a great act of physical bravura leading to, or emanating from, political independence, and it got it in Israel. But how long can one live on bravura alone? I don't hesitate to declare that up to recently Israel has done nothing for me spiritually. It has, if anything, destroyed some of my spiritual illusions. Maybe the expectations were too big, but how could they have been anything but big after all that has happened to us? These expectations—and I am speaking of the spiritual expectations, mind you,—were greatly boosted by the 'six days' war.' It was a war which has opened, in my opinion, new frontiers not only for the land of Israel, but for the spirit of Israel and of Jewry in general. It is a matter of historic record that on the eve of the six days' war, Jews in Israel and in other lands were gripped by a feeling of prophetic fulfillment. I, myself, went to Israel a few months after the war, and I suddenly discovered that to the Israelis, even the non-religious Israelis, the Bible has become a document as contemporary as a tourist guide, while it gained enormously in power as an eternal guide for the perplexed. I am still under the impression, and impact, of something which I cannot help but describe as a spiritual reality. I am referring to the confidence which prevailed in religious Jewish circles in Israel and abroad on the eve of a war—a war in which Israel stood alone and which Israel's neighbors promised to turn into another Auschwitz. The confidence in religious Jewish circles on the eve of that war was one which transcended reason. When the war ended in Israel's victory—a victory which arose out of a Biblical cataclysm she had brought upon her enemies—non-religious Jews in Israel didn't hesitate to describe the victory in terms similar to those that were used by religious Jews during, and prior, to the war. 'Something has happened to us,' a student at the Hebrew University in Jerusalem told me, 'which I find it almost impossible to define. But this, as far as I know, is the first case in history when a great military *victory* arouses spiritual cravings. Up to now only *tragedy* could do it.'

"I couldn't agree more. Wherever I went in Israel, I have heard young men, even Kibutzniks as they are called, posing questions and seeking answers which I have never associated with young Israelis, with Sabrahs, who never really liked the idea of being an integral part of one Jewish people. What I discovered, following the six days' war, was a realization of *Oneness* in Israel—a desire, both sincere and humble, to be a part not only of an *eternal people,* but of the *eternity* of a people. And it is this desire, born in the sands of Sinai and on the heights of Golan, on the west bank of the Jordan and in the old city of Jerusalem, which now places young Israelis in the same boat of *spiritual restlessness* in which I, and many thousands of other young Jews outside Israel, have found ourselves for years: 'What makes Jews out of us?' Young Israelis now ask—almost following in our footsteps—and I speak of Israelis who only a short time ago wouldn't hesitate to say that they were Israelis, not Jews, 'Are we Jews'—they now ask—'just because we were born Jews and live in a Jewish land? We have witnessed our irreligious comrades, during those incredible six days of war, jumping joyfully into the fire that raged between them and the liberation of the old city of Jerusalem, the Wailing Wall, Rachel's grave in Bethlehem, the tombs of the Patriarchs in Hebron and other holy places, and grave questions arose in our minds as to what all this really means. Does it mean that our brave young comrades, the flower of our youth, have died for the liberation of places which are nothing but historic monuments? Is that all which those places represent to us—*historic monuments*? Do people die like *that* to liberate monuments? And if there is something else behind those monuments and behind the ecstasy of dying for them —of living for them—what is it? What lies behind all this? Are we in Jericho, and in Bethlehem, and in Gaza and in Hebron as *occupiers,* as the Arabs say, or is there something about Israel's undivided geography *which is one* with her undivided history, her eternity, her mission and her meaning? And if that *is* the case, if Israel is the expression of a craved spiritual reality to which every stone, every tree in it bears witness,—is it enough for us to know Bialik's poetry, Mendele's prose, Sholem Aleichem's lovely 'shtetel' stories, or Shlonsky's excellent translations from the Russian classics, in order to be called Jews? And what does it mean a Jewish state, or a Hebrew state, anyway? Is a Jewish state Jewish just because it has ministers who were born as Jews, speak Hebrew in addition to their original Yiddish or any other language, and feel a kinship to Jews in other parts of the world? Is that what makes Jews out of us in Israel?' These are some of the questions which young Israelis are bothered by following the six days' war—questions which echo some of my own. They don't know the answers any more than I do—I who was bothered by similar questions long before they were. But one thing seems clear to me as a result of their, and my own, unanswered questions: "normalization"—that hallowed word which the Zionist uttered as if it were a panacea to all ills of the Jewish body and soul—*is hardly the answer to alienation,* nor is cultural peoplehood, of which there is so much talk now, or, even, experimentations in social justice. Political normalization, cultural peoplehood and experimentations in social justice are vitally important things, to be sure, but how do they answer my search for a *meaning*—not for an *ideal,* mind you, but a *meaning*? The idealists' problems are mainly of a social or political nature; *mine*—and this holds true of many thousands of others in Israel and abroad—are existential. I believe that the Jew was bothered by existential problems more than anybody else in the world. That, in fact, was the vital thing that set the Jews apart from other peoples. Do I believe in chosenness, you will ask, in differentness? *Differentness* may not be the answer, but *sameness* after Auschwitz, on the one hand, and the six days' war, on the other, sounds like a curse. And suppose I accept differentness, what does it mean, anyway? *Chosenness,* of course, but chosenness for what? Not for greater privileges, we are told, but for greater responsibilities. I buy that answer, but how is one to define the *differentness* of our responsibilities? What do they oblige me to? What am I to do with that *burden,* or *treasure,* or *burdensome treasure,* of my Jewishness which God, or history, or faith, have placed on my shoulders? Is this Jewishness of mine an accident of birth or a providential summons? Have we learned anything from our unbelievable disasters and incredible triumphs? Have Auschwitz and the six days' war, for example, done anything to us, and if yes—what? How does Christianity really look today? And Judaism? And God? And Man? Where do we go with the momentous load of such problems on our shoulders? To others? They will never understand us, and, what is worse, they will regard any plea for understanding the meaning of our search for a meaning as a symptom of weakness. To ourselves? But aren't we constantly avoiding the main issue—the issue of meaning—by supplementing it with 'culture,' on the one hand, and with materiality, on the other? Let's face it: material considerations have taken the overhand in Jewish life no less than in the lives of other peoples, while the results of this materiality—vulgarity, showiness, ignorance—oh, that ignorance!—are often more disastrous to us than to others. In the world we live in, and in which we actively externalize and banalize our values, what is all this talk about Jewish survival—or survival of Jewishness—but a self-deception? What exactly do we want in and of our Jewishness to survive, particularly in the Diaspora, if most of the things that would make this Jewishness survivable are about to *cease* surviving? And if, as it seems to be the case, all we want to survive here is a little Hebrew, a Saturday morning sermon, a Sunday school, a charity donation for Israel or local needs, matzo balls and some Yiddish jokes—may one not ask the question: survival for what?"

The following chapters represent an attempt to answer these questions.

PART ONE

WARNING ON THE MOUNT

Chapter One

THE SINAI DETERRENT

In his *Conversations with Hitler,* a book first published at the beginning of the war, Herman Rauschning, former Nazi Gauleiter of Danzig, tells of an unusual discussion with Hitler that took place only a couple of years after his rise to power. It was a conversation in which Nazism revealed itself, for the first time, as an attempt at an anti-spiritual revolution—which to Hitler was the same as an anti-Jewish revolution—on a global scale. This is how Rauschning relates the form and substance of the discussion:

". . . Suddenly I heard Hitler scream in his well-known manner. He was standing in front of his desk, leafing through a scrapbook with newspaper clippings about him from the time of his struggle for power. 'No,' Hitler yelled at Goebbels and Streicher, who were standing before him, 'I am not interested. Whether German Christians or Roman Catholics or God knows what kinds of Protestant sneaks, I am not interested.'

" 'Give them an inch and they'll take a yard,' Goebbels agreed. 'The enthusiasm of those "German Christians" for our movement is as big a lie as anything that has come from Protestant quarters. By misusing us for their miserable "Away from Rome" movement, they consider themselves particularly smart.'

" 'But don't you think we ought to support the German religious movement of Professor Hauer and others?' Julius Streicher asked.

" 'All this is cramped,' Hitler replied contemptuously. 'It is false and deceitful and without strength.'

" 'And Chamberlain's book, *Words of Jesus?* Couldn't one cut the German churches loose from their connection with the Jewish Old Testament in the same manner?' inquired Wagner, Gauleiter from Munich.

" 'Houston Stuart Chamberlain has had the right attitude toward many of our most urgent problems,' Hitler answered. 'But what he has been trying to do with this "non-Jewish Christianity" idea of his is completely nonsensical.'

" 'Marcion already tried to separate Christianity from Judaism,' Goebbels interjected. 'It never worked. It couldn't possibly work.'

" 'Historically speaking, the Christian religion is nothing but a Jewish sect. It has always been and it will always remain just that, as long as it will exist,' Hitler went on.

" 'We don't fight only the Christian circles, we fight against Christian ideas. They constitute the real poison in our blood,' Streicher said.

" 'That's right. After the destruction of Judaism, the extinction of Christian slave morals must follow logically.' Hitler began to pace up and down in his room, 'I shall know the moment when to confront, for the sake of the German people and the world, their Asiatic slave morals with our picture of the free man, the godlike man.'

" 'There is no difference between Freemasonry and Christianity,' Streicher exclaimed. 'Both are the instruments of secret Jewish world domination.'

" 'There is much more behind this,' Hitler began frantically. 'It is not merely a question of Christianity and Judaism. We are fighting against the most ancient curse that humanity has brought upon itself. We are fighting against the perversion of our soundest instincts. Ah, the God of the desert! That crazed, stupid, vengeful Asiatic despot with his powers to make laws! That slavekeeper's whip! That devilish "Thou shalt," and that stupid "Thou shalt not!" It's got to get out of our blood, that curse from Mount Sinai! That poison with which both Jews and Christians have spoiled and soiled the free, wonderful instincts of man and lowered them to levels of doglike fright.'

" 'The youth is on our side,' Goebbels exclaimed triumphantly. 'The youth of the whole world is no more interested in those old ideologies.'

" 'The time for false considerations has ended. This is true: We no longer need to be considerate,' Hitler went on. 'Whatever is against nature is against life itself. That's why nations die out. They kill themselves under the curse of that "Thou shalt" and "Thou shalt not!" '

" 'Honor thy father and thy mother? No!' Goebbels interrupted. 'Every boy revolts, and hates his father, and must do so to start his own life. It's an immortal law of nature!'

4

" 'Thou shalt not steal? Wrong!' Hitler's voice was loud in the small room. 'All life is theft! Yes!'

" 'Thou shalt not desire thy neighbor's this and that . . . Thou shalt not commit adultery . . . Thou shalt, thou shalt not . . . what not?' Goebbels laughed derisively.

" 'I am the Lord thy God! Who? That Asiatic tyrant? No!' Hitler shouted. 'The day will come when I shall hold up against these commandments the tables of a new law. And history will recognize our movement as the great battle for humanity's liberation, a liberation from the curse of Mount Sinai, from the dark stammerings of nomads who no more could trust their own instincts, who could understand the divine only in the form of a tyrant who orders one to do the very things one doesn't like. This is what we are fighting against! The masochistic spirit of self-torment, the curse of so-called morals, idolized to protect the weak from the strong in the face of the immortal law of Divine nature.
. . . Against the so-called ten commandments, against them we are fighting. . . ."

This frank discussion is without parallel in modern history, for it tells in a few clear sentences the entire background story of a war which claimed the lives of fifty million human beings and declared it a crime to be born a member of a particular human race. Hitler, with satanic instinctiveness, points the finger at the real basic issue: deterrent! Three and a half thousand years ago, the Jews, emerging in the desert in front of a mountain called Sinai, became the recipients, and the protagonists, of a law aimed at deterring man from yielding to his natural, evil instincts. It is a Judaic article of faith that man was not born good. It was for this reason, according to the legendary Rabbi Judah Loeb (Maharal) of Prague, that the Bible did not characterize the creation of man as "good." After each act of creation there follows in the Bible the statement that "the Lord saw that it was good" (Genesis I), but no such characterization is given after the creation of man. The reason is that "all other creatures were perfected at the time of their creation, but man was born imperfect." He was born imperfect, but with a craving for perfection which, according to Rabbi Judah, is the source of his restlessness (or anxiety, to use a modern existentialist term).

On another occasion, evil, or sin—the two are often identical in the Bible—is described not as an accident that happens to man, as

5

something extraneous to him, but as an innate reality, terrifying and indestructible, with a life of its own. Jean-Paul Sartre remarks somewhere that those who, like him, as a member of the anti-Nazi French underground, had witnessed the unbelievable sight and sound of "entire blocks screaming," are bound to regard evil as something akin to an independent and ineradicable reality in man. The Bible says it even more forcefully. In the Bible, evil is compared to a ravenous beast lying in wait at the door to jump on man's throat. Not that man desires evil, but evil, an invisible power at the door of every man's heart and mind, desires man. "If thou dost well, shall thou not be accepted? And if thou dost not well, sin lieth at the door, and unto thee shall be his desire, but thou mayest rule over him." (Genesis 4:7). Man's uniqueness, according to the Bible, thus doesn't lie in his being born good, but in his ability to choose it in freedom. Aggression is an inborn trait in man and it is neither a result of frustration nor environmental deprivation. "The imagination of man's heart is evil from his birth" (Genesis, 6:5). This first Biblical statement on the naturalness of aggression in man is mentioned after man's discovery of sex and man's murder of his brother. The idea behind it is as modern as space exploration, namely, that aggression is a drive as innate and as powerful as sex. Modern psychologists and sociologists, even the most outstanding among them like Konrad Lorentz and Anthony Storr, who recently published some very profound studies on human aggression, make the mistake of thinking that aggression when described as an inborn human trait is offensive to the religious ear. It is not offensive to the Jewish ear. The Jews have claimed it all along and, while doing so, clashed head on with the Christian view of man, a view which attributed to faith *per se* the same qualities which Marxism claims for "environment." Judaism's belief in the innate nature of human aggression can hardly be described as pessimism, however, for the aggressive urge, or the evil urge, is created in order to make man's efforts to rid himself of this urge an achievement of an elevating nature. The very existence of this inborn urge, which bears testimony to man's imperfection, proclaims, at the same time, the inevitable advent of an age of perfection "at the end of the days." That age, the Messianic age, will be distinguished precisely by the *change it will introduce in human nature,* a change which will mark the end of aggression as an innate trait in man. What else could the Prophet have had in mind if not the end of aggression as a natural human trait when he spoke of a period, at the end of the days, when "the wolf and the

6

lamb shall feed together, and the lion shall eat straw like the bullock"? What else could He have had in mind but the end of the urge to do harm when He spoke of a time, at the end of the days, when "they shall not hurt nor destroy in all my holy mountain, said the Lord"?

This is Judaism. Pessimistic about man's inborn traits, optimistic about his efforts to overcome them, when an effort is made; pessimistic about man's natural reliability, optimistic about his final destiny; pessimistic about his professed faith, optimistic about his practiced *deterrent*.

And by the "deterrent" we mean, of course, the law of Sinai. According to Maimonides, the great teacher of Judaism, in *The Guide for the Perplexed,* this law has two objects: the love of God and the fear of God. The love of God is the result of the eternal truths taught in the law of Moses, and especially the truth of God's existence and activity; while the fear of God, which is the highest form of love, is produced by the practices prescribed in the law. There are thus religious acts as well as religious knowledge. The religious acts, the pillars of the deterrent, are disciplinary and educative. They train the soul to reverence. Religious knowledge tells us about the subject of that reverence, and inclines the mind to love. The sanctions of the law are thus for the purpose of spiritual education: the fear of God is the beginning of wisdom. It is not, however, its end. Its end is the all embracing love of God, which is its own end, for it is life's meaning.

This is Judaism. St. Paul, Judaism's first great adversary, by expounding the theory about man's goodness and about the law begetting sin—a theory which sounds today as false as the naturalistic utopia of Rousseau—was not only the first monotheist to throw a stone at the Hebrew concept of the Deterrent, but he was the first post-biblical Hebrew to renounce the biblical concept of man by declaring the law as "fulfilled". In other words, St. Paul, too, believed that only with the coming of the Messiah will a change take place in human nature which will make the deterrent of the law superfluous, but since he believed that the Messiah has come already, that Jesus was the Messiah, the continuation of the practice of the law was regarded by him as a denial of Jesus' messianity. It was either the law *or* Jesus. The fiery barrage which Christianity of old unleashed against the "Pharisees," for example, was a declaration of war against the uncompromising exponents of the continuing validity of the great Hebrew deterrent. The fact that the "Pharisees" and their faithful disciples, the compilers of the

"Talmud," clung even more desperately to the law *following* the emergence of Jesus, was regarded by the early teachers of Christianity not only as heresy, but as soulless formalism at its worst. There wasn't a vestige of truth, or of soul, in the incredible accusation of "soulless formalism" hurled against a people who, as the Talmud tells us, didn't hesitate to call their Supreme Judges, members of the Sanhedrin, "murderers" if they sentenced a man to death *once* in seventy years! But the accusation of "soulless formalism" had to be made because its opposite, "soulful charity", the most typical Jewish trait down the ages, had either to be described as "Christian" or the claim to moral superiority of Christianity had to be abandoned.

That is why, for centuries, Christian theologians spoke of the adherence of the Pharisees to "the letter of the law" as if it were a major crime against God and man. Even in recent times, Karl Adams, a widely read German Catholic theologian, describes the world of the Pharisees as follows: ". . . A world which was falling in ruins. . . . A world of ossified belief in the letter. . . . Of a narrow-minded cast spirit and materialistic piety."

Why "materialistic piety"? (The expression is as typical as "soulless formalism.") Because the Pharisees, rejecting the negation of life—a typical component of Christian creed—believed that with the coming of the real Savior, His kingdom will be of *this* world as well as of the other; that His reign will be as manifest in the world of *matter* as in the world of the spirit and, hence, that a Messiah who claims that his kingdom "is not of this world" is suspect! Let's dwell for a moment on the Messiah idea for it leads us straight into the realm of the "Sinai Deterrent." In the Pharisean era, the era of Jesus, "man's thought began to be preoccupied with two concepts: 'this world' and 'the world to come'. The Messiah belongs to the 'world to come', the true world; when He appears, however, 'the world to come will have been realized here below, and this world and the hereafter will become *one*. The Messiah, just like the Torah, the Hokhmah, the Logos, or the congregation, becomes a cosmic entity, a cosmic principle dwelling in God from the beginning of time, ready to descend on the day of fulfillment." (Dr. Leo Beack, *The Pharisees*).

What this means is that the Messiah, the true Messiah, not the Messiah whose kingdom is of another world, must be the Messiah of matter as of spirit, of this world as of the other, of the body as of the soul, of the mind as of the heart. It was thus the duty of the Law to see to it that the bridges—pre-messianic and preparatory

8

to his coming—between the temporal and the eternal, the spiritual and the material, the body and the soul, be saved *particularly* from the raging fires of a faith which presented itself as "pure spirit", "pure soul" and "pure eternity."

This firm conviction, and uncompromising attitude, of the adherents of the Law aroused the wrath of St. Paul whose belief in the innate goodness of man was so great that quite often it emerged as totally disconnected from his belief in the divinity of Jesus. The divinity of Jesus, on the other hand, was totally predicated upon the insistence on the outlived usefulness of the law. The Law to St. Paul, as Dr. Leo Beack rightly points out, meant the entire Bible, every commandment of the Bible, and not merely the so-called "Ritual Law." "Hence," Dr. Beack writes in his excellent essay on the Pharisees, "this question to him became one upon which everything turned. If redemption had, in fact, taken place, if faith and baptism made it manifest, it followed that the law had ceased to exist; if the law were still in force, it was proof that the hoped for time of fulfillment was not yet at hand. Either the law or redemption! Whoever maintained that the law was still binding was an unbeliever, for he denied the redemption. Hence for St. Paul it had to be the case that Judaism had ceased to be a religion, either of the present or of the future, and the Bible had ceased to be the Bible, that is, the book of the present and the future."

And so it came to pass that St. Paul, like Augustus and Luther after him, went to the very extreme of his views. In his frantic attempts to cut to shreds the deterrent of the law, he denied the value of human activity and made everything exclusively dependent on grace (*sola gratia, sola fide*). The pathetic efforts of contemporary Paulist apologists, which include such erudite thinkers as Jacques Maritain, to describe St. Paul as "the greatest Doctor of freedom" whose "heart was melted, and all barriers broken by the vision of Christ in glory" cannot change the fact that, vision or no vision, the barriers which St. Paul had broken were those of Sinai. This fact cannot be altered by all the intellectual and dialectical hair-splitting in the world—an art in which Mr. Maritain, for example, is a master. ("And so it happens that love is the fullness of the law, and that we are saved by faith, not without works, but with charity and the works of charity. . . . With charity whence proceeds works, and without which works are nothing. . . . With the works of charity which, being the active and living completion of our liberty suffused with grace, are the very workings in us of the grace which has been given us. . . ."—Jacques Maritain,

Saint Paul). St. Paul relegated the commandments, the great Hebrew deterrent, to insignificance, and he believed that thus he had
rendered the faith more unshakable. He went, in fact, to such
absurdity as to consider a belief in the religious value of moral
conduct as impiety, a sin against the Holy Spirit.

St. Paul set himself not only against the law of Sinai as binding
after the emergence of Jesus, but also against the very spirit of
Sinai as a timeless revelation of the godly. For what expresses the
spirit of Sinai more than the two eternal words uttered by the
people who witnessed the revelation of the Godly than *naase ve-
nishma?—"we shall do and we shall hear!"* First—and that's the
greatest lesson of Sinai—comes *doing*—works, deeds, the law—
then, second in importance, comes *hearing,* which, to Paul, stood
—and rightly so—for faith: "Therefore faith is by *hearing,* and
hearing is through the word of Christ." (Romans 10:18).

And don't let anybody tell us stories as does Mr. Maritain and
many others before him, that hearing means "a return toward the
inward and the spiritual. . . . The life of the soul is no more
centered in the visible—on works and on the law—but on the
invisible, and on that eminently invisible thing, the mystery of God
in us." (*Saint Paul*) The truth, not of theological wishful thinking,
but of recorded human history, is that the Jew, because of strict
adherence to the law, sacrificed the visible for the invisible; just
because he placed *doing* above hearing, his hearing, his faith, has
become unshakable; he didn't have to *return* toward the inward
and the spiritual—the inward and the spiritual, which to the vast
majority of Christians was just idle, irrelevant talk, was the thing
that kept him alive; "that eminently invisible thing," the mystery of
God, became the main spiritual preoccupation of the Jew *precisely*
on account of the law, for it was the law, which, by setting him
apart from others, made the mystery of his apartness a part of the
mystery of God!

But if to the Jews, St. Paul had brought a dangerous distortion,
to Christians he brought a much more dangerous illusion. If he
really was, as many Christian historians like to present him, "an
apostle to mankind," then mankind must ask itself, eighteen centuries after Paul's death, whether "the great Doctor of freedom",
by declaring that the cross will make it free, had not actually
contributed to its enslavement.

Of course, the Paulist view of man is no more predominant in
contemporary Christian thought. The changes which the Christian
view on the nature of man underwent since Paul (There was no

10

need for a change in the Jewish view!) are described by Jacques Maritain as follows:

"In broad outline, the image of man which reigned over medieval Christendom depended upon St. Paul and St. Augustine. This image was to disintegrate from the time of the renaissance and the reformation—torn between an utter Christian pessimism which despaired of human nature and an utter Christian optimism which counted on human endeavor more than on divine grace. The image of man which reigned over modern times depended upon Descartes, John Locke, the enlightenment, and Jean Jacques Rousseau."

"Here we are confronted with the process of secularization of the Christian man which took place from the 16th century on. Let's not be deceived by the merely philosophical appearance of such a process. In reality the man of Cartesian rationalism was a pure mind conceived after angelistic pattern. The man of Natural Religion was a Christian gentleman who did not need grace, miracles, or revelation, and was made virtuous and just by his own good nature. The man of Jean Jacques Rousseau was, in a much more profound and significant manner, the very man of St. Paul transferred to the plain of pure nature—innocent as Adam before the fall, longing for a state of divine freedom and bliss, corrupted by social life and civilization as the sons of Adam by the original sin. He was to be redeemed and set free, not by Christ, but by the essential goodness of human nature, which must be restored by means of an education without constraint and must reveal itself in the City of Man of coming centuries in that form of state in which 'every one obeying all, will, nevertheless, continue to obey only himself.' "

"This process was not at all a merely rational process. It was a process of secularization, of something consecrated, elevated above nature by God, called to a divine perfection, and living a divine life in a fragile and wounded vessel—the man of Christianity, the man of the Incarnation. All that meant simply bringing back this man to the realm of man himself ('Anthropocentric humanism'), keeping a Christian facade while replacing the Gospel by Human Reason or Human Goodness, and expecting from Human Nature what had been expected from the virtue of God giving Himself to His creatures. Enormous promises, divine promises, were made to man at the dawn of modern times. Science, it was believed, would liberate man and make him master and possessor of all nature. And automatic, and necessary progress would lead him to the earthly realm of peace, to that blessed Jerusalem which our hands would build by transforming social and political life, and which would be the kingdom of man, and in which we would become the supreme rulers of our own history, and whose radiance has awakened the hope and energy of the great modern revolutionaries."

All this is true. The illusion of man which Paul implanted in Christian Theology, lived long after him in philosophy, even in the philosophy of Reason and Science. It lived, in fact, till the middle of last century. But suddenly, in the second half of that century, something very ominous began to creep into the heart of man: anguish and despair. It was not only, as Mr. Maritain believes in his above-quoted *The Range of Reason,* that man, "having given up God so as to be self-sufficient, has lost track of his soul", but that man, having been fed for centuries on the grand illusion of his redemption in Christ, suddenly felt himself cheated. Man began to see himself as what he was, and got scared at what he saw. An abyss opened up between what he was told for centuries about his redeemed self and the self that had emerged stripped of its misleading philosophical and theological ornaments. Dostoyevsky described the nihilistic reaction to open and sublimated Paulist optimism in *The Possessed,* but the earth-shaking wrath at the feeling of being cheated by an impossible promise of fulfilled redemption, he expressed in that unique masterpiece "The Grand Inquisitor"— a chapter of his book *The Brothers Karamazov.*

We shall come to that remarkable chapter a little later. It will be better introduced, and understood, if we dwell a little more on that crucial period in European history, the second part of the 19th century, when people started to realize how woefully unredeemed they were almost two millenniums after the emergence of a faith which attributed to itself redeeming qualities and which promised salvation through the sheer act of embracing it. The disillusionment of man in these optimisms, and in the other, more secular optimisms they produced, was so great that a wave of irrationality, in the very midst of an age which prided itself with "reason"—a wave which was later to become tidal—swept the world. It was an irrationality which soon expressed itself in hatred of intelligence, and in the awakening of an increasingly violent clash between life and the spirit. In Germany, where the philosophy of nature brought forth rich fruit in many realms, especially in the natural sciences, it soon burst into noxious weeds which filled the entire garden of German thought and produced the arrogance and aggressiveness of its racist thoughtlessness. More than a century ago,

Heinrich Heine, displaying a prophetic sense for historic developments in Germany and in Europe in general, spoke of a period when German philosophy will mould the minds of German executioners. "Revolutionary forces which only wait for the day to erupt, will fill the world with terror and amazement. . . . Then there will appear Kantians who even in a visible world will know nothing of reverence and who will mercilessly plough up the soil of European life with sword and axe and extirpate the last roots of the past. . . . Armed Fichteans will enter the battle who in their fanaticism of the will are not restrained by fear or self-interest, for they live solely in the spirit and defy matter. . . ." (*Germany*) Just a little later in the same country, Nietzsche, to overcome despair, proclaimed the coming of the superman of the will to replace God whose "death" he announced not with ignorant joy, but with learned pain and sorrow. Then the inevitable followed. The vacuum left by the unfulfilled Christian promise was slowly but surely invaded by forces which promised kingdoms that were of *this* world, but which could be attained through fire and blood and total ruthlessness. "More terrific voices, the voices of a base multitude whose baseness itself appears as an apocalyptic sign, cry out: we have had enough of lying optimism and illusory morality, enough of freedom and personal dignity and justice and peace and faithfulness and goodness. Let us give ground to the infinite promises of evil, and of swarming death, and of blessed enslavement, and of triumphant despair!" (Jacques Maritain, *The Range of Reason*).

Yes, that was, that is, the outcry. It is primarily the outcry against a faith which, though rarely mentioned by name, is on the minds of millions of thinking people who compare the grandeur of the promise with the *totality* of the unfulfillment. Not that they are bothered by the fact that a religion which taught rejection of all earhly goods, abject hang-dog humility and angelic patience, often resorted to despotic means, but that the sheer impossibility of such teachings made the advent of despotism, even anti-Christian despotism, inevitable. Dostoyevsky, who was torn to pieces between his love for and his anger at Christianity, gave to this anger an expression of unequalled power in his "Grand Inquisitor." In that much discussed and much misunderstood story, the great Russian writer tried to tell Christianity things which no Christian dared say before or since. He chose Jesus as his target—not Christianity in general, but Jesus in particular—for otherwise the great drama of the confrontation would have been reduced to a treatise on theological confusion. Actually, Jesus himself was infinitely less the cause of Dostoyevsky's incomparable "J'acuse!" than some of His main interpreters, particularly St. Paul, for it was him, St. Paul, as we all know, who had attributed to the good man from Nazareth many qualities which he, Jesus, never attributed to himself and which the Grand Inquisitor pointed out as outright deceptions.

A whole literature was written about "The Grand Inquisitor." Dostoyevsky, it seems certain, mystical believer that he was, wrote this chapter with fear and trembling. He had to say certain things to Christ, that is to Christianity, but afraid lest what he says is interpreted as outright heresy, he put the words, which were uppermost on his tormented mind, in the mouth of a Grand Inquisitor in 15th century Spain in the most terrible times of the Inquisition "when fires were lighted every day to the glory of God, and 'in the splendid act of faith,' the wicked heretics were burnt." What kind of man was this Grand Inquisitor? D. H. Lawrence, who wrote one of the most penetrating studies on the "Grand Inquisitor," rightly points out that no matter how desperately, and movingly, Dostoyevsky tried to make him appear diabolic, he was actually as far from, or as close to, diabolicism as Dostoyevsky himself. For the unmistakable impression is received that the Grand Inquisitor, speaking through the mouth of Ivan Karamazov, who is no other but Dostoyevsky himself, actually *is* Dostoyevsky himself. By attributing to the Grand Inquisitor some diabolic traits, according to Lawrence, and by making him talk admiringly of "the Prince of Darkness," Dostoyevsky "showed his epileptic and slightly criminal perversity. . . . The man [the Grand Inquisitor] who feels a certain tenderness for mankind in its weakness and limitations is not therefore diabolic. The man who realizes that Jesus asked too much of the mass of men, in asking them to choose between earthly and heavenly bread, is not therefore satanic." No, the Spanish Inquisition could not have produced a Grand Inquisitor whose fury at Jesus was as great, if not greater, than the fury he had shown to those who refused to believe in him, nor could such a Grand Inquisitor have been a product of 15th century Spain. The fury of the Grand Inquisitor was a 19th century fury which Dostoyevsky, for reasons of artistic impact and spiritual convenience, placed in 15th century Spain. It was a 19th century fury because it was typical to an age in which mankind began to realize that it was gravely deceived by an unfulfilled promise of redemption. It was not, as D. H. Lawrence claims, the fury at Jesus because he asked too much of man, but that *He promised man too much!* And it was

14

this promise—which was never kept, which could have never been kept—that aroused Dostoyevsky's fiery wrath.

For what does Dostoyevsky's Grand Inquisitor actually tell Jesus? He tells him—sometimes in very ambiguous terms—not that man has failed him, but that he has failed man. He has failed him by promising him the miracle of inner freedom—not only the freedom to choose, but to choose right—through the very act of recognizing him as the redeemer. "Didst thou not often say to them: 'I will make you free?' But now thou hast seen those 'free men'! Yes, we have paid dearly for it, but at last we have completed that work in thy name! For fifteen centuries we have been wrestling with thy freedom, but now it is ended and over for good. Dost thou not believe it is over for good? Thou lookest meekly at me and deignest not even to be angry with me. But let me tell thee that now, today, people are more persuaded than ever that they have perfect freedom, yet they have brought their freedom to us and laid it humbly at our feet. But that has been *our* doing. Was this what thou didst? Was this thy freedom?"

These are terrible words, and they strike at the very heart of the grand illusion which Christianity presented to man in the wrappings of a magic formula of faith—a formula which was supposed to contain the magic of redemption and salvation. The illusion of man's redemption in and through Jesus, the illusion of soul-saving through a confession of faith in the cross, outraged the old man, the Grand Inquisitor, who for almost ninety years watched both the so-called "saved" souls and those whom he came to "save" by burning them alive, and was disturbed by what He saw. And it was against this illusion, this promise, that the Grand Inquisitor directed his fury: What kind of promise did you make in Palestine fifteen centuries ago?—the Grand Inquisitor was actually asking—"Bread from heaven?" Isn't that what you promised people? And what does "bread from heaven" mean, I am asking you, what does it mean but the arousal, through the sheer act of believing in you, of the soul's hunger for food other than earthly? Isn't that what it means? You haven't given them a new law which would discipline their souls to a point where spiritual hunger would become consequential. On the contrary: "In the place of rigid, ancient law, man must hereafter with free heart decide for himself what is good and what is evil—*having only thy image before him as a guide.*" But thy image, the confession of faith in thee, has proven woefully insufficient! The trouble with you was that you have entertained too high an opinion of man, otherwise you wouldn't have believed that he can be elevated to perfectibility just by believing in you. This belief, as a redeeming and saving act of faith, I dare tell you in your face, was sheer seduction! "Behold! Instead of giving a firm foundation for setting the conscience of man at rest forever, thou didst choose all that is exceptional, vague and puzzling. Thou didst choose what was utterly beyond the strength of men, acting as if *thou didst not love them at all.*" Fifteen centuries after your emergence as the Savior of men—look at them and tell me whether there is a trace of saving redemption in them and whether their souls have become any less corrupted by believing in you. "Thou didst crave for free love and not the base raptures of the slave before the might that has overawed him forever. But thou didst think too highly of men therein, for they are slaves, of course, though rebellious by nature. Look around and judge! Fifteen centuries have passed. Look upon them. *Whom hast thou raised up to Thyself? I swear! Man is weaker and baser by nature than thou hast believed him.*"

You read these lines and you can't help feeling that Dostoyevsky wanted to say much more. He namely wanted to say, nay, to ask, the following: if you are the Son of God, the healing Prophet, the saving Messiah, how come you showed such a poor judgment and knowledge of man? Of course, there is that outburst of charity, of the purest morality, that typifies your teachings. But have you prepared man for receiving it or is it just that you simply didn't know man—you who are described as the Son of God? Could it be that you came only to the elect? That you who have spoken with such endless love of the poor, and the meek, and the downtrodden, and the sinners, that you have come only to the elect, to the best, the saintly souls whom you helped, I admit, to make saintlier than they were, not to *create* their saintliness?

"If so, it is a mystery and we cannot understand it. And if it is a mystery, we, too, have a right to preach a mystery, and to teach men that it is not the free judgment of their hearts, not love that matters, but *a mystery which they must follow blindly, even against their conscience.* So we have done. We have *corrected* thy works and founded it upon miracle, mystery and authority. And men rejoiced that they were again led like sheep, and that the terrible gift that had brought them such suffering, was, at last, lifted from their hearts."

". . . In truth, Thou didst Thyself lay the foundation for the destruction of Thy kingdom, and no one is more to be blamed for it."

16

And what is *Jesus'* reaction to the grand accusation? The Grand Inquisitor longed for Jesus to say something, "however bitter and terrible, but He (Jesus) suddenly approached the old man in silence and softly kissed him on his forehead. . . . That was his answer. The old man shuddered. His lips moved. He went to the door, opened it and said to Him: 'Go and come no more. . . . Come not at all, never, never!' ' "

The kiss which ends the great confrontation can have only one meaning: Jesus, stripped of a divinity he had never sought, wanted to say one thing which he couldn't really say: "you are right!"

Christianity, because it couldn't free man from his inborn evil urge, has demanded from him the "bricks" of faith without providing him with the "straw" of works. That too was implied in the Grand Inquisitor's words to Jesus. But what was implied, above all, was the inevitability of despotism, in the name of Christian love, to keep the faith alive. The rest was consequential. When the great illusion of Christian redemption was shattered, along with its despotism, the disillusionment, while abandoning Christian hopes, was bound to feed itself on Christian prejudices. That was the easy way out: if we cannot love anymore what Christianity told us to love, let's at least hate what Christianity told us to hate! If the Grand Inquisitor didn't succeed to discipline the people, long live the Grand Executioner! If the promised Messiah failed to mould us in his image—for he failed to be a Messiah—let us find a Messiah whom we shall mould in *our* image. We shall mould him in our image so that he moulds us in his, that he does with us what the promised savior has never done: change us to his liking!

And this process was inevitable. It was inevitable that the "Messiah" who failed to manifest himself in man's promised goodness, inadvertently paved the way for unpromised "Messiahs" who easily manifested themselves in his innate badness. For two millenniums Christianity, in the name of a saving faith, fought so desperately against the spirit of Sinai and against all those who clung to it, that when the disaster struck, the ground was ready, in a world woefully lacking in works, for the unleashing of forces of undeterred evil primarily directed against the people of the deterrent. The Germans, we must never forget, built Auschwitz in the very heart of unshakably faithful Catholic Poland, where even Communism couldn't frighten its pious populace away from the Church. There was plenty of "hearing" in Poland, but no—no *doing*! Plenty of kneeling, and praying, and confessing, and kissing the cross, and carrying it like a banner, but no, no works. And the works we are referring to very specifically in this instance are the works of *charity*. Charity is a favorite Christian term. "Faith gushing forth in charity." But there was no charity when the thunder struck! Not even the Pope in Rome would risk his security, let alone his life, when the thunder struck. Christian charity has developed a queer tendency to mute itself whenever a tragic reality demands that it resorts to deeds. It was silent in the face of the fires at Auschwitz; it was silent when the Arabs spoke of the total annihilation of Israel; it was silent when millions were starving to death in Biafra; it was silent when the Russians murdered Czechoslovakia's new-born freedom. Christian charity was never real, never! It is not that Hitler made a mockery out of Christian charity, but that Christian charity, made into a mockery by the fact that the Christians have never really practiced it, made it easier for a Hitler to emerge!

One of the gravest accusations which Dostoyevsky's Grand Inquisitor hurled in the face of Jesus was that he, Jesus, may have come only to the elite, not to the large masses of people. Superficially, it may look the other way. Wasn't it to the masses of people, to the poor and the downtrodden, to the humiliated and the persecuted, to whom Christianity has brought the hope that there is a reward for suffering? Yes, Christianity may have brought to these unfortunates the hope that there is a reward for suffering, that one doesn't suffer in vain. But this hope, this promise, was brought in almost as a theological "package-deal" along with the insistence that the greatest suffering of them all, that of the Jews, —"the agony of the Jews",—far from being subjected to the hope for a supernatural reward, was actually the execution of a supernatural punishment. This alone turned prejudice into an article of faith, so that when man's innate aggressiveness caused Christianity to falter, the prejudice—appealing greatly to this aggressiveness—grew alongside with the fading away of the faith. The masses subscribed easily to this trend, for nothing pleases them more than the thought of a supernatural confirmation of their natural, evil urges. Christianity thus succeeded in making the elite— better, and the plebe—worse. And it made the plebe-man worse because it constantly catered to his prejudices without at all trying to elevate him above himself, something which cannot be achieved without elevating him above his prejudices. Christian love has thus turned, at best, into pity. And pity when shown to souls religiously regarded as "unsaved" and, even, "damned", is nothing short of mockery. Christian pity was the cause for making Jews, in certain prejudiced areas of the world, constantly apologize for their existence. This kind of pity is morally inferior to hatred.

The undermining and, indeed, perversion, of Christian charity was thus accomplished as much by sincere prejudice as by insincere pity. But neither sincere prejudice nor insincere pity would have been possible had Christianity not contributed to man's terrible helplessness by making him, even in his own eyes, much tinier than he is.

And the Christian diminution of man went hand in hand with Christianity's denunciation of the Jewish deterrent. The entire philosophy of the deterrent is man-centered: it is not that "nobody can come to the father but through the son", but that "nobody can come to the father but through himself", which is another way of saying that "nobody can come to himself but through himself." The philosophy of the Jewish deterrent regards man as the self-endowed subject of history who, by a concentrated effort of his free will, can become the creator of justice and, consequently, the recipient of grace. But when a destiny called, "Divine", the destiny of Jesus, and the belief therein, is the sole criterion of the human soul and its final destiny, "the essence of history becomes a drama between below and above which really takes place beyond the human sphere which it enters only in the miracle of grace or in the victory of the demonic." (Dr. Leo Beack, "Judaism and Christianity")

The result of this attitude is that the vital "wrestling with God", at once the most dramatic, the most agonizing and the most heroic trait of Judaism, (or the "wrestling for the truth" which Lessing prayed for) is supplanted by the submission to an illusion which, no matter how lovely and sentimental, is bound to diminish man's spiritual horizons and reduce them to sacraments and dogmas. This is particularly evident in modern Protestantism. In Protestantism, much more than in Catholicism, a completed story of the "Unique" personality of Jesus is all that remains of the Christian faith. The relation of Protestantism to religion thus becomes, as Dr. Leo Beack rightly points out in his above mentioned book, "a relation to a story."

In such a state of diminution of religious spirituality, the diminution of man becomes consequential. The man created by Christianity,—and we are not speaking of the elite,—is a very small man indeed. And not only that his spirituality–his spiritual absorptive capacity that is—is diminished but, as a result of his tiny spirituality, based more on prejudice than love, his humanness, too, is diminished. In a state of denominationalization, the diminution of humanness is consequential. Since love becomes a word reserved for a divine mystery of old, and man becomes good only to the extent of his belief in a miracle that was once performed, this sole way of loving God often leaves very little room for loving man. Such a state is inevitable when the glory of God no longer fills the world, but only the church, and everything outside the church is given over to the dominion of the devil and is seething with damned souls. "Mankind is cut in two; the deep abyss passes right through it and separates the elect and the damned unbridgeably. As far as the world extends, everything falls apart into heaven and hell. The conception of the unity of mankind is thus broken up. Ahead of man is placed the believer; ahead of love, the denomination." (Dr. Leo Beack, "Judaism and Christianity").

In such a state, moreover, a clash between faith and ethics becomes inevitable. When the sacraments accomplish the miracle of salvation, and nothing but the sacraments, religion becomes condensed and "materialized." It becomes like a biological substance, a magical tonic taken with the ease of a cough syrup, and thus contributing not only to man's narrow-mindedness and ignorance, but also to his *passivity*!

And it is in this inherent passivity where one must look for the reason of Christian toleration of evil. No matter what well-meaning Christian teachers and preachers declare from all the pulpits in the world, Christian faith, be it that which was promulgated by Saint Paul, or that which was vehemently advocated, fourteen centuries later, by Martin Luther, introduced into western civilization an element of spiritual passivity which makes it easy for evil to emerge. For if the Word is received "not by your strength, but by the grace of God which makes the Gospels bear fruit in you that you may have faith in it" (St. Paul), man is a mere object who is totally incapable of climbing the mountain of the Lord with his own strength, and who totally depends on an external thing—not an internal—to help him achieve this task. Luther spelled out this dependence very clearly and, by doing so, aroused the wrath of the Silesian reformer Kaspar Schwenckfeld who accused his master that "he will not let anybody become blessed without an external thing."

Luther's bitter denunciations of the Law, his regarding of the law, of the Jewish deterrent of the law, as something "befouling", paved the way for the rise of Nazism. There can be no doubt about it. Luther, more than any other Christian reformer (going, of course, in the footsteps of St. Paul), replaced the *Fides Qua Creditur,* the faith *with* which one believes, with *Fides Quae Creditur,* the faith *in* which one believes. Thus the *obedience* of faith is the thing, not the faith itself. "Obedience," to use Dr. Leo Beack's words again, "becomes the substitute for experience," even the experience of justice. For if you say that "whoever believes in him is just," justice is now an act performed *on* man, by some miracle, not *by* man. And the amazing thing was that Luther didn't hesitate to openly downgrade justice. "We are called just" he declares, "not when we do what is just, but when we believe and trust in God." What such a statement actually implies is, that believing and trusting in God must not be seen as something which prevents one from doing evil, but which actually makes the doing of evil more permissible. The opposition to ethics as a result of the theological divorce between justice and faith is implicit in another well known saying by Luther: "Let life be the earth and the doctrine—heaven." That was the principle from which he started. The rest followed without difficulty. "I live as I live—that does not make the doctrine false. We must not consider the life, but the doctrine." Or: "You do not owe it to God to do anything, except believe and profess. In all other matters he releases you and leaves you free as you please without any danger of conscience." In the demand for good deeds as something decisive in, and for, man, Luther perceived the tempting voice of the devil who would pit human activity against grace. "At times," Luther writes, "one must commit some sin out of sheer hatred of and contempt for the devil so that we leave him no room at all for making petty things matters of conscience; otherwise we shall be vanquished if we shall regard too anxiously against sin . . . Being so threatened and vexed by the devil, *we must banish the whole decalogue completely from the sight and mind.*" ("Dr. Martin Luther's Briefwechsel," ed. Enders.)

We don't know how successful Dr. Luther was in banishing the devil by banishing the Decalogue, but we do know of some occasions, for which the word "devilish" is much too mild, which arose precisely as a result of the complete banishment of the Decalogue. Was it devilish or devotional—or both, since there is no real contradiction—for Nazi officers to sing "Holy Night" on Christmas in Auschwitz? Jewish concentration camp inmates remember also the sound of another tune, that of the "Wiener Waltzer"—the "Wiener Waltzer" in Bergen Belsen!—but when asked how they

21

had felt when the sound of the two above mentioned songs had reached their ears in the death camps—the answer was as follows: "The 'Wiener Waltzer' added to the mockery, while 'Holy Night' confirmed a suspicion."

What suspicion? The suspicion, which no Christian apologist will ever eradicate, that Christianity, in some devious manner, paved the way for Nazism. The denunciation of Sinai was the beginning of Auschwitz. There is a twisted, indirect line, but a line nevertheless, between Luther's declaration that "we must banish the whole Decalogue from the sight and mind" (for the sake of grace,) and Hitler's declaration that "it's got to get out of our blood, that curse from Mount Sinai!" (for the sake of *race*.) When justice is divorced from faith, the ascent of evil is inevitable.

And it is against the irrelevancy, impotence and, indeed, *danger* of this kind of faith, that Judaism puts forward the power and the glory of its concept of Justice. It is a justice conducive to faith and a faith leading to justice. In Judaism, from one God come both mystery (Faith) and commandment, (Law). They come as one from the One, and the soul experiences both as one. "Every mystery means and suggests also a commandment; and every commandment means and suggests also a mystery. All humility also means and suggests reverence, and all reverence, humility; all faith—the law, and all law—faith. All consciousness that we have been created means and suggests the demand to create, and every demand to create means and suggests the consciousness that we have been created. What is evident is here rooted in what is concealed, and what is concealed has its evident aspect for man. The profundity of life cannot be grasped without its also speaking to us of duty in life; and not a single duty of life is perceived truly without at the same time proclaiming the profundity of life. We cannot have knowledge of the foundation of our life without at the same time beholding our way, and we cannot understand this way without penetrating to the foundations of our life. We cannot fully take to heart that we are the creatures of God without apprehending also that we ought to be the creators of our own lives; and we cannot be in full possession of this commandment to create unless we remain aware that we, ourselves, have been created—created by God—that we ourselves may create, and creating because we have been created by God. This unity of both experiences in the human soul constitutes Jewish piety and Jewish wisdom; the meaning of life reveals it-

22

self here in this form." (Dr. Leo Beack, "Judaism and Christianity")

The unity of heaven and earth, of mystery and commandment, of faith and justice and, above all, *the belief that this unity constitutes the essence of God,* was epitomized by Rabbi Pinhas of Koretz in a saying unequaled for power and simplicity: "Whoever says that the words of the Law are one thing and the words of the world—another, *must be regarded as a man who denies God."*

But this state, the state in which the words of the Law and the words of the world become one—the state of the great triumph of the deterrent following which man emerges free from within—cannot possibly be the lot of all men. It is too much to ask it from all men. But from a small, exemplary minority, it could be asked in the hope that many will follow. This minority were always "separatists" (*Perushim—Pharisees*). Separateness was not an aim in itself, only a means to achieve a greater triumph of the deterrent through not exposing it to the inevitable banalization of mass contact. That's why the sages of Israel, while convinced that the Hebrew concept of God and man will one day be adapted by all mankind, never aspired to impose this all-embracing deterrent of the law prematurely. That is also why the teachers of Judaism distinguished between the great and the small deterrent—advising sincere adherents of the smaller deterrent, when advice was sought, to continue adhering to it. When in 1895 a Catholic from Lyon, by the name of Aimé Palliere, approached Rabbi Elie Benamozegh, of Livorno in Italy, asking him to convert him to Judaism, the Rabbi strongly urged him to remain within the faith of his birth. "Christianity," he told him, "as seen in the Jewish tradition, represents the universal aspects of monotheism, equally acceptable to the Gentile. This rather unknown Christianity is based upon an accord with Noah and is called Noahism. According to this agreement between providence and Noah, at the same time unchangeable and progressive, and which embraces all humanity, man must live at least by a minimum deterrent against evil." This minimum deterrent consists of seven principles, one of which is positive and the rest negative. The positive one is the promotion of justice; the six negative ones are cruelty to animals, blasphemy, theft, murder, idolatry, and immorality. "The Nazarene," Rabbi Benamozegh writes, "was in the right and deserves every praise when he freed the Gentiles from the obligations of the Mosaic law. But his disciples erred when, in later years, they demanded the very same freedom for the Israelites."

And why not the same "freedom," the same minimum deterrent, for the Israelites? Because "Judaism," in Rabbi Benamozegh's words, "sees a distinction between Jew and Gentile. The former, as the Priests of humanity, are subjected to the priestly rules of Judaism. The latter, as the laymen of humanity, are subject only to the one ancient and eternal universal religion, in whose service the Jews have been placed. Christianity, however, has given birth to the most regrettable confusion. But without any doubt, any layman has the right to become a priest; it is up to the individual to embrace the Jewish faith if he so desires, as long as he is fully aware that he is not required to do so."

This approach to Christianity as to Noahism was rarely used by teachers of Judaism for the simple reason that they were afraid lest the description of Christianity as a lesser deterrent against evil than Judaism, unleash even greater forces of evil against the Jews. But Judaism remained silent too long, as Hyacinthe Lyoson, the great Christian who attempted in vain to reform Catholicism, has expressed himself. Now it is the time to speak up, for something has transpired in our day and age which has put to a test of fire some of mankind's longest held moral, spiritual, and religious concepts. And one of the main concepts that was put to the most fiery test was the Christian concept of its superior morality. This superior morality was supposed to present a most formidable barrier against evil in the world, but it didn't. Why? *Because this morality was too aloof and too remote from reality to be able to direct it in any way.* In order to create a superior morality for man, man had first to be made spiritually ripe to receive it. And that precisely was Judaism's main preoccupation: man and the gradual change in his nature through the application of a deterrent which alone would prepare him for grace, make his faith pure and his kind—chosen.

Christianity resented Judaism's claim to be "chosen" (which actually means chosen for a greater responsibility) because it considered *itself* chosen. Christianity entertained such a high opinion of its own moral code that it did not hesitate to assert that the absolute excellence of this code was the best proof of its own divine origin. "But is this pride of superiority well founded?" the A. M. Rabbi Benamozegh asks in his remarkable *Jewish and Christian Ethics.*

Judaism, he answers, finds her true reflection and it glories in the unquestionable manifestations of basic Jewishness which issued from her fold. Among these manifestations are: the overturn of the altars that were still reeking with human blood; the closing

24

of dens where prostitution was regarded as a sacred duty; the proclaiming of the common origin and universal brotherhood of mankind; the effacing of the brands that egotism, pride, brute force and wealth had put on the brow of the poor, the unhappy, the conquered and the enslaved. But this real basis of Christianity, its Judaic basis, has served, in Benamozegh's words, "as a base of enormous pretensions. . . . Without justice, without logic, its ethic has been declared superior to the Hebrew's. Christianity itself, with a wonderful blindness, has given free reign to prejudice and permitted the worship of this intoxicating incense; Nay! It has formally instituted a comparison between the ethics of Moses and Jesus and it has struggled, as in the medical or legal competition, to show the superiority of its receipts to those of its rival. What has actually taken place in the great discussion between the two opposing world views is this: Christianity, a system of *abstract morality*, was juxtaposed with *a Hebraic system of civil government*. But how could a system of civil government, no matter how pure, ever compete with a system of abstract morality?"

"Of course," Benamozegh continues, "there is unity in Judaism. Its civil code blends in a thousand ways with its moral. But this civil code, which is politics, at times clashes with its ethical, as it is bound to. *The ethical has come into being in order to control, restrain and dictate the political.* One must distinguish the ethics of Judiasm from its politics; the civil code from the religious; the citizen from the monotheist, or, to be more specific, the Jew from the Hebrew—the member of a state government by the Judaic dynasty from the Hebrew, the son of Abraham, the disciple of his faith. Example: try to apply to the life of nations the moral perfectionism of the gospels: tell nations to allow their cheeks to be smitten, to be spit upon, or to requite with benefits the most atrocious injuries, and see if a nation can maintain itself with such a code." If a nation must live, it can never live on the moral code of the Gospels which is, therefore, not a deterrent—for a deterrent must be relevant, and, no matter the effort, *realizable*—while this moral code (Christianity never suggested a *civil* code) is sheer abstraction and unattainability under any circumstances. Christianity, therefore, either through the extravagance or the exclusiveness of its ethics or through its ultramundane aspirations, ever on the point of realization, lacks a vital side, the social or political side. With its ethics, strange as it may sound, *it had no jurisprudence!* Christianity therefore, is only a religion, while Judaism, which actually had no Hebrew word for "religion", is a way of life. "The law of Christianity, its state policy, its throne, were respectively the dogma, the worship of God and the altar." Rabbi Benamozegh writes, "It never tried to give ethics the same rank as public virtues. There was an immense gap, an unbridgeable void, in Christianity, the gap between dogma and life which often made its existence embarrassing and embarrassed in the world. Its beautiful morality, exquisite as it appears when preached from the pulpit, could not, from its very refinement, evade the consequences of this blank, this want of the socio-political element which constitutes at once the weakness and the glory of Judaism. In Christianity, therefore, the great principle of charity destroyed itself, and thus lost any contact with and any bearing upon life, as it was bound to, because it was not allowed to play its legitimate part with its kindred justice. In vain did it fix its gaze upon the Kingdom of God when it was to reign supreme! This world kept on going its way—a world for whose political and social interests Christianity failed to provide."

Judaism, by contrast, had a socio-political system which covered all walks of life from the cradle to the grave. Everything was part of this system, even food, even sleep, even small talk. It did not disdain to mix in the minutest affairs of man and the world for it was never divorced from man and the world, it only tried to elevate them. To compare Christian moral code and Hebrew civil code—and that's precisely what Christianity has always done—is, therefore, not only an injustice but an impropriety. It exposes the nakedness of Christianity—exposes that void which has led charity to be less than just in not reserving a suitable place for the duties and concerns of life. And it was this same void which provided fertile ground for *forces of darkness whose subsequent abhorrence of Christian charity was originally fostered by Christian abhorrence of the Hebraic law.* This process was as inevitable as the one which followed the disillusionment with Christian "messianity": the dismissal of works in the name of faith had to give rise to evil men whose evil was enhanced by what they and their forefathers were told for centuries by the prejudiced exponents of faith versus works. And what they were told was that the exponents of works versus faith—of works *leading* to faith—were damned souls.[1] This theological verdict added to anti-Semitism a "supernat-

---

[1] Pastor Hall, a Canadian Protestant missionary in Jerusalem, was permitted by the government of Israel to visit frequently Adolf Eichmann in his prison cell where the good missionary tried in vain to save the arch-murderer's soul.

ural" dimension, and this is probably Christianity's greatest sin against Judaism—a sin which was soon to be punished by wicked irrational forces which subscribed readily to *Christian hatred while regarding Christian love as a Jewish invention.* Thus it came to pass that evil men, whose evil was fed by theological prejudices against the bearers of the Law, turned also, as they were bound to—though with much less violence—against the very faith that was supposed to replace the Law. Rabbi Elie Benamozegh prophetically foresaw such a cataclystic development when almost a century ago, he asked: "When the Gentiles, who knew nothing of the Law of Moses, hear that a revelation which had provided for ethics as well as worship is about to give way for the law of grace, of freedom, (St. Paul's freedom from the law as freedom from sin)—who does not see that morality is struck down with doctrine, worship and legislation? *Where shall reason take refuge when the great catastrophe arrives?*"

We don't know where reason took refuge when the catastrophe came, as Benamozegh predicted. We have no reason to believe, moreover, that reason, in its frantic flight from evil, fared any better than others of God's creations who found out that when catastrophe strikes, seekers of refuge are neither welcome nor popular anywhere. What we do know, however, is that when disaster struck and reason was running for its life, the world of Christianity with its accent on faith, on grace, was caught both faithless and graceless, for it was caught, almost two thousand years after St. Paul, without an effective deterrent against evil.

Only now, after Auschwitz, do we realize why this was bound to happen and why the seeds of Auschwitz were planted long before Hitler. A thousand small things pointed to this development. To mention just one of them which so many of us have witnessed in Eastern and Western European cities: prostitutes walking the streets proudly displaying gold crosses on their exposed necks. Didn't these prostitutes see a contradiction between the crosses they displayed and the profession they practiced? Not necessarily! They had *faith* in the cross and that was enough to justify the

---

After Eichmann's execution, Pastor Hall, on a visit to his native Canada, was asked at a press conference whether Eichmann, had he "embraced Christ" would have saved his soul, and gone straight to heaven. The pastor's answer was in the affirmative. He was then asked what of the six million Jewish men, women and children—a million children!—who died in Nazi Europe without having embraced Jesus? "Would you classify their martyred souls as 'unsaved, damned' "? The pastor sighed, nodded and replied, "May God have mercy on their poor souls . . ."

display of their profession. Their faith didn't interfere with their "works," nor did their "works" with their faith. The two were things apart.

This is just one little instance, and maybe not so little. It all started out with faith making holy works unnecessary and it ended up with unholy works making faith useless. Another example, the opposite of the above mentioned, one that comes to prove the long lasting, almost hereditary impact of the Hebrew accent on holy works, on the total deterrent, on moral purity, is taken from Jean-Paul Sartre's little book *Antisemite and Jew*. In that interesting, though by no means profound, book the famous French existentialist tells of a typical reaction of a Jew upon finding out that the prostitute he had chosen in an Argentine brothel was a Jewish girl: he was attacked by nausea and was rendered temporarily impotent. . . . Dostoyevsky, more preoccupied with evil than any other great author of the last century, has a cute little story, or story detail, which tells more than any long story what faith without works (the famous Council of Trent came too late to correct the error of fifteen hundred years!) is capable of: it's the story about a peasant who piously crosses himself before he slaughters his sleeping neighbor in an inn so as to take his watch away. He mutters faithfully: "Forgive me, Lord, for Christ's sake!" and draws the knife. That is faith in collusion with evil, faith *plus* evil. This is faith without works, bare, sterile, ignorant faith making evil easier to commit. It was the same faith without works that had induced the good Christian women of Warsaw to kneel down in prayer on that terrible Sunday morning when the Warsaw ghetto was going up in flames on fifty thousand burning Jews. They did not pray, these Christian women, for the unfortunates behind the ghetto walls, oh, no! They thanked God—so eyewitnesses say—that the wind, fanning the flames, wasn't blowing in the direction of *their* houses!

And don't let anybody try to repudiate this by pointing at the thousands of good Christians—priests, nuns, and simple folk—who died in concentration camps or put their lives in danger to save Jews. These good Christians and what they did only prove the truth of our thesis. For what do we say? We say that the Paulist concept of faith without works has inadvertently paved the way for the destruction of the deterrent against evil which the Hebrews of old were about to introduce into the world. But what did these good Christians do when the terrible test came? *They resorted to works, to deeds, to doing dangerous things that would make their*

28

faith relevant. But it was their faith, you would say, which prepared them for such deeds? Yes, it was! *It was their faith in as much as it didn't repudiate, malign, and defame the grandeur and the validity of the Jewish deterrent that served as its basis;* their faith, in other words, which, from the top of the smaller hill of Noahism, to which they faithfully adhered, they saw and admired from a distance the great and eternal Sinai! What this means is that Noahism, as Rabbi Benamozegh has referred to it, could have served as a sufficient minimum deterrent only if it did not look upon the maximum deterrent of Sinai as heresy and if Christian charity did not disdain its older Jewish companion—Justice! But what happened was that the hatred for the carriers of the maximum deterrent was greater than the fear of no deterrent at all! And so it came to pass that the deterrent of faith without works—or, at best, little works—became hateful to those who regarded *any* deterrent as a Jewish invention. The same contempt that the teachers of Christianity showed to the great Jewish deterrent—the Nazis soon showed to the small Christian deterrent which they inevitably had to regard as a derivative of Judaism and which they found it easy to destroy. Less than twenty-five years before Rabbi Benamozegh asked the great question: "Where will reason take refuge when the great catastrophe strikes?" Another great Jew, one who remained spiritually Jewish even after his conversion to Protestantism, asked the question—"Where will *faith*—the faith symbolized by the cross—take refuge when the thunder strikes?" He may not have used these exact words, the unhappy Jewish poet, Heinrich Heine, but he implied it when he warned France and Europe against a German revolution which would be unleashed, as quoted earlier, by her philosophies of nature—philosophies, by the way, based on the very opposite of the thought of the Jewish deterrent which is, first and foremost, an attempt to tame instincts, to curb nature, and finally, to transcend it: "But even more terrifying than all of these will be the philosophers of nature once they actively enter upon a German revolution and actively identify themselves with its destruction. For if the hand of the Kantian strikes firmly and surely, it is because his heart is moved by no traditional reverence. If the Fichtean boldly defies all danger, it is because it has no real existence for him. But the natural philosopher will be terrible indeed, because he has allies in the forces of nature, because he will be able to invoke the demonic energies of the old German pantheism, because that ancient love of war we find among the old Germans will once again awaken in them and they will fight not to

29

destroy or conquer, but for the sake of fighting. Christianity—and this is its greatest merit—has somewhat mitigated that brutal German love of war, but it cannot destroy it. Should that subduing talisman, the Cross, be shattered, the frenzied madness of the ancient warriors, that insane, berserk rage of which Nordic bards have spoken and sung so often, will once more burst into flames. The talisman is rotting and the day will come when it will break into miserable fragments; the old stone gods will arise from long-forgotten ruins and rub the dust of a thousand years from their eyes and Thor will leap to life with his giant hammer and smash the Gothic cathedrals!" (H. Heine, *Germany*)

And it was of this very day, the day of the mad rebellion against the deterrent of Sinai, that Hitler had spoken to his henchmen in the recorded conversation with Raushning. It wasn't difficult for him to complete the destruction of a deterrent which Christianity itself began to undermine many centuries prior to Hitler. Hitler was thus perfectly aware that no matter how much he attacked Christianity, many of those with a cross on their necks or chests would come to his side, as they did. And they did it because they believed, as he did, that by attacking Christianity they would actually help to eliminate Judaism which Christianity, alas, was the first to make hateful to them! And that's how it happened—exactly as the prostitute on the big-city streets doesn't necessarily see a contradiction between her displayed cross and her equally displayed profession—that millions of Christians in Nazi-occupied Europe didn't see the contradiction between faith in the cross and worship of the swastika. (The same, let's add, is true, of course, in related fields: take, for example, the great urge for social justice which was responsible for the so-called "social revolutions." Social revolutions, to use an expression by Charles Peguey, are supposed "to be moral or not be." But the revolutions, which called themselves social, came to certain unhappy lands without being moral at all. They may have had a moral faith, but no moral works. They had an end which, as many thought, sanctified the means, but they didn't use means that would sanctify the end! So what happened? The inevitable: "social justice," as it is called, made alliances with mass murder; love for the oppressed closed ranks with oppression; execution became the handmaid of equality). That is why we shall not be wrong when we state that in a world in which ends count more than means, faith more than works, hearings more than doings, and faraway ideals more than immediate deterrents—new Auschwitzes are possible, be they racial Auschwitzes or class Auschwitzes. And do not let anybody pin his hopes on "culture" and "progress" and similar big words. In certain leftist lands, "progress" is now a close ally of murder and genocide, and as far as "culture" is concerned, we must never forget, we shall never forget, that some of the most furious madmen of the Nazi era were scientists.

We have to say all this most emphatically now because in an era following that of Hitler and Stalin, the old, and undying, Hebrew concept about the nature of man, on the one hand, and of the Messiah who is yet to come for the sole purpose of changing that nature, on the other, has been so terribly vindicated. Only now do we begin to see this much maligned, much vilified, much distorted, and much suppressed religion in its true light. We begin to see it, along with many thinking, searching, feeling Gentiles all over the world, whose aroused interest in Judaism testifies to their aroused hope in the survival of the human spirit. Eugene Ionesco, the famous French playwright, gave clear expression to this interest, and to this hope, in a remarkable article published in the August 1968 issue of *Figaro Literaire*: "What keeps us alive now if not the hope that one bright morning the world will change; that everything will undergo a radical change and a new era of happiness will come to mankind?"

"Without the Jews there will be no faith in such a change, and there will be no waiting for the coming of the redeeming Messiah. We are waiting endlessly in the knowledge that the Messiah is already around the corner. We are waiting and we are expecting that one bright morning Messiah will open the door and the world will be flooded with joy and with light. We are all waiting for the 'Ideal State'; we are waiting for a 'New Jerusalem' to emerge out of the deserts of devastation and death. We are hoping that this world will acquire a new image, and this hope will live only as long as there will be Jews in the world. Without the Jews, a craze of crime will grip the world; without the Jews, darkness will prevail."

When the Jews adhered "to the letter of the law" (that, according to the Christian theologians, or to most of them, was supposed to be the curse of the Pharisees, who by doing so, refused to recognize the divinity of Jesus) they adhered to the letter of the *hope*. And the combination of the two did something to the Jews which, in retrospect, is short of a miracle: under circumstances which would have made delinquents out of other peoples, they kept up a life of works, of belief, of study, of knowledge, of compassion, of decency, of humility, of charity, of morality and,

31

very often, of gaiety which set them apart from the rest of mankind. It was this apartness which caused the finest among the Gentiles to admire them, and the scum of the earth to hate them, persecute them and put them to death. The Jews, accused of carnality and materiality, were the people of the spirit *par excellence*; they became carnal and material only to the degree that they abandoned that spirit or traded it for the carnal and material convenience of conversion. The great Heinrich Heine, who, even in his unhappy conversion, never ceased to see the beauty of Judaism which he had expeditiously abandoned, knew exactly what he meant when he wrote that "the Jews are the people of the spirit, and whenever they return to their principles, they are great and glorious, and they shame and conquer their clumsy oppressors. . . . Rosenkrantz [Karl Rosenkrantz (1805–1879), a follower of Hegel and professor at Berlin University] profoundly compares them to the giant Anatheus, except that the giant was strengthened whenever he touched the earth while the Jews gain new strength whenever they touch heaven. Strange phenomenon, this, filled with the most amazing contrasts! At the same time that you find among them some caricatures of vulgarity, (we shall deal with this vulgarity in another chapter), you also find among them the very purest ideals of humanity. As they once led the world to new paths of progress, the world may still expect them to open up others."

The path of Jewish progress, both old and new, is the path of the great deterrent aimed at the ennoblement of man through *works*. "The Law is created for the purpose of man's refinement," the Talmud says. Faith is as good only as the works that lead to it. And these are *works, and works alone,* which determine man's ability to refine and transcend himself.

By this we don't want to say that without the Jewish deterrent no self-change or self-transcendence is possible. There were, as there surely are today, exceptional men and women in all religions who successfully apply other deterrents in their strivings to perfection. What is so particular about the Jewish deterrent, however, is that it is the only one known to man which, at one time or another, *has created spiritual mass movements*. The terms "mass" and "spiritual" are almost contradictory, yet there were periods in Jewish history when the deterrent was practiced by the majority of people, or, at least, a very large minority, not just the elect. In those periods, juvenile delinquency, murder, arson, rape, incest, robbery or any other kind of immorality was practically unknown among the Jews. And it was unknown among them at a time when

32

they lived a life bogged down with poverty, and harassed by persecutions and hatred. Take the Eastern European period in Jewish history—not to speak of the Babylonian period of the "Golden Era" in Spain—a period of misery and oppression bitter enough to drive anybody to lawlessness. How did he really look, that poor Jew of the "shtetel"? We know, we read, a great deal about his poverty, about the shabby clothes he wore, about the miserable houses he dwelled in, about the knee-high mud streets through which he strode, about the impression of submissiveness and fear which he conveyed—all these we know. We are great masters when it comes to the description of externals that don't induce us, because of prejudice, hostility, or ignorance, to look at what lies behind them. Of course, there was no glitter and glamour in the "shtetel", but, underneath an exterior, often unpleasant to the eye, there palpitated a life which the strict adherence to the law of the deterrent had turned utterly pure and good.

An Apollonian mind would have been appalled at what he saw, but "the pattern of life of a people" in the words of Abraham J. Heshel, "is more significant than the pattern of its art. . . . What counts most is not expression, but existence itself. The key to creativity lies in the will to cling to spirituality, to be close to the inexpressible, and not merely in the ability of expression. What is creative comes from the responsive merging with the eternal in reality, not from an ambition to say something. . . . To appraise adequately the East European period in Jewish history, I had to inquire into the life-feeling and life-style of the people. This led to the conclusion that in this period *our people attained the highest degree of inwardness.* . . . Phoenician craftsmen had to be brought to Jerusalem by Solomon the King to assist in erecting the temple for the Lord. But there were Jews who knew to lay bricks in the soul, to rear holiness made of simple deeds, of study and prayer, of care, of fear and love. They knew how to pattern and raise a pyramid that no one could see but God."

"He was a unique type of man, the Jew in Eastern Europe, one whose habits and tastes did not conform to classical standards of beauty, but who nevertheless was endowed with a wistful charm; one whose physiognomy was not like a passage in an open book—a static picture of uniform lines with a definite proportion of text and margin—but like a book whose pages are constantly turning. . . . The charm came from the inner riches of their being—from the polarity of reason and feeling, of joy and sorrow, from the mixture of intellectualism and mysticism which is often bewildering to analytical observers. Their spirit was not like the luster of a sedate pearl, but rather like the tremulous gleam of light, like the twinkle of cut gems. . . . To be gay, carefree, relaxed, was an art few of them ever learned. A Jewish child would be taught that life was too earnest to be wasted on play. Joy, when felt, was always for a serious reason, the trimming for a happy occasion, justified like a logical conclusion. They were taught to care for the most distant in the most immediate, knowing that the passing is a reflection of the lasting, that tables in their humble homes might become consecrated altars, that a single deed of one man may decide the fate of all men. Characteristic of their piety was the unheroic sacrifice—unassuming, inconspicuous devotion rather than extravagance, mortification, asceticism. The *purpose was to ennoble the common, to endow worldly things with hieratic beauty.*" (*The Earth Is The Lord's*)

And for this purpose of ennobling the common, of endowing worldly things with hieratic beauty, the Cabalah has a word: "Tikun": The process of mending and repairing one's imperfect self and, consequently, the whole world around him. Something which is purposely torn in man from his very inception craves for mending, for repairing, for the great "Tikun," and it is with the attainment of this "Tikun" that man attains his own self and sets himself free. That is why the sages describe the messianic era as one in which the world—*this* world—will find its "Tikun" in the revealed Kingdom of God.

Survival for what?
For the sake of the universal "*Tikun*"!

Chapter Two

JUDAS, MY BROTHER

Ever since I first read about Judas Iscariot and what he did to Jesus, that he sold him to the seekers of his soul for thirty pieces of silver, I couldn't quite help feeling that there were, there must have been, other reasons for Judas' betrayal of his master, and for the subsequent decision of the "teachers of contempt", as Jules Isaac rightly refers to the prejudiced Church fathers, to turn this brave man into a monster. And the kind of monster Judas has been made to look like is well known to us by now: the man of Cariot, his true image as suppressed as the true history of his time, has become a symbol of all the evil things which were supposed to be typical of the Jews who rejected Jesus in his lifetime and, even more so, of those who refused to recognize him as the Messiah after his death on the cross. There were twelve apostles, as we all know, all of them Jews; but while Simon became Peter and Levi became Matthew, Judas was the only one whom the teachers of contempt have decided to leave forever with his manifestly Jewish name. For a Jew, whose identity could not be mistaken, was badly needed to provide prejudice with a prototype of perfidy, treachery, avarice, greed—all in one. "Look at the Jew, Judas,"—so went the cry of hatred which paved the way for pogroms and concentration camps, "and what he did to our Lord! Look at the cowardly way he betrayed him to his mortal enemies—a kiss! And for what? For thirty silver coins! That is Judas, the perfidious, treacherous, greedy, damned Judas!"

There were, of course, difficulties in explaining Judas' strange deed—the greatest of them being his famous, or, to be more exact, infamous, kiss. Why did the heartless traitor choose such an astoundingly unlikely, and unnecessary, means to denounce his master? A kiss! Couldn't he have denounced him, if denouncing alone was the aim, with something less cowardly than a kiss? Wouldn't a discreet nod with his head in his master's direction have sufficed? Or a slight pointing with the finger? Or a simple description of Christ's face, manner, and robe in advance? Why did Judas have to kiss Christ at the moment he was clearly delivering him to his executioners?

Christian theology is almost unanimous in its explanation that on the night prior to his betrayal, Satan entered the soul of Judas. His kiss, according to this convenient version, was an arch act of satanic mockery, the epitome of whatever is ugly, cowardly, sinister, base and cruel in man.

Many Christian authors, poets, and painters have elaborated a great deal on the subject of the diabolically possessed Judas. But an Italian poet of the 19th century by the name of Ferdinando Tirinnanzi, the author of *Catilina* and *Canossa,* was the first to consider the problem of the kiss of Judas. According to Tirinnanzi, Judas who kisses Christ is Satan who kisses God. In the tragedy of the Passion, in other words, there was another meeting between the redeemer and the adversary, a bodily contact in which hate was forced to kiss love. Satan was drawn to the kiss of God, to *kiss* God, like to a magnet that was, at least for a fleeting moment, stronger than all his dark powers combined.

Judas was thus portrayed as the bearer of hate as much as Jesus was as the bearer of love. This simple juxtaposition went on for almost twenty centuries, and with considerable success. The teachers of contempt succeeded enormously in this publicity task, as, indeed, in any other they set before themselves in the realm of the theological interpretation of history. The Pharisees are another typical example. A strictly religious, uncompromisingly pietistic, profoundly moralistic and humanistic popular movement—not sect—in the times of Jesus, it became in all literature, be it Christian or secular, as synonymous with hypocrisy as Judas is with perfidy. The term "Pharisee" has become, in fact, an integral part of our negative vocabulary, and is used by Jew and Gentile alike as another word for "hypocrite."

But let us return to Judas. Albert Schweitzer was the first great Christian thinker who felt that there was something contrived about the official Christian version of the Judas story, and that there were much deeper, and purer, reasons that motivated Judas to do what he did. His historical and psychological analysis of the Judas enigma was published (in *The Quest for the Historical Jesus*) about fifty years after a similar assertion made by Thomas de Quincey. The great Englishman claimed, namely, that Judas' object in betraying his master was not due to selfishness based on avarice, but to a desperate urge, growing out of an even more desperate faith in Christ's messianity, to compel him, as quickly as possible, to perform the miracle of his emergence *as a redeemer of mankind.*

These views, which left little imprint on Christian thought in recent times, must assume a different nature now in the era of Auschwitz and the Dead Sea Scrolls. And we mention Auschwitz and the Dead Sea Scrolls in the same breath because Auschwitz to us is the place which symbolizes man's failure as man, while the Dead Sea Scrolls, discovered only two years after Auschwitz, bring to light a period in history, in which the struggle for man's emergence and delivery, *through the most rigid application of the Sinai deterrent,* became the only raison d'etre of an entire people. And it is in the context of that tremendous era in Hebrew history, to which the Dead Sea Scrolls have opened a wide avenue of understanding, that the Judas figure can be seen in all his historicity.

What kind of a period was it really, the period of Christ and Judas Iscariot in old Jewish history? By now we can state without hesitancy that it was a period of *spectacular spiritual grandeur,* more enhanced than undermined by political oppression. Political oppression, on the other hand, or the tolerating thereof, was regarded, for the first and only time in human history, as a *violation of a divine law, the law of Sinai.* Thus the unjustly maligned "Sicariis" ("Zealots") saw in the toleration of Roman rule over their land—a rule based on the belief that Caesar was vested with divine powers—a forbidden perpetuation of a state of idolatry. Since Sinai, so argued Hizkiya the Galilean, an early philosopher of the Zealots, when Jews swore allegiance to God, any submission to man who claims divine powers is an idolatrous crime. It was, in other words, either God *or* Caesar. God *and* Caesar could not possibly dwell together, each of them getting their separate dues. . . . The moral level of the people of Israel was at an all-time high in spite of violent inner struggles which centered around questions of a spiritual nature much more than around struggles for temporal power, which were confined to a complacently collaborationist minority. The mood of the period was unique in the history of mankind in general, for it was distinctly eschatological in nature—a mood of cataclystic expectations which, according to the belief of most, if not all, the Hebrews were to herald the imminent Messianic era. As time passed, however, and paganistic Rome strengthened its hold on occupied Israel, the Jews began

37

pinning their hopes more and more upon a direct intervention by God in the unhappy affairs of His subjugated people and, indeed, in the bloody affairs of all peoples and all nations of the earth. The conviction was growing amongst the Jews that nothing short of a divine take-over on a cosmic scale would unseat the present hold of idolatrous evil on the world. But how soon and by what means this divine take-over would come about was a question which divided the nation into powerful religio-political movements and sects: the Pharisees, the Sadducees, the Essenes and the Zealots. These warring groups, except, perhaps for the Sadducees, believed in a divine intervention which was bound to come. This irrevocable conviction in the establishment of God's Kingdom on earth following a cataclysm on a cosmic scale was particularly shared by the Essenes and the Zealots. The Pharisees, on the other hand, the fathers of the interpretative law, of the Mishna and the Talmud, while their messianic creed was as fervent as that of the others, didn't think that this creed, a basic tenet in Judaism, must in any way be affected by the possible, and even inevitable, delay in its realization. The Pharisees thus put more stress on the long-term survival of the law under adverse conditions than on Messianic expectations of an immediate nature. The Essenes, at the same time, reading the signs of the times from the holy scriptures— almost a national pastime in those days—believed that the end, or the great beginning, can be brought about without delay by abstinence, purity, prayer and watchfulness. The Zealots, on the other hand, who were later to dominate Jerusalem and the Temple in the crucial days of the final showdown with Rome, hoped, as John Allegro puts it in *The Treasure of the Copper Scroll,* to "force God's hand with armed revolt and martyr's blood." This belief— the belief, that is, that God's hand can be forced by self-sacrifice— was as alive just before the destruction of the Temple, thirty-five years after the execution of Christ, as during Jesus' lifetime when he himself was convinced, as we shall discuss later, that his own blood could force the issue. There was, by the way, more than one self-sacrificial "suffering servant" of God, to use the famous Biblical term which Christian theologians apply to Christ, in those dramatic days. One such servant, referred to in the Dead Sea Scrolls as "the Teacher of Righteousness," was put to death in Jerusalem about a hundred years before Christ.

The messianic restlessness was universal. Large segments of Jewry, scholars and laymen alike, were frantically reading their own wishful thoughts in enigmatic Biblical sentences and interpreting them in a way that made them feel increasingly confident that "the day of the Lord, great and terrible" was at hand. This belief was enhanced by deeds—by a vitality and profundity of the religious life in Israel which was not diminished even by the complacency of some collaborationist priests, corrupted officials, and pro-Roman assimilationists of Sadducee leanings. "Pre-Christian Judaism," Jules Isaac writes in his *Teachers of Contempt,* "far from being paralyzed, was imbued and animated by tremendous currents of intense piety and mystical spirituality. . . . Christianity arose not from a decadent, but from a living Judaism, as is proved by the wealth of Jewish literature, by the indomitable resistance of Judaism to Paganism, by the spirituality of the religion practiced in the synagogue, by the spread of proselytism, by the incorporation of new beliefs, and by the multiplicity of sects." A small, but fiercely proud nation, the only iconoclastic people on earth serving a One and Invisible God, and scorning graven images—the old Hebrews, while attributing their misfortunes to their sins ("Only you have I known from all the families of the earth, I shall therefore visit upon you all your iniquities"—Zechariah) thought it unthinkable that the Lord God of their fathers would tolerate for long a situation in which His honor, along with that of His people, was willfully debased by evil doers. There was, moreover, a universal conviction in those days that God was *committed* to the redemption of Israel and that this redemption would materialize through the coming of a promised Messiah. The exact nature of the Messiah as well as the conditions that would make the time ripe for his coming were under constant discussion. The Essenes, for example, unequalled in the practice of an extreme moral purity which amounted almost to renunciation—something the Pharisees denounced and fought against—believed that the Messiah would have to die in order to bring about the new world order. This belief gained strength after the violent death of the man who must have been the cherished founder and leader of the sect and who is constantly referred to in the Scrolls, as already mentioned, as "the Teacher of Righteousness". This thought—the thought, that is, that the death of the Messiah, or of a first Messiah, would herald the redemption of Israel—was already considerably developed, as it now seems certain from the Scrolls, when Jesus later emerged on the restless scene and gave his attention to it. Nor was Jesus the only one who had given to it his attention and saw in it a summons of a personal nature, as was bound to happen in a land that seethed with Messianic fever. Jesus, as it seemed clear to more objective theologians and historians long before the discovery of the Dead Sea Scrolls, never regarded himself as a founder of a new faith—the living, vibrating faith of his people reached unequalled heights in his time—but as the longed-for Messiah of the Jews. Dr. Schweitzer expounded this most likely theory as far back as 1906 in his *The Quest for the Historical Jesus,* as mentioned earlier. According to Schweitzer, Jesus expected his "Parousia"—his revelation as a redeemer and deliverer of man in *this* world—to be imminent. Jesus, at a certain stage of his preaching, was, in fact, so convinced of his Messianity that when he sent out his disciples to proclaim the coming of the Israelite Kingdom of God, he warned them that before their mission was completed, the Kingdom of God on this earth would already have appeared. His command to them, according to the Gospels, was clear: "Go not in any way to the Gentiles, and enter not into the city of the Samaritans, but go rather to the lost sheep of the house of Israel." In other words, since his "Parousia" was at hand there was no more time, in Jesus' mind, for long, external missions. But the imminently expected "Parousia" did not materialize. "And when it failed to happen," A. Powell Davies writes in his comprehensive *The Dead Sea Scrolls,* "there came a change upon Jesus so that, as the record describes it, he was 'transfigured': he began now to talk of going to Jerusalem and of undergoing suffering and death." According to Schweitzer, again, this metamorphosis was due to Jesus having adapted—perhaps he had tended toward it all along—the view already mentioned that the Messiah must be "the suffering servant of God," long ago prophesied by Isaiah (who may very well have had in mind the entire people of Israel), so that only through his agony could he precipitate the appearance of the Divine Kingdom on earth.

The Dead Sea Scrolls lend to this interpretation, as already indicated, a unique air of historicity. Messianic movements, such as the Essenes', with thousands of members throughout the land, who behaved as if they had actually heard the footsteps of the deliverer around the corner, expected that the coming of the Messiah of Aaron, who would be a priest, and of the Messiah of Israel, who would be a descendant of the house of David, would be heralded by a Prophet. This role, so his followers undoubtedly thought for a while, was the one which Jesus was fulfilling. This was both in the spirit of the epoch and in the tradition of the sect—the Qumran community of the Essenes whose influence on Jesus seems, in view of recent discoveries, decisive. But when

40

Jesus, following his disappointment and subsequent "transfiguration," began to speak of his Messianity and to claim that this Messianity would manifest itself in suffering and even death, something must have happened among his followers, or at least among the more daring, less patient of them, which led straight to the "perfidy" of Judas.

What caused Judas Iscariot, ardent and long time disciple of Jesus, to inform the authorities that Jesus regarded himself as the Messiah—the King—of the Jews? And did he really do it for thirty pieces of silver, as the teachers of contempt maintain? Was Judas really a traitor, a lecherous, greedy villain? Judas, so Schweitzer claims, bolder than the others, saw himself as acting out a part that was essential to Jesus' plans. For on the basis of Jesus' own disclosure, Schweitzer maintains, the man of Nazareth sought death, expecting that it would inevitably bring on his "Parousia"—his revelation as the immediate redeemer of his people. The later expression, attributed to Jesus, that "my Kingdom is not of this world", was, it seems clear, only one side of his Messianic coin, on the other side of which there was, displayed like a banner, the constant warning of the Baptist: "Repent, for the Kingdom of God is at hand!" The Romans, moreover, little concerned with kingdoms which were not of this world, would have never condemned Jesus to death, nor would they have executed him, if they did not regard him, on the basis of his own words, a threat to their rule in *this* world. Jesus, in fact, was so confident of his forthcoming "Parousia", which will manifest itself at the very moment of his apparent physical death, that when it failed to manifest itself in the terrible moments of his agony, he felt abandoned. "God, my God why hast Thou forsaken me?" are, no matter what theological hairsplitters claim, shattering words of disillusionment as the bitter realization of failure had set in.

So what did Judas, after all, do? He did something which, as Schweitzer put it, was supposed to "act out a role that was essential to Jesus' plans": Jesus craved the Golgotha as the arena of his "Parousia," and Judas thought he had found a terrible yet hopeful shortcut to the craved end. This is Schweitzer's opinion. To this author, however, going in the ineradicable footsteps of Thomas de Quincey—footsteps made even more distinguishable by the Dead Sea Scrolls—it seems certain that Judas did much more than that. Judas namely decided to put Jesus to a final test of his Messianity. Up to a point he believed in Jesus by *hearing*. Now the time had come for *doing*. Faith alone, no matter how deep, no matter how strong, was not enough when the very earth was burning under the feet. *Works* were needed to prove the Messianity of the man he so loved and worshipped and who claimed that his revelation was at hand. Thus Judas' crime was that he decided to put his Christ's Messianity to the test of *works,* something for which early Christianity couldn't forgive him!

That early Christianity shrunk from the test of works is evident yet from another instance in the theological account of Jesus' life. We are referring to the story in the Gospels about Satan testing and tempting Jesus in the wilderness. We have no difficulty in subscribing to the mystical thought that only Satan could have tried to tempt Jesus by promising him all the kingdoms of the world if he would yield to his power. However, when it comes to the story of the man, also described as Satan, who tried to test Jesus in the same wilderness by asking him to prove his Messianity through the performing of miracles—we are at a loss to discover the satanicity of this request unless, of course, we subscribe to the thought that *testing*—works, deeds, proofs—is tantamount to blasphemy. . . . Thus Satan took possession of Judas' soul on the night prior to his putting his master to a test. Testing, according to this theory, is evil.

But Judas putting his master to a test was both in line with the Messianic emergency that characterized that era and with the great Hebrew accent on *works.* Not that Judas doubted Jesus' purity and sincerity—nobody doubts that—but following his master's "transfiguration," when his promised "Parousia" failed, as aforementioned, to manifest itself, the tiny seeds of a terrible doubt were planted in Judas' fiery soul as to Jesus' Messianity—his divinity wasn't then even under discussion. Judas, in other words, while convinced in Jesus' own conviction of his Messianity, and frantically eager to see this conviction triumph, was suddenly determined to let *works* confirm without delay the veracity of his faith. If Jesus was the Messiah of the God of Jacob—Judas must have fearfully reasoned with himself—and if this Messiah is so utterly convinced that only out of the depths of his agony can he emerge as the redeemer—if Jesus himself, in other words, sought works—superhuman works—to prove the truth of a faith he personified—let this saving agony come at once. Neither Jesus, nor his disciples, nor the suffering house of Israel can bear waiting any longer. False hopes can be fatal. If Jesus is the Messiah, let his Messianity appear now. If not, let *him* at once *disappear.* Along with the great modern Hebrew poet, Ch. N. Bialik, Judas could have cried out:

> And if there is justice, let it appear right now.
> But if only after I am annihilated under God's eyes,
> Justice will arise—
> Let it be annihilated, too!

The great heart which cried thus about justice, must have loved justice above anything else in the world, and only because it loved it so much, it simply couldn't bear the thought that all one might hope for when evil reigns supreme, is for some survivor, some day after the deluge, to plant the exalted flag of justice in the midst of the valley of the bones.

Judas must have harbored similar thoughts about Jesus: if He is the Messiah, let Him come to life now through the very death He so craves, and redeem his people. But if he is not the Messiah— even if he wholeheartedly believes that he is—let him die now, for his own sake as well as for the sake of His people. A Messiah must either prove his Messianity or disappear. There is no third way.

So what did Judas do? He denounced Jesus as the man who regarded Himself as the Messiah and King of the Jews—a crime punishable by death. It was probably one of the most purposeful, most hopeful, yet most desperate and fearful denunciations in the history of man. It was an act of perfidy integrally connected with boundless personal love and devotion, yet it had to completely transcend personal love, even personal worship, for the sake of a general truth which had to be proven or disproven at once. It was a denunciation as tragic and dramatic as any in history, as tragic and dramatic as the kiss—supposing there was one—which Judas had planted on his master's pale face when the Romans had come for Him. What Judas wanted to say with the kiss couldn't be anything else but this: "I love you, Master, and I believe in You as I believe that You believe in You. If, however, I decided to put You quickly—more quickly than anticipated by You—to the test of death which You Yourself crave, it is only because my love for the tormented house of Israel, whose need for a redeemer is so great and whose outcry for redemption so strong—is even greater and stronger than my love for You. And it is because of this love for Israel, oh Master, because of the frantic fear of misleading her in her distress, of giving her false hopes in her pains, that I denounced You to the seekers of Your soul, so that if we are both right and You are the Messiah, You will bless me for precipitating Your revelation; if, however, we are both wrong, oh great friend and teacher of mine, and You are not the Messiah we have prayed and hoped for, let my kiss tell You that the greatest of all hopes, the hope of redemption, which will die with You, and because of You, for a very long time, will never mar the love I harbor for the pure man whose death I precipitated because of a Messianity that had to be proven, but wasn't—alas!"

That was, it seems most likely, the real, the tragic man called Judas Iscariot. He may have very well been under the influence of the Zealots, as some historians suggest, for "forcing God's hand through a martyr's blood" was clearly an idea borrowed from the spiritual fathers of Eliezer Ben Yair of "Massada". But whether Zealot or not, Judas was a Messiah-struck Jew to whom redemption was the only absolute thing in the world, and the Messiah only relative to the mission he was supposed to fulfill. He was so Messiah-struck, in fact, this great, unhappy Judas, that when Jesus' death convinced him of his error in believing that the Nazarene was the Messiah—he committed suicide. He killed himself—a self-killing which is so much in line with his Messiah-struck character —out of disillusionment, of course, but also out of guilt. The death of Jesus as a Messiah wasn't his, Judas', fault. But didn't he hasten Jesus' death as a *man* just because he wanted to test him as a Messiah? Jesus Himself might have craved, as he did, a martyr's test of blood, but who could precipitate such a test—and such a failure—and remain remorseless!

But this feeling of guilt and disillusionment wasn't all. There was, there had to be, in addition to it, the inevitable sense of futility, meaninglessness and hopelessness that seized Judas when his Messiah was dead. He hanged himself, because a Messiah-struck Jew cannot live in a world whose hoped for Messiah is dead!

Jesus' death on the cross without his "Parousia" was to Judas the dreadful sign of his master's non-messianity. To the other apostles, however, it was soon to become the sign of his newly proclaimed divinity. Since Jesus failed to establish His Kingdom in *this* world, his Kingdom was soon declared as the exclusive property of the next. The "Parousia" which failed to manifest itself at Jesus' death, soon gave birth to the story of His Resurrection three days *after* His death—a resurrection which was supposed to make even clearer that Jesus' Kingdom is of another world. Eternal salvation in the world to come now substituted for the redemption that failed to materialize through Jesus in this world. Soon the very consideration of this world as an actively redeemable entity became abhorrent to the Church fathers who didn't hesitate to label the belief in the redemption of, and in, the physical world as "materiality" and even "carnality". Thus Judas, of course, who betrayed his master so as to test his Messianity of *this* world—was described as the epitome of materiality and carnality; hence also the obviously contrived story about the thirty pieces of silver.

But Judas Iscariot was vindicated in our day and age, and he was vindicated because our day and age has heard the loudest professions of the faithful—social, national and political, let alone the religious faithful—about the messianity of their faiths, and it has witnessed, at the same time, the failure of those faiths as soon as they were put to the test of works. To such faithful, Judas has a message, and his message is simple: *beware of kingdoms which are not of this world!*

For what does it mean "not of this world"? It means in the light of our experiences, the belief in a promise whose fulfilment is not really attainable and is, therefore, trying to present itself as fulfilment that has already taken place. And this is true not only of Christianity. Whenever a theory, which sounds messianic in its promissory stage, pretends to possess the panacea for its messianic *fulfilment,* it actually talks of a kingdom which is not of this world. (As, for example, Lenin's belief in the coming of a "classless society" in which "the state will wither away.") Whenever, in other words, an idea regards itself as messianic just because it is convinced that it has so proven itself in *theory*—it actually deals with a kingdom which is not of this world. Or to reduce it from the plane of ideas to that of individuals: whenever an idealistic guerrilla fighter anywhere in the world picks up arms and goes to the mountains to kill and be killed for a revolutionary idea which is presented to him, and which he regards, as messianic, world-saving, etc., he is actually killing, and is being killed, for a kingdom which is not of this world. A messiah is either of this world, which means that he has to prove his messianity by improving man's lot and man himself right here, or he is not the *Messiah,* period. The proof of the Messiah, of the Savior, is in his *saving.* When Maimonides tries to answer the question as to how one would recognize the true Messiah, he says in fact that if a man will appear—wise, pious, inspired—who will *save* and *redeem*—he *is* the Saviour and the Redeemer. The belief that just the *promise* of redemption, if you believe in it, *is* redemption, and the stress that was placed on this belief by countless theologians, is the great tragedy of Christianity and the reason for its failure as a fearless, fighting and spiritually redeeming moral force in the world. Some Christian theologians, particularly Germans, realize it now more than ever before, for never before was there such an abyss stretching out between the "Saviour" and the soul that was supposed to be saved through faith in him and in his other worldly kingdom. That is why the apocalyptic prophecies of the real Jesus, announcing that the Kingdom of God was at hand, as he undoubtedly believed, and his grand vision of the imminence of a "new heaven and a new earth", are being now reinterpreted by some young, restless German theologians the only way they could be interpreted, namely—Judaically. The stress is no more on the saving power of faith—faith that the Messiah has *already* come—but on *hope*. In his *Theology of Hope* the German theologian Jurgen Moltman states bluntly that "there is only one real problem in Christian theology: the problem of the future." He believes in the resurrection of Jesus and says that "Christianity stands and falls with the reality of the rising of Jesus from the dead." And from his point of view he is absolutely right! That was what Judas was actually trying to find out; the only difference being that while Judas' belief in the messianity of Jesus stood or fell with his, Jesus', *not* dying AT ALL—in the case of some modern Christian theologians it hinges upon the belief in his resurrection *after* death. But that new approach—the stress on hope rather than "faith"—would make theological sense only if it did not clash head on with the history of Christianity, or, if you will, Christian peoples, which is far from being one of moral and spiritual *redemption*. Mr. Boltman, as some of his fellow theologians in Germany, like Bloch and Pannenberg, are bothered by this incompatibility. The question which must be bothering them is the one which is now haunting Christianity in general: if Jesus was the Messiah, and if this messianity is experienced through faith—what evil has this faith, or this messianity, prevented from happening in a world to which a messiah was supposed to have come already? Boltman doesn't pose this question directly, but, instead, he resorts to his theology of hope instead of faith. This theology may be new to Christians, but it is a basic spiritual and religious tenet of Judaism. The main difference between Christianity and Judaism lies in the unbridgeable gap between a faith which insists that the Messiah has already come (though he may appear again), and a hope, which is the quintessence of faith, that the Messiah, the true Messiah, whom man has never known yet, is still to come. This hope, and this hope alone, so Judaism preaches, gives direction, meaning and purpose to history, for what it actually says is that humanity, woefully unredeemed as it is, is moving *precisely on account of its unredemption,* toward a goal, which is the messianic age, and in which man's oneness with God, the universe and himself will be accomplished. One may not believe in the coming of a Messiah the way messianic Judaism—*and there is no other Judaism, but messianic Judaism*—believes, but how, on earth, can one fail to believe in his *not—having—come—yet?* To the Jews, the belief that the Messiah hasn't come yet is as basic as the belief in his promised coming. The Jews would rather die than declare their belief in a Messiah who has come already. But it was in this dying that they saw a prerequisite to the coming of the *real* Messiah. The theology of hope is bound to be eschatological. Whenever there is an abundance of evil and bloodshed in the world, the believing Jew saw and sees in it, or hopes to see in it, a sign of the approaching messianic age. That was also what Judas hoped to see in the eschatologically interpreted events of his day and age. It is here, of course, in the process of the eschatological crises, that people are most prone to fall prey to delusions, and they always do. Eschatological, as apocalyptic events are thus not only a preliminary to the messianic age, but, often, a condition to the emergence of a Messiah. But it is precisely this condition which inevitably gives birth to the false Messiah as well as to the ideational hysteria which regards it a crime to doubt his messianity. We live now in an era of dead Messiahs whose followers are ready to kill in order to "prove" that their Messiahs are immortal. To put a Messiah, who is supposed to be immortal, to the sincere test of mortality, requires superhuman strength. Such a test, particularly when administered by a Messiah-struck man, is by no means a result of infidelity and disloyalty to the Messiah in question, but of loyalty to, and concern for, the last great hope of humanity. Jesus, in Roman-occupied Israel, in the midst of great sufferings brought about by the oppressor and by equally great yearning for God's Kingdom on earth, had plenty of eschatological "proofs" for the construction of his messianic edifice; nobody doubts that. But the same is true of other "eschatological" periods in history, even if they were not of a spiritual nature. Take Marxism, for example. It emerged in 19th century England amidst terrible sufferings caused by the transition from an agricultural to an industrial economy. This transition provided Marx with plenty of material for constructing an "eschatological" analysis of primitive capitalism, now as defunct as primitive Christianity. But when both Christian and Marxian messianisms were put to tests and failed to save, the word "faith" (sometimes called "party discipline" or "dialectics") was, and is, invoked as the only condition for "grace." Albert Camus rightly remarks in *The Rebel* that "it can be said of Marx that the greater part of his predictions came into conflict with facts as soon as his prophecies began to become an object of increasing faith." It is, in other words, the temptation, and the test of faith, nay, the TRAP of faith, which now determines the ultimate value of man's hopes. Faith can be as much a trap as a test, and it is definitely wrong to believe that people, particularly young people, nowadays are faithless. The very opposite is the truth. Never in the history of mankind were so many people having so much faith in so many false Messiahs. The Messiahs may be false, but the faith is there and is unshakable. The faith in such Messiahs is so great, in fact, that murder is justified through ideation. Krishnamurti is right when he says that our present crisis is graver than any in history because "it is in the field of ideation. . . . We are quarrelling with ideas, we are justifying murder; everywhere in the world we are justifying murder as a means to a righteous end, which in itself is unprecedented. Before, evil was recognized to be evil, murder was recognized to be murder, but now, murder is a means to achieve a noble result. Murder, whether of one person or of a group, is justified because the murderer, or the group which the murderer represents, justifies it as a means of achieving a result which he says will be beneficial to men. That is, we sacrifice the present for the future—and it does not matter what means we employ as long as our declared purpose is to produce a result which we say will be beneficial to man. Therefore, the implication is that a wrong means will produce a right end and you justify the wrong means through ideation. In the various crises that have taken place before, the issue has been the exploitation of things or of man; it is now the exploitation of ideas, which is much more pernicious, much more dangerous, because the exploitation of ideas is so devastating, so destructive. . . ." (Krishnamurti, *The First and Last Freedom*). And why is the exploitation of ideas so devastating, so destructive? Because ideas, like Messiahs, tend to lend to their followers a faith which increases in strength the more it clashes with the facts of truth. Ideation is therefore the state of mind which prevails when man is in love with a kingdom, be it political or social, which is not

48

of this world, which can never be achieved, that is, but which man believes that he achieves through the frantic process of willing it.

This has been true with political and social movements as it is or was true with movements of a distinctly religious and spiritual order. The faithful masses, once bitten by the messianic bug, so to speak—by the bug of a Messiah who is already here, and must only be recognised, are victims of messianic delusions (which is another word for "ideation"). It takes a truly great man, a truly great soul, to realize not only that a "Messiah" can die, but, which is even more important, that a Messiah who refuses to die though forced to do so by a spiritual or socio-political reality which belies his messianic claims, may become a danger to man. Man would have been much closer to redemption had he mastered the courage to recognize the death of his "redeemers." To be capable of such a recognition, however, a world of courage, and stamina, and selflessness, and sincerity, and fearlessness is needed, for there is nothing more agonizing than a messianic reappraisal. And it was precisely this agony of reappraisal which was the mark of greatness of Judas Iscariot. Judas may very well have been, as so many believe, the most Messiah-struck among the apostles, but it is precisely this passionate nature of his devotion which raises his ability to recognize the non-messianity of his "Messiah" to the heights of unparalleled spiritual grandeur and spiritual tragedy alike. This grandeur and this tragedy are particularly relevant today because the age we live in is one which is distinguished by the inability of man to differentiate between redemption and deception. Judas Iscariot was redeemed in our day and age because exactly as the Golgotha of the one innocent man which he had precipitated proved to him that Jesus was not the redeemer—the Golgotha of millions of innocent men, women and children, nineteen hundred years after Jesus, and in the heart of Christian Europe, proved beyond any shadow of doubt that precisely the part of mankind which believes that the redeemer has come already *is actually the least redeemed.*

Let's talk frankly about it, lest we suffocate of overdoses of pious pleasantries. Free mankind, living, as it does, in the shadow of the bomb and looking everywhere for sources of moral strength that will enhance its chances for survival, finds itself, following the last World War, incapable of invoking God's name without sounding hypocritical. What do such words as "God," and "love" and "brotherhood of men" and "fatherhood of God" mean after Auschwitz, particularly when invoked by Christians? Let's face it,

49

for God's sake! If it will be very long before mankind after Hitler and Stalin regains its dignity, let it at least try to regain its sincerity. Let's stop for a moment our self-flattery and God-flattery. Let's have a good look at what has actually happened even if the real truth will hurt false brotherhood. Sören Kierkegaard, one of the most sincere and profound Christians who ever lived, speaks in his remarkable *Fear and Trembling* of a possibility, dialectically speaking, of religious suspension of ethics. We do not want to go so far as to speak, dialectically, of the moral suspension of theology —of a certain theology that is. But we do say without hesitancy *that Christian theology clashes head on with morality when the claim to soul-savings is maintained after Auschwitz!*

And not only that it clashes head on with morality, but, as it became apparent after the discovery of the "Dead Sea Scrolls"— with history! When the Christian Church claims that what was essential in all events which preceded the emergence of Jesus was ended once and for all with a particular revolutionary occurrence, the life and death of Jesus, (which the "Dead Sea Scrolls" irrefutably proved to be *evolutionary*!)—this one event becomes not only the quintessence of a religion, but a dogma of history. The past,—the past called "historic",—turns into a dogma, and one is not supposed to see it any other way but the way the dogma sees it.

And this dogma stands and falls not only with the belief in the divinity of Jesus, but with the carnality of the Jews in Jesus' time, —with their "corruption", their "legalism", their "casuistry" etc. An amazing, indeed incredible thing has happened: the self-criticism of the Jews—a criticism nowhere more vehement than in the so-called "Old" Testament—was described by Christianity as the exclusive trait of the era of Jesus. It was with the ascent of Jesus, according to Christianity, that a fiery attack was first unleashed against the establishment in Jerusalem whose downfall was prophesied by Jesus. This downfall, in turn,—the downfall of an establishment which the Gospels describe as "corrupt",—was supposed to prove the revolutionary, messianic and, indeed, divine nature of Jesus' appearance on the scene.

But it is precisely here where Christian theology clashes head on with history and with historic truth. For the truth of the matter is that Jesus, *imitating the Prophets, tried to speak their language.* The Prophets were angry men. Whoever tried to talk their language was bound to be angry. Jesus was no exception. If the sins of the Jews are visited upon them more than upon other nations,—as the Prophet Zecharia cries out,—precisely because they are the chosen among nations, the divine wrath at their transgressions, as expressed by *all* the prophets, beginning with Moses, was bound to be the very *language* of the Prophets. And that's what it was. When dismay is not the companion of greatness, there isn't much greatness to talk about. And nothing typified the language of the Prophets—of all the Prophets—more than dismay. But the trouble is, as Prof. Krister Stendahl of Harvard rightly remarked (in "Christian news from Israel", May, 1968) "that this prophetic language fell, so to say, into the hands of the Gentiles . . . Once the Jewish context and identification were lost, the words of Jesus received a new setting. They were no more operating within the framework of Jewish self-criticism. They hardened into accusations against 'the Jews', the synagogue across the street, and against the people who claimed the same scripture, but denied its fulfillment in Jesus Christ."

But that is only part of the story. The words of Jesus, or those attributed to him, hardened, in the new setting, not only into accusations against 'the Jews', but into the *character assassination of a people*. For if the misinterpretation of the most vital part of Jewish history became an article of faith,—and if Christianity still persists in this misinterpretation—what is all the talk about a dialogue between Christians and Jews but a renewed attempt at the conversion of the Jews?

But if there was a distortion of history after Golgotha, let there not be a distortion of truth after Auschwitz! For after Golgotha—for centuries after Golgotha—Christian theologians, in order to maintain their claim to soul-saving, insisted upon the "carnality" of the Jews. The Jews were carnal—an incredible, indeed perverse, accusation—for two major reasons: first—so the theory went—because they were already in a state of degenerate carnality when Jesus appeared on the arena and tried to save them, but they refused his redeeming touch. Second, following this refusal, the Jews brought upon themselves a permanent state of non-redemption. Messianity equals spirituality. Carnality is thus not only the result of non-spirituality, but the punishment thereof. And the punishment included, according to this theory, the destruction of Jerusalem and the eternal dispersion of the Jews.

But such a sweeping theory needed badly the help of history. It was impossible to admit to the truth that Jesus had appeared in the midst of an era unequalled for spiritual grandeur in spite of adversity, for had such an admittance been made, the revolutionary nature of Jesus' Messianity, let alone divinity, would have been put in jeopardy.[1] That is why Christian theologians, paving the way for historians and philosophers, even of our own day, succeeded in portraying the Jewry of Jesus' day and age as a corrupt, carnal society devoid of spiritual grandeur or moral fiber. The picture of Jewry in Christ's days the way it was drawn by hordes of dogmatic theologians was of a people that reduced its creed to a mere formalism and cold ritual, to a desiccated, ossified, stale and sterile legalism without a soul, without fervour, without love and without any deeper longings for God. "This contention," writes Jules Isaac in *The Teachings of Contempt,* "has its source in the earliest Judeo-Christian controversies over the Torah—the law of Moses—and its observance. The Christian apologists maintained that with the coming of Christ the law had been fulfilled and superseded. They taught that the Jews were attached to the letter and not the spirit of the law because they were 'carnal' beings blinded by Satan, incapable of understanding the real meaning of their own scriptures."

The Early Church fathers not only return constantly to this theme, but return to it in an almost violent manner. Thus Saint Jerome, discussing the Jews, does not hesitate to declare that "their prayers and psalms are like the inarticulate cries of animals," and Saint John Chrysostom, a particularly vicious Jew-hater, preaching in Antioch in the fourth century, refers to the Jews as to "those unclean and savage beasts," and to the Synagogue as to "the house of the devil."

And it was the poor devil, as already mentioned, whose mythological image Judas had assumed in the writings and paintings of Christian theologians as well as artists for close to two millenniums. The devil, the mythological arch symbol of carnal sin, was depicted as the treacherous power with whom Judas had entered into a pact in order to destroy a human, or superhuman nature that was utterly spiritual. That great nature—Jesus—had emerged, according to the Teachers of Contempt—even teachers whose contempt was bearable, like Pope Gregory the Great—from amidst people "who have been faithful only to the letter of the Divine commandment. . . . A people more dedicated to the world than to truth,

---

[1] It is for the same reason that the Communists never admit that the Russian Tsar was actually overthrown by a democratic, humane and liberal movement headed by Kerensky, and that they, the Communists, have actually overthrown not the Tsar, but his democratic overthrowers!

who had but a *fleshy* understanding of the incarnation of God, and refused to see in him anything but a man."

"A material cult," "corrupt priests," "Scribes copying out formulas," "hard-hearted and hypocritical Pharisees," "people who sought to find happiness in silver and gold, in base sensuality, in vain display, dispute and revenge. . . . Their only desires: the enjoyment of riches, pleasure and power." "The Scribes and Pharisees had not the slightest concern for moral and spiritual purity. . . ." "The Pharisees are hypocrites, their religion—a farce. They overload the law of God with countless minutiae and elaborate rites. But underneath, their hearts are full of pride, ambition and malice."

These are just a few excerpts of textbooks of Christian instruction taught to children and adults for centuries and with such a vehement persistence that they inevitably penetrated the main blood stream of Christian thought and became as unquestionable by Christians as the treachery of Judas. The Hebrews who came after Christ and who refused to recognize his divinity were thus put in the same inferior class as those who didn't recognize his divinity in his lifetime [2]—the class of the unredeemed, the blind who didn't see the light as seen by the redeemed Gentiles. Thus a strange, indeed incredible situation was perpetuated before the eyes of God and man for almost twenty sorrow-laden centuries, a situation that can be best described as a theological suppression of history, on one hand, and of truth about the men who are forever a product of that history, on the other. And so it came to pass that one of the most spiritually stormy periods of man—the period leading to the violent Hebrew revolt against Rome—of which the historian Dion Cassius says that "the whole world trembled because of it"—was described, denounced and decried as corrupt. The Hebrew himself, of that or any other age that followed, the spiritual man *par excellence,* whose manner of working thought, when he fully subscribes to it—that is, "rebels against the very idea of a distinction between the secular and the religious aspects of life" (John MacMurray)—was portrayed as the epitome of non-spirituality, as carnality personified. And all this because the Jew,

---

[2] A divinity, by the way, to which Christ himself never laid claim. There was, in fact, a sect of Jewish Christians after Christ's death which regarded him as a prophetic figure or a teacher of righteousness, as the Essenes would have called him.

in the midst of a violently hostile, flagrantly unredeemed world, refused to believe that the redeemer had come already! [3]

We have spoken before about the messianic emergency that gripped Israel prior, during, and after Christ, and we are not going to repeat what we have already said. All we would like to stress now is the fact that that entire period in Hebrew history, covering a span of more than two hundred years, from the revolt of the Maccabees to the destruction of Jerusalem, was marked by a unique and almost universal craving for redemption through *purity*. Suffice it to say that one of the main differences between the Pharisees and Essenes—spiritual Zealots, if there ever were any—was the question of *impurity* and what constitutes it. While the Pharisees maintained (according to Professor David Flusser in his essay on the Essenes) that defiled man (defiled in the Biblical sense) can still be morally pure—the Essenes went so far as to insist that sin defiles the sinner even *physically,* let alone spiritually. There was such an obsession with moral purity amongst the Hebrews, that Greek homosexuality, common even among its great philosophers, would have surely been branded as defiling if only on the account of the apologetic tone of those who promulgated it. But it was this very age—the age of obsessional purity—which the teachers of contempt have branded as "carnal," "material" and "corrupted to the core." [4]

---

[3] It will not be a digression from our main theme if we mention, in this context, the profoundly meaningful, and profoundly tragic case of a good and brilliant Christian priest who, when faced with the horrors of a German concentration camp, began to think in terms of a philosophy which later served as the basis of the so-called "Death of God" movement. What Dietrich Bonhoffer had actually realized in a concentration camp was what the Jews have known, and insisted upon, for close to 2000 years, namely that the world is a terribly unredeemed entity. Because the concentration camp had confirmed this belief, it is, in our opinion, much more difficult to remain a Christian after Auschwitz than a Jew. But that is something else again. To the good, thinking Christian, the discovery of the concentration camp in the midst of Christian Europe was intolerable on theological, let alone moral, grounds. In 1936—the Nazis were already in power, but Auschwitz was not yet in sight—Bonhoffer, still a free man, writes as follows: "By the temptation of Jesus Christ, the temptation of Adam is brought to an end. . . . As in Adam's temptation all flesh fell, so in the temptation of Christ all flesh has been snatched away from the power of Satan. For Christ wore our flesh, he suffered our temptation and he won the victory from it. Thus today we all wear the flesh which in Christ vanquished Satan." How do such words sound *after* Auschwitz?!

[4] Who, then, were the corrupted Jews? "Rome ruled Palestine not only through Pontius Pilatus, but also through a small minority of royalist Jews. These fought amongst themselves for the fat crumbs of position and privilege that their masters threw them." (Nelson Glueck, *The River Jordan*)

And the Zealots—cruel, merciless, unyielding, uncompromising, unforgiving as they were—what corrupt nation on earth has ever produced men like these? What corrupt, carnal nation on earth has ever put up a fight for freedom like that which the Zealots, drowning in their own blood, mastered against the legions of Rome? When Titus, in charge of the Roman forces, exhorts the Zealots to surrender—starving Jerusalem has already paid for the uprising with six hundred thousand lives and is still fighting!—he asks them simply what on earth makes them go on fighting under such conditions. "On what do you rely now?" he asked them according to Josephus, "On your wonderful physique? Yet you know that the Germans are our slaves. On the strength of your walls? What wall could be a better obstacle than the open sea that is the bulwark of Britain? But Britain was brought to her knees by the arms of Rome! On your invincible determination and the wiles of your Generals? Yet you know that even Carthage was overwhelmed!"

And the defeated Hebrews—what kind of men were they? Men are judged not only by the way they fight, but the way they surrender when the fight is lost. The Germans, brave in attack, are cowardly in surrender. No, not so the Hebrews. When the war was lost and the Temple went up in flames, the surviving Zealots, about a thousand of them, retreated to the mighty rock of Masadah on the shores of the Dead Sea, and for three years they held their ground against the elite of the Roman forces—ten thousand of them. When the Romans were finally about to break through the mighty wall, the entire group—men, women, and children—committed suicide. No purer, prouder, deeper words about freedom and the dignity of men facing death were ever spoken than those pronounced by Elieziar Ben Yair, the Commander of Masadah, exhorting his doomed garrison to commit suicide en masse.

But let's return to Judas. Judas, living less than half a century before the destruction of Jerusalem, was, after all, a product of that age of mighty men who faced death with the same determination with which they could cause it when necessary and who didn't see any reason to remain alive when their Messiah was dead or when freedom was dying. This Judas—and let us say it now with all our strength—was vindicated in Auschwitz, and he was vindicated there because Auschwitz has proved to the whole world—or, at least, should prove to the whole world—what Golgotha had proved to Judas, namely, that the *world we live in and all those who dwell therein are still woefully unredeemed*. It has, moreover, proved something which Judas may have never anticipated: Judas knew how mortal the pain can be of having had a savior and lost him. What he didn't know was how much more mortal can be the damage of *not* having lost and renounced in time a "savior" who failed to save! Auschwitz may have been launched by Godless Nazis, but Auschwitz wouldn't have worked if the Godless Nazis hadn't subconsciously consoled themselves in their brutality with the thought that no matter what they do to the Jews, they do it also because the Jews have killed a Christian God in whom they, the Nazis, didn't necessarily have to believe in order to hate in his name. Yes, for the sake of Auschwitz it was convenient for many of them to believe in him—not the other way round!—and, consequently, to accept without reservations all the vicious things which the teachers of contempt have said about the "God-killers," while killing the same God a thousand times over. For what Auschwitz has proven is also that when people who regard themselves as "redeemed," deal with people whom they regard as "unredeemed," they are bound to resort to, or at least tolerate, flagrantly unredeemed deeds and regard such deeds, deep in their hearts, as the punishment for unredemption. And when we say "tolerate" we have in mind the silence of the entire Christian world in the face of Auschwitz. And it is this toleration, more than anything else, which has further proven, in line with Judas' agonized realization, that a faith, no matter how noble, must never be taken by its word. A faith, unless it is put to the test of deeds and *proven* by works, must be regarded as suspect. It may even turn out to be a danger to man's hope for compassion and a menace to whatever is left of his morality. A faith, moreover, which had originally placed itself above works and arbitrarily pinned the label "damned" on a multitude of dissenting souls, can lead to the tacit toleration of murder. For Auschwitz—let's not forget it—was confidently placed by the Nazis not only in the very heart of heartless Catholic Poland, but in the very midst of a Christian world whose silence and indifference, amidst heart-rending professions of faith, was as taken for granted by the Nazis as the perfidy of Judas by the Christians.

Judaism and Christianity had first clashed on the question of works versus faith, the law versus grace. Time and pain may have blunted the edges of this discussion, but the prejudicial powers that were unleashed by the Christian part to this controversy, rooted in the much more crucial question as to whether the Messiah had already come, are still very much at work. The Christian world, even after Auschwitz, and after the terrible moral beating it had taken in World War Two, feels itself kind of cheated—by way of example—by Israel's stunning victory in the six days' war and may still be very active in its future attempts to deprive the brave little nation of the fruits of her victory. Had Israel lost that war, the Christian world—a master of charitable post-mortems—would have shed big tears over its grave—a mass grave to be sure—and would have said how unjust we were to permit the downfall of Israel and how un-Christian was the behavior of the Christian world toward the Jewish State which was permitted to bleed herself white. But since Israel had won that war, and had won it in a manner to cast a grave doubt upon a certain article of Christian faith according to which the Jews cannot be redeemed, and Jerusalem can not be rebuilt, unless they embrace Jesus as their Messiah —the Christian world, its respect for the gallantry of the Israelis nothwithstanding, finds it difficult to swallow the pill of Israel's victory. They would have forgiven the Israelis a tiny little victory, they may have even prayed for a tiny victory, but a victory with Jerusalem as its main price—that was too hard to take! This hardship expressed itself very clearly in the unanimity of the United Nations vote on Jerusalem following the unification by the Israelis of a city which represented the essence of their soul, their hopes, their agonies, their longings and their prayers since David first ruled it as King.

Yes, there is a certain Christian inability to overcome the attitude toward the Jews as to "unredeemed" people, and it is this inability which makes the clash between Christian theology and human morality inevitable. Unless this inability is overcome, a theological dialogue between Christians and Jews on equal moral footing is as good as impossible. But if and when such a dialogue does take place, an inevitable topic of discussion must be this: "In a manifestly, and progressively unredeemed world, can the thought that the redeemer has already come, and that salvation of the soul depends on the confession thereof, be possibly conducive to good deeds?" Or: "In a world marked by evil deeds which seem natural with man, does the promise that redemption is a matter of professed faith conducive to grace, help to make man better or worse?"

The Jewish side, confused as it is, will at least be in a position to add to such a discussion, conducted on a moral as much as a theological platform, a vital third dimension: the dimension of hopelessness leading to hope following an era in which promised Christian hope didn't prevent—or maybe even led to—despair. Let us be more specific: If Auschwitz was tolerated, let alone perpetrated, in a world to which a redeemer had already come—a world which had had already the taste of redemption that is, and which is thus composed of millions of "redeemed" and "saved" souls—there is no hope for humanity but the grave, and it doesn't deserve any better lot either. If, however, this most foul and heinous of all crimes against God and man was perpetrated and tolerated in an admittedly *unsaved* world, and by the hands and minds of admittedly unsaved and unredeemed men—and be these men active murderers or passive onlookers or plain, indifferent "believers"—there is still hope for the long ago promised redemption to come "at the end of the days." The abnormality of the evil, moreover, makes this hoped-for redemption of the future—*provided we dismiss the thought of a redeemer in the past*—theologically, psychologically, ontologically and morally *relevant*. The very hope for redemption coming on the heels of two thousand years of suppressed—and vindicated—Hebrew warnings that no redemption has taken place yet, and that when it *will* take place—*man's very nature will undergo a provable change*—this hope thus becomes a moral necessity as much as a theological inevitability.

If the Messiah has come already and if that's how man looks *after* his coming—there will never *be* a Messiah; if, however, the Messiah hasn't come yet—as we have always insisted—there *is still hope for a Messiah to come.*

If man is saved, he is woefully unsaved; but if he believes he is unsaved, he'll be saved!

Blessed be the unsaved, for they shall save the earth!

Survival for what?

For the spreading of the gospel that the Messiah hasn't come yet!

Chapter Three

"FOUR WHO ENTERED A VINEYARD"

The story in question is of four great men, sages of Israel, pillars of wisdom, who were groping for an ultimate reality, for a final answer to life's riddle, and what happened to them in the course of their search. Few stories in theological literature, if any, are briefer or more meaningful than the one entitled "Four Who Entered a Vineyard." The Talmud tersely relates:

"Four who entered a vineyard . . . Ben Azzai, Ben Zoma, Elisha Ben Abuya and Rabbi Akiba. . . . Said Rabbi Akiba unto them: 'When you reach the place of pure marble stones do not (look at it and) say: 'Water! . . . Water! . . .' (But they did not listen to him). . . . Ben Azzai looked and lost his life; Ben Zoma glanced and lost his mind; Elisha Ben Abuya vandalized the plants . . . Only Rabbi Akiba entered peacefully and left peacefully."

That is the story. It has both baffled and fascinated Hebrew sages and scholars throughout the ages. What kind of "vineyard" was it that the sages of Israel had entered in search for an ultimate meaning? What had Rabbi Akiba warned them against upon entry? What did he mean by "the place of pure marble stones" and what would have induced them, at the sight of such a place, to say "Water! . . . Water! . . ."? What did Ben Azzai see that made him lose his life? What drove Ben Zoma out of his mind? Why did Elisha Ben Abuya "vandalize the plants"? And, finally, how can it be explained that only Rabbi Akiba entered the vineyard peacefully and left it peacefully?

Before attempting to answer this question we must acquaint ourselves, no matter how fleetingly, with the towering personality of Rabbi Akiba. Rabbi Akiba, to use a modern term, rose from spiritual rags to riches. He was a spiritual success—story unsurpassed in Jewish history. He climbed the ladder all the way—from ignorance to genius of heart and mind, and has left behind, for almost two thousand years, traces of a deedful faith as pure and unshakable as the foundations of heaven. Up to his fortieth year, Rabbi Akiba worked as a shepherd for Kalba-Shabua, a wealthy and respectable man in Jerusalem. Not only was Akiba an ignorant man up to that mature age, but his ignorance was aggressive —so aggressive, in fact, that, according to the Talmud, he would say, "hand me a 'Talmid Hacham' "—(which means "a spiritual man," not merely "a learned man")—"and I'll tear him to pieces." It is worthwhile to note, at this point, that in those great eras of Jewish history—the Tanaic and Talmudic eras—there was a consciousness of a spiritual class struggle in Israel and it reached such unsurpassed heights, that the sages permitted themselves to say that "a man who has no knowledge (meaning spiritual knowledge) must not be pitied. . . ." The villain was the ignorant as much, if not more, than the sinner, and the evil of ignorance was stated in unmistakable and merciless terms: "He who doesn't teach his child the knowledge of the sacred law—teaches him banditry." The contemptuous hatred of the ignorant, however, is best expressed in the Talmudic warning against marrying a man for any other reason but his knowledge: "He who marries off his daughter to an ignorant, may as well have bound her and placed her before a lion." It will not be a digression from the Rabbi Akiba subject if we state here that Jewishness begins with contempt for ignorance. The Jew in the ghetto, deprived of rights, of means, of security, of protection, had only one great aspiration: knowledge. There was not enough bread at home, but a child had to acquire knowledge. The acquisition of knowledge was a must, and the poorer a man, the more knowledge was expected from his children. "Watch out for the children of the poor for they will produce knowledge!" But, let us come back to Rabbi Akiba.

It must have been her contempt for the ignorant, and adoration of the knowledgeable, that caused the beautiful daughter of Kalba-Shabua, Akiba's employer, to spurn the advances of the unusually handsome shepherd who fell in love with her. As his love persisted, Rachel made her marrying him contingent upon his acquisition not of wealth or independence, but of knowledge—the knowledge of the Torah. What a spiritual creature—not only a beautiful one—Rachel must have been if she could make the love of the Ultimate exercise in her heart so much power over the Immediate! Rabbi Akiba was swayed by this grandeur and accepted the challenge. After seven years of relentless study he came back to Jerusalem

60

with scores of devoted disciples. But when Rabbi Akiba was told, even before reaching the house of his beloved, of what she had said, namely that she would wait for him another seven years as long as he kept on ascending the scale of perfection—he turned around and, without seeing her, went back to his place of learning. When he finally returned, after seven more years, to marry Rachel, she was the princess of an all-conquering love, and he—the recognized spiritual giant of his generation of Jews and of generations to come.

Rabbi Akiba's inducement to the acquisition of wisdom—a woman—is, theologically speaking, non-Christian or, at least, non-Paulist. In St. Paul's view, this kind of love—the love of a woman —or any other kind of earthly passion, had to be completely eradicated before one could hope to achieve a full realization of the Godly. The Paulist approach, in other words, advocated the suppression of the normal as a condition for the attainment of the supernormal, or the purely spiritual. Rabbi Akiba's story, however, as is the story of Job, presents the opposite view. It is the *Jewish* view, which is based on the *total* affirmation of life, lived unignorantly and daringly to the very brim.

In the cases of both Job and Rabbi Akiba, "normalcy" is underlined. Job, after his ordeal, is restored to success and gives birth to beautiful children. But for Rabbi Akiba, finite human love—the love of a woman—is exalted as the inducement to infinite and ultimate love. This inducement, however, is of a very unusual nature: both Rabbi Akiba and his beloved bride waited for each other fourteen years before they married. We do not know how old Rachel was when she met Akiba, but we do know, since the Talmud tells us, that Rabbi Akiba spent the best years of his life—from forty to fifty-four—preparing himself for two great encounters with his earthly and unearthly loves without seeing a contradiction between them. And not only that he did not see a contradiction between them, but he saw these two loves as completing each other. Thus when he finally returned to Rachel after fourteen years of yearning, and his beloved fell to his feet—something his disciples were trying to prevent—he told them: "Let her do what she wants: mine and yours is hers!"

Ever since I've first read this story—both deeply human and superhuman—of Rabbi Akiba's great love affair with God and with one of His fairest creatures, I could not quite free myself from the thought that had Sören Kierkegaard known the story of Rabbi Akiba—the immortal Dane would finally have found an historic

61

archetype of the man who, as he confesses in *Fear and Trembling,* he had spent a lifetime searching for in vain: "the Knight of Infinite Resignation." Kierkegaard, let us add, was very eager to know the Hebrew sources in their original. I know of no other great man in religious literature who understood almost intuitively that the original Hebrew of the Bible—and only the Hebrew—might provide a clue to its ultimate, and higher, understanding—something which is in line, by the way, with Rabbi Akiba's interpreting every *letter* of the Torah. "This man," Kierkegaard writes in his preface to *Fear and Trembling*—meaning himself—"was not a learned exegete, he knew no Hebrew; perhaps, if he had known Hebrew, he would have easily understood the story of Abraham!" By the same token we might say that had he known the story of Rabbi Akiba, he might have seen before him a Knight of Infinite Resignation personified. Kierkegaard had made repeated attempts to clarify the existentialist meaning of "infinite resignation" (which can also be called "resignation to the infinite"). In trying to explain this much misunderstood term, he resorts, time and again, to the example of love. And a fine example it is! But before we quote from him, let us dwell for a moment on Kierkegaard's dialectical conception of what he calls "infinite resignation":

The highest passion of mankind, according to Kierkegaard, who found himself in a state of constant clash with Christendom, is faith, not love. It is a faith, however, as we shall explain more fully later, which to Kierkegaard meant not a profession of belief—as conducive to grace—he was, if anything, allergic to professions—but a total deedful commitment, growing out of a total and constant spiritual effort. Nothing has a deeper meaning than true, tried faith, for the whole of life and the whole of life's meaning is contained therein—including works, including love. Faith, however, is challenged by life's vicissitudes—by cruelty and misery, by the existence of evil, by ugliness, by sickness, by death—that is why absolute faith cannot possibly sustain itself on its own constantly undermined strength, unless it draws on the source of "resignation." This resignation, however, is not a negative attribute. It has nothing to do with despair, passivity or hopelessness, but with a higher, utterly spiritual, "ontological" state of mind in which faith and infinite resignation become identical. In such a state man, transcending the tragic, reaches out for the heroic, and it is on this exalted plateau that he is able to attain the inner glory which, in Kierkegaard's words, (in *Fear and Trembling*) is "reserved for the Knight who becomes the familiar of God and the friend of the

Lord; one who, to speak humanly, can say 'Thou' to God in heaven, while even the tragic hero may address Him only in the third person."

The thought that one has to go through the tragic before reaching out for the heroic was as typical to Rabbi Akiba as it was to Kierkegaard. Rabbi Akiba, seeking love and loving life, nevertheless regarded suffering as of divine origin and, even, as divinely inspired. Thus when he visits another sage, gravely sick and in pain, he doesn't hesitate to exclaim: "Havivin Yessurim!"—"Suffering is beloved!" Rabbi Akiba, moreover, placed suffering on the same level as learning and regarded its impact on the soul as purifying and uplifting. That, however, doesn't mean that the great sage had in any way a "Christian" attitude to life, that he was obsessed with the fear of the flesh or that he was trying to extinguish in him all earthly desires. Christianity, we all know, in its higher theological expressions, couldn't conceive of saintliness without renunciation. The Christian saints were thus enemies of their flesh. In order to experience the spirit in its totality, so went the argument, the body must be immunized against its "earthliness." The body is the villain. Down with the body!

Not so Judaism, and not so Rabbi Akiba. Rabbi Akiba didn't try to extinguish the passions of the body, but to make them harmonious with the strivings of the soul. He didn't regard earthly love as a ladder that leads down to a cellar, but as stairs leading up to the top of a citadel. The experience of love did not tie him down to the earthly, but lifted him up to the heavenly. Simone Weil, the great, poor Jewish girl—not Jewish soul!—from France who sought refuge from her "vertigo of the infinite" in Christianity (though she hesitated to officially embrace it), was, of course, very Christian when she said that "the bird cannot fly whether it is tied to earth with a chain or with a silk-thread." The point she totally missed here is the definition of "earth" and what constitutes it. If love—not lust—is "earth" just because it engulfs in its marvellous flame bodies and souls alike, then love, of course, is an impediment to grace and, as such, must be regarded as a thread, and be it only a silk thread, which prevents the bird from taking off. But if love, truly and fully experienced, instead of unnaturally and forcefully suppressed, is an uplifter, sharpener and purifier of all human senses and strivings, including the unearthly ones, as Rabbi Akiba must have believed, then the thing that ties it to earth, and which then becomes not a thread but a chain, is not the experience thereof but the sanctimonious branding of this experience as sin. That must have also been the reason why Rabbi Akiba rejected as outrageous the opinion expressed by some overzealous contemporaries that there were doubts in the minds of earlier teachers as to the sanctity of "The Song of Songs." Rabbi Akiba did not regard the metaphor of human love, of man's love for a woman, when used to describe the superhuman, the Godly, as debasing in any way. At the same time, however, he warned against being misled by the metaphor and using the great love song of the pure spirit, so grandly expressed in the "Song of Songs," as a means of shallow entertainment. When love is demoted, it is also vulgarized. The only antidote to vulgarity is spiritual nostalgia. The truly great loves of history bear witness to a grandeur of soul that made the Godly and the poetically nostalgic almost identical.

And it is the Godly when merged with, and enhanced by, the spiritually romantic—not the sentimental—which draws upon the sources of a faith that makes love consequential. In the case of Rabbi Akiba, the experience of the Divine and that of the divinely romantic went hand in hand—a privilege enjoyed by a very few of his kind or any other kind. It went even more hand in hand in moments of grave crisis when affliction tried to shake the foundations of faith. Thus the Talmud relates the unique manner in which Rabbi Akiba behaved when his son was dying. All through the long hours of his son's agony the great man was studying the Law, the Torah, and refused to be interrupted in his studies. He interrupted it only when he was told that his son was dead. "Up to this moment," Rabbi Akiba said to his disciples, "the only thing to do was to study the Law; now it's time to mourn the loss."

What is the relation, one might ask, between the study of the law,—of "the ossified letter of the Law", to use the famous expression of the teachers of contempt—and a loving father's frantic attempts to arouse God's mercy on his dying son? But in this story about Rabbi Akiba, as typical as any in Talmudic literature, the essence of Judaism is hidden like a treasure. Here the Law becomes a prayer. And not just a prayer, not a prayer like any other prayer, but an ecstatic prayer of love and devotion, of strength and supplication, such as only the very great invoke in very critical moments of their lives. Man here is trying to arouse God's mercy not by pleading with Him—anybody can do that—*but by speaking His language,* for the language of God Almighty, so the believing Jews believe, is contained in the study of His law. "Though usually the ways of God are remote from the ways of man," in the words of Franz Rosenzweig, "the way of Israel's God and the

way of His people meet on Mount Sinai, which is ever aflame."
("God and man") In that flame, the flame of the Law, man's
great purifier, God and man draw as close to each other as they
can ever be. It is a flame which both illuminates and elevates
man to a point from where eternity is within sight and an "I–Thou"
relationship becomes not only possible but inevitable. Such a relationship, which is one of intimacy with the Maker, turns the
study of God's Law into an experience of His will. And when
man is in a state of experiencing God's will, his whole being *is*
prayer. Not that he has a prayer to invoke, he is *all* prayer.
Prayer invokes *him*. Every bone in him, every vein, every fiber,
is a string in the violin of eternity. Thus when tragedy strikes, the
thing to do is to face God in purity. And purity is the Law.

That was Rabbi Akiba, rising from the tragic to the heroic on
the mighty wings of the Law which he helped define. But when
even the most potent form of prayer didn't help and the son
died, the thing to do, according to Rabbi Akiba, was "to mourn
the loss". The Knight of faith is overcome by grief, and lets himself be overcome by it. It's not only that to "mourn the dead"
is also a part of the Law, but that *the law of the heart is a part of
the law*! But in Rabbi Akiba's case, the Law of the heart, a heart
made stout by the Law, is a different law and a different heart.
It's not a heart which questions God's ways.

Personal tragedy could not induce a knight of faith like a Rabbi
Akiba to question His ways. Personal tragedy to a Rabbi Akiba
was not the thing that would make God's existence, or His justness, questionable, but something that would only deepen His
unfathomable mystery. And it is only when one keeps his faith
in God while His mystery deepens on account of tragedy that he
becomes a dweller in the house of the Lord "not as a stranger." He
then becomes, in Kierkegaard's above-quoted words "the familiar
of God and the friend of the Lord, one who, to speak humanly,
can say 'Thou' to God in heaven. . . ."

To prove his point, Kierkegaard, as aforementioned, repeatedly
resorts to the example of a love which is fulfilled through the passion of an ideal, the power of which is enhanced precisely by the
remoteness of the reality: "A youth falls in love with a princess
and the whole of his life is bound up with his love, although the
relation is such that it is impossible for it to realize itself or to
translate itself from ideality to reality. . . . The slaves of the
finite and those frogs which inhabit the swamps of life will naturally cry out: 'What a stupid love story! The rich brewer's widow

65

would make just as good a match.' Let those who are in the swamps croak undisturbed. The Knight of Infinite resignation does not follow their advice. He refuses to surrender his love even for all the glory in the world." (*Fear and Trembling*)

When Rachel and Rabbi Akiba decided to wait for each other fourteen years, during which he would attain a state of familiarity with the Torah, there must have been many frogs in the social swamps of Jerusalem who croaked: "How stupid!" Yet, both Rachel and Rabbi Akiba *resigned* themselves to a love which could not have lasted without a final movement toward ideality. There is really no difference between Kierkegaard's fictitious example about the princess and Rabbi Akiba's actual love affair with Rachel which was, for fourteen years, "fictitious." And it takes a Knight as well as a Princess, of Infinite Resignation—pure faith untouched by despair or frustration—to wait fourteen years for the first touch of a finite, human love. For the princess and the Knight of infinite resignation, in their adoration of the infinite, had by no means lost their taste for the finite. On the contrary: "The taste of the finite is as pleasing (to them) as if they had never known anything higher. (They) rejoiced in it with so much assurance that for (them) there appeared to be nothing more certain." (*Fear and Trembling*)

That must have been the nature of the relationship between the equally enjoyed finite and the infinite in the love affair between Rabbi Akiba and Rachel on one hand, and between Rabbi Akiba and his beloved God on the other. And that was also the nature of Rabbi Akiba's life and death. We shall soon discuss his "existentialism"—which we do not hesitate to call Divine—but before we do so, let us mention the way this giant gave up his soul to his Maker. He was apprehended by the Romans, against whom he had revolted in fearless pursuit of freedom for his people, and, along with other "Cedars of Lebanon"—as they were referred to—was put to death. Rabbi Akiba made his final movement of infinite resignation just before the Romans literally skinned him alive. He told his pupils, who had come to part with their great teacher, that he had waited all his life for this hour of sanctification of God's name. He further told them that thrice a day when he would invoke the prayer "And thou shall love the Lord, thy God, with all thy heart, and with all thy soul and with all thy being," he would ask himself: "When shall I have the final opportunity of proving my love of God with all by *being*?" "Now," he concluded, "when I have this opportunity shall I not rejoice?"

Thus spoke an incomparable "witness to the truth," a martyr and saint of Israel who expired with the holy word *"one"*—*"echad"!*

Denis de Rougemont rightly remarked that Kierkegaard's entire career as an author had no other meaning in his eyes than to establish the concept of a "witness to the truth," which is another word for martyrology. Kierkegaard once felt violently outraged when this term was used to describe a man posthumously whose life was blessed with titles, honors, success as a prelate—and worldly goods. Bishop Mynster, the primate of the Danish Church, was a good man, a pious man, a beloved man, but a man whose faith, throughout his lifetime, was routinely Christian—unchallenged that is either by adversity or by "fear and trembling." To call such a man "a witness to the truth," Kierkegaard declared, was to commit a crime of "aggravated lèse Majeste" against the absolute. It was the same as to recognize and sanction usurpation. Professor Martensen, another prelate, who was the one to call Mynster a "witness to the truth" and who later succeeded him, came under Kierkegaard's bitter attack: "A witness to the truth," he said, "is a man whose life, from the beginning to the end, is familiar with every kind of suffering, with inner struggles, with fear and trembling, trepidation, scruples, agony of the soul, torment of the spirit, with all the sufferings the world has known. . . . A witness to the truth is a man who witnesses in penury, in poverty, in abasement and humiliation—a man who is unappreciated, hated, loathed, insulted, outraged, mocked. He is a man who is scourged, tortured, dragged from prison to prison and then finally —for it is indeed about a genuine witness to the truth that Professor Martinsen speaks to us—and then finally crucified, beheaded, tossed by the executioner into some out of the way place, without being buried."

"There you have a witness to the truth, his life and existence, his death and burial—and Bishop Mynster, so Professor Martinsen says, was one of the genuine witnesses to the truth!"

"Verily there is something more contrary to Christianity than heresy or schism—and that is *to play at Christianity,* to brush aside its danger, and then to pretend that Bishop Mynster was a witness to the truth!"

Kierkegaard's rejection of ignorance was so total, that even "success," or non-suffering, seemed to him connected, in some devious way, with not-knowing the truth. He was not satisfied with the "fact" of his being born a "saved" Christian: he felt that in order to be one, in order to be a man of faith, which is much more than being a man of love—for faith compromises love, while love does not always compromise faith—one has to spend his life in preparation thereof and he can do it only through the constant exercise of *deeds*. Kierkegaard did not take his Christianity for granted. He did not believe in the myth of "Christian peoples," or in the saving power of "conversions." He wanted to discover Christian *individuals* whose lives and works are in a constant affirmation of what he regarded as "Christian." The antithesis to this profoundly spiritual attitude is contained in what the Grand Inquisitor is compelled to tell Christ in the previously discussed chapter of Dostoyevsky's *The Brothers Karamazov*: "We are concerned with the masses whose minds crave a disciplined standard of consolation, a spiritual conformity to which they can subscribe, but we cannot achieve this by telling every man that he should be his own church, his own uplifter, as you did!" Kierkegaard's contention, however, was the very opposite: he was convinced that unless man, every individual, is his own church, his own uplifter—religion is a mockery of spiritual truth. Thus a document like "The Grand Inquisitor"—for a document it is!—had it been written before, not long after, Kierkegaard's death, would have only caused the Danish colossus, who did not recoil from constantly attacking the Church, to officially confirm a thought that must have been on his mind all his life: and this thought could best be expressed thus: "In the fight between God and the Church I am on the side of God."

For the side of the Church in Kierkegaard's writings (under the pseudonym "Klimakus") was once expressed by a woman neighbor of his. "How can you doubt, how can you think even for a second that you are not a Christian?" She asks him, "Aren't you a Dane? And didn't we study in geography that the Lutheran Christian religion is the official religion of Denmark? You are not Jewish, after all! What are you then? Idolatry was banished in Denmark hundreds of years ago, and I know you are not an idol-worshipper. Don't you do your work in the office as a good clerk? Aren't you a good subject of the King? Then you are a Christian!"

But Kierkegaard rejected this silly reasoning. Religion to him was, in his own words, like a store that sells very precious things. A large crowd gathers before the store, eager to enter and buy, but the store owner has arranged it in such a way that only a costumer at a time can enter it. So it is with religion the way he saw it: God Almighty is the storekeeper; He sells the most precious merchandise, which is eternity; He bestows it upon individuals because they are individuals, not because they belong to a certain community of "believers," and the currency He accepts in exchange for the merchandise is Faith. And faith, the way Kierkegaard understood it, was something which is bought for deeds, and works, and sighs, and pains, and sorrows, and cannot, therefore, be sold for all the gold in the world. It is the faith that can make one survive, or survivingly succumb, to the supreme test of being "a witness to the truth."

And, as we may realize by now, this chapter is dedicated to one such witness to the truth: Rabbi Akiba. From the moment this spiritual giant stood up to witness the truth of craved wisdom, which was the very same moment he stood up to witness the truth of his craved love, he lived a life of danger. It started out with the danger of acquiring love—love of God—at the price of losing his beloved, or of acquiring his beloved at the price of losing his love. Then, when this danger was overcome through a blessed reunion, other dangers began. Rabbi Akiba, during this long period in his life, had to walk a tight rope that stretched out between the finite and the infinite. At the outset of his dangerous love life—love in all respects—he had to tell himself that even if life and earthly love passed him by in the finite world where his beloved waited for him—his and her faith in the overwhelming worthiness of the infinite would enable them to wait for each other, to dream of each other in love and faith even if they never met again.

The same was true of Rabbi Akiba's other great, nay—greatest love—and we mean, of course, his *dangerous* love of God. Here too, there was not only the realization that there is little consolation for the just in this world, but that justness and sorrow are often inseparable. Rabbi Akiba defined man's visit to this world as a continuously dangerous proposition. When we read the terse, powerful sentences in which he describes life's meaning, we are overcome by a feeling of holy emergency—a feeling that must have characterized the entire life of Rabbi Akiba. "Everything is given on lease, and the net is spread over the entire span of our lives; the store is open for customers, and the shopkeeper sells on credit, and the book is open, and the hand writes, and he who desires to borrow comes and borrows; and the supervisors are always around, and the customer is finally made to pay whether he wants it or not, and the data is there on which to base all accounts, and the judgment is made in truth, and everything readies itself for the banquet."

Another statement dealing with the same subject is even more terse: "Everything is foreseen, and the choice is free, and the world is judged in goodness, and all depends on deeds."

This was Rabbi Akiba. The style—urgent, brief, haunting—was the man. No pessimism, but seriousness; no renunciation, but responsibility; no sadness, but serenity. The main idea behind existence is the divine essence of man. This essence must be felt even more than understood. The carrying of this essence is a challenge which tests and strains every fiber of man's soul and body. It is a difficult proposition, as is existence in general, but all leads somewhere. "Everything readies itself for the banquet." And the banquet, of course, is the final stage of redemption, the messianic age. Life, moving inexorably toward this blissful goal, has to be accorded the treatment one would give to a poor man who is going to get rich. And how should the real poor man be treated? Rabbi Akiba's ethical convictions are as clear, and as pure, as his religious, "Like a free man who *was* rich and has lost his possessions."

With the treasure of such convictions safely stored in the chambers of his heart, Rabbi Akiba was ready to go into what Saint Paul might have called "the terrible night of contemplation." Rabbi Akiba's friends, Ben Azzai, Ben Zoma, Elisha Ben Abuya, swept by the spiritual torments typical to "tragic heroes," as Kierkegaard would have called them, present him both with the great doubt and with the fear thereof, and demand clarity. Neither of the three had reached the high state of resignation to the infinite that was typical of Rabbi Akiba, for they were still devoured by the questions of "why?" and "how?" and "until when?" Rabbi Akiba, however, the Knight of Faith, was already above and beyond these questions. He resisted the temptation of "reason," avoided its trap, and rejected its claim to be the sole judge of man's life and thought. He subscribed wholeheartedly, as he must have done, to that famous axiom attributed to Rabbi Eliezer the son of Hyrcanos, "Don't over expose your children to 'Logic' "—an axiom which precedes another, at least as important, and consequential: "And make them dwell among men of wisdom." For the wisdom of the "Talmid Hacham" transcends logic and knows the barrier which logic cannot cross. The wisdom of the "Talmid Hacham," the wise man, the sage, is distinguished precisely by its knowing that there are certain things which we cannot, we must not, know, for these are things the data of which is unobtainable here below. To obtain such data one has to wait, in love and in deeds and in faith, for an encounter with the infinite. Rabbi Akiba, having waited fourteen years for his beloved, had learned the great art of resigning oneself to the holy thought that a love endlessly craved is a love partly realized and that the beautiful expectation is in itself an act of experiencing beauty. During these years he must have experienced, in Kirekegaard's words, "the voluptuous pleasure in allowing love to run shuddering through his veins, yet his soul remained as solemn as the soul of a man who had drained the cup of poison and feels the liquid mingling with his blood. . . " It was this experience, moreover, which enabled Rabbi Akiba to feel a similar sensation, only infinitely more profound, toward God. In his love of God, in his love of wisdom, in his love of faith and in his love of love he knew no compromises. "He plunged deeply into it and did not lack the courage to attempt anything and risk all." (Kierkegaard)

This was the state of Rabbi Akiba's mind and heart when, along with his three great colleagues, he had entered the Vineyard, as the Talmud says, "peacefully" and had left it the same way. What kind of "peace" was it, however? Kierkegaard, in his inimitable fashion, defines for us the meaning of the peace that comes to the Knight of Faith as follows: "In infinite resignation there is peace and rest; everyone who desires it, who has not humiliated himself by looking down upon himself, which is even more terrible than being too proud, can discipline himself to make this movement, which, in its pain and suffering, reconciles one with life. Infinite resignation is like the shirt in the fable: the thread is spun with tears and sewn with tears, but, afterwards, it is better armour than iron or steel. . . . The one imperfection in the fable is that a third person could weave the linen; the secret of life (however), is that everyone must sew it for himself, and the curious thing is that a man can sew it as well as a woman."

In the case of Rabbi Akiba, both he and his beloved sewed their own linen for themselves, and each separate piece turned out to be "a better armour than iron or steel." And it turned out to be so because for a woman, even more than for a man, it is almost unimaginable to wait fourteen years for the craved touch of the beloved without tears and pain and sorrow and despair. But the cloth of love that was spun with the threads of suffering, and waiting, and yearning, and praying, indeed proved as irresistible as armour. And it was the very same armour, turned into another direction, which enabled Rabbi Akiba to enter and leave the terrible Vineyard peacefully.

"Four who entered a Vineyard . . . Ben Azzai, Ben Zoma,

Elisha Ben Abuya and Rabbi Akiba. . . . Said Rabbi Akiba unto them: 'When you reach the place of pure marble stones don't shout: Water! . . . Water! . . .'"

What does this mean? The four sages, we realize by now, had entered the "Vineyard of Wisdom," which is another, much more tender expression for what Saint Paul calls "The Terrible Night of Contemplation." The "Vineyard," we imagine, spreading over areas as vast as the universe, was marvellous and terrifying to behold. Its branches were loaded with the dark grapes of wrath as well as of luminous love, with fruits of clairvoyance as well as of stupefaction. . . . The tree tops, drinking the waters from above, were proudly piercing the clouds, while the plants, blossoms of eternity, had their roots wetted by the deep dark waters from below. But between the waters from above and those from below, which irrigated and fructified this endless area, there were stretches which deceptively looked like water, but were not. These were isolated areas which had all the polish, glitter and sparkle of wavy waters, but were only immense, polished, darkly scintillating blocks of marble stones. So Rabbi Akiba sounded a warning. "Brethren," he said, "I know how thirsty you will become in the course of exploring this endless region, and how great will be your need for water to quench your thirst, so I want you to make sure, before you take any plunge, that what you see is really water, not marble stones that look like it. If, God forbid, you fail to distinguish between the two, you may spell your own doom. I must warn you, furthermore, that the temptation which the marble stones present is very great and that more than one fine swimmer, mistaking its wavy polish for water, has broken his neck on it. Remember that!" So the three sages turned to Rabbi Akiba and asked for an explanation. The Master answered, or must have answered, as follows: "The waters I am referring to, my friends, those which look like waters I mean, but are nothing but deceptively polished marble, are precisely the waters we feel we must brave at any price if we are to reach a heaven of certainty in this world. But these waters, I warn you, are the forbidden marbles of the great, dark questions which we cannot and, therefore, we must not try to answer. If we do try to answer questions whose data is simply unobtainable in this world, we are guilty of lying before God and man. The unobtainable data, oh, brethren, is the infinite, and he who is deceived by the glittering reason of his finite mind into believing that he can understand the infinite with the finite means at his disposal, works deceit. It is about this deceit that the Psalmist talks to us when he says, 'he that worketh deceit shall not dwell within my house.' Let's therefore not try out our rational ability to swim on the superrational zone of pure marble stone that may look like water. You know exactly what I am referring to. . . ."

"The origin of evil." Elisha Ben Abuya said tersely. "That's the most important question of them all."

"It is." Rabbi Akiba answered. "But if you walk the great vineyard and you reach the marble of this question, you must have the strength to circumvent it."

Elisha Ben Abuya disagreed. "The great vineyard," he said, "is not interspersed with, but undermined *by* the marble of these questions, and we know what these questions are: if God is the Prime and Only Cause of the creative cosmic movement; if whatever lives and exists and breathes—lives, exists and breathes through Him, in Him and because of Him—then the deeds of all individuals are only occasional incidents to God's will. And if their deeds are only occasional to God's will, men are not autonomous in what they do. But if that *is* so, if we are not autonomous in our so-called 'free will,' then our spiritual and intellectual light is a way of cognition implanted in us by the Supreme Power. Consequently, whatever picture we may perceive of Him, or the not-Him, comes from Him, and if that is so, God Himself is the source and reason of all conscious and unconscious sin, evil and ugliness in the world. And if God is both the prime source of sin as well as the prime cause of its pursuit, then there is no such thing as human responsibility before God, and there is no free choice either. For if our choice between good and evil is free, we must conclude, against everything we were taught, that God, if He really exists—His non-existence, I admit, opens as many questions as His existence—has made Himself absent from the most important areas of our lives where His presence is most vital. And, which is even more grave, He has made Himself absent from these vital areas without seeing to it that we are ready and equipped to face the issues by ourselves. In either case the question is as hard as black marble."

"It is," Rabbi Akiba answered. "And while I may not agree with the harsh way you phrased the question, I agree that the origin of evil is the largest block of insurmountable marble in the seas of God. What I say, however, is that at a certain stage of our braving God's seas we know intuitively and revelatorily that there *is* an explanation for everything, only that the human mind is too small to grasp it."

"If the human mind is too small to grasp the explanation," Ben

Zoma asked, "why did *He* make it large enough to pose the question?"

"It is not that He had made it large enough to pose the question," Rabbi Akiba replied. "Not all minds pose the question. But the very posing of the question makes it large enough to seek an answer, and the seeking itself is a way of cognition. The answer, however, cannot be found here below, and let's get used to the idea before we go any further."

"What you preach, in other words, is resignation." Elisha Ben Abuya exclaimed.

"No." Rabbi Akiba answered. "What I preach is faith—a faith made so strong through deeds and works that the resignation to the Ultimate is the ultimate in consolation."

"Life, in other words," Ben Azzai asked, "is bound to be meaningless in rational terms?"

"The superrational," Rabbi Akiba replied, "includes the rational, but the rational is that which not only doesn't include the superrational, but often rejects it. That is why I say unto you that if life is not meaningless in superrational terms—and these are the only terms that ultimately count—life isn't meaningless even in rational terms. The difficulty, therefore, is not in enduring the meaninglessness of life—for life *isn't* meaningless!—but in bearing our incapacity to grasp its meaningfulness. And only the man of faith can bear it. The marble stones, my friends, which look like water, and which we must not, we *cannot* brave, symbolize this incapacity. Man is made deeper, stronger and better by realizing it. Let us therefore resign ourselves to the thought that at a certain point in the endless vineyard of wisdom there are waters which are nothing but marble."

"And when, oh, when will the marble turn into water?" Ben Zoma asked.

"At the end of days." Rabbi Akiba answered confidently. "When the Prophecy will be fulfilled 'and the earth shall be full of the wisdom of the Lord like the waters that fill the sea.' We have seen the fufillment, to the letter, of dark prophecies, and we shall see—we or our children's children—the fulfillment of the good ones."

So they all entered, and what transpired in the course of their agonizing exploration we all know. Crazed as they were by the thirst that seized them under the intense heat of the fiery craving for answers, they saw the polished marble stones and they shouted: "Water!" "Water!" One of them, Ben Azzai, dived and died; another, Ben Zoma, as crazed by the same thirst, went out of his mind; the third, Ben Abuya, revolted against the Vineyard, and, in his fury, vandalized its plants. "If it's in the nature of God to tolerate evil for reasons that are beyond me," he must have exclaimed, "I shall not tolerate the God that tolerates it unless I know the reason." Only Rabbi Akiba, the Knight of Infinite Resignation, the Prince of Faith, the Master of Love, the beloved of God, the Giant-killer of ignorance, entered peacefully and left peacefully.

That was, to be sure, a "terrible night of contemplation." The Christian saints, always more occupied with sin than with evil, emerged from it with completely deadened desires of the flesh, and they were "at peace." But can one also emerge from such a night with completely deadened sorrows of the spirit—sorrows caused by general evil, not necessarily by personal sin? Never! The preoccupation with sin is a matter of man's holy egotism. The preoccupation with evil, however, is a matter of his holy altruism. And suppose one emerges sinless after his terrible night of contemplation—does it mean that he is, that he has the right to be, less preoccupied with evil? "The terrible night of contemplation," in other words, can answer the question of sin by mercilessly extinguishing the fire of lust in the body, but can, or may, such a night also extinguish the dread preoccupation with the existence of evil in the mind of him who is free of sin? Can such a night ever answer questions of both an immediate and ultimate nature such as "If there is a God—why did my child die? What wrong did he do? And if he had to die so soon—why was he born in the first place?" Or, to come back to our terribly "enlightened" age, "how can you reconcile Auschwitz with the existence of a God, let alone a Loving Father in Heaven?" To these questions no answer is possible, not only because if an answer *were* possible, God would first have to be reduced to our size and thus become an explicable, provable, defined Deity, which is another word for a *finished* Deity ("A defined God is a finished God") but also because it is *the very unanswerability of these questions which turns faith into a mounting and endless spiritual challenge and expands the mind, in the words of Nikos Kazantzakis, "to a point of cracking."*

Faith—grand faith which nourishes itself on deeds—is the triumph of the spiritually remote over the physically likely, and it is this "remoteness" which moulded the souls of whatever was great, beautiful and enduring in man. It is, in other words, the very realization of our inability to understand God which makes our thirsting for Him both creative and unquenchable. And what would man's soul, or whatever is left thereof, be without this thirst? Alfred North Whitehead defined the nature of this thirst very exactly when he said (in *What is Religion?*) that "to be in the service of God is not a security-precaution of any kind, but an adventure of the spirit, a flight into the inconceivable." And it is in the spirit of this terrifying adventure that we must understand what Kierkegaard meant when he said that faith—not confessional, ritualistic faith, but one which is painfully achieved—much more than love, is man's greatest passion. Love can be easy, as easy as the pocket-God of Love with whom a thousand preachers are playing around as with a little toy, but faith, real deedful faith, as the highest-altitude flight into the inconceivable, connotes works, often dangerous works, fear and trembling, and above all, a very stormy takeoff. This kind of faith arms one for a battle when all the odds are against him, and though he may step into this battle as on air, it is this Faith, as Whittier expressed himself, which provides him with a rock under his feet. It is the rock which enables spiritual faith to triumph over the *physical* fact. And that is precisely what God, and man, and life, and death are all about. Take away the grandeur of soul that makes such a spiritual triumph possible, and man is a reasoning animal. Take away the adversity that makes faith possible, and man is a coward. Take away the danger that makes faith necessary, and man is a weakling. Take away the deeds that lead to real faith, and man is a hypocrite. And what did Garibaldi speak of if not faith when he promised his handful of warriors, fighting for a just cause—faith in an unjust cause, when we know it is unjust, is in the long run unthinkable!—misery and hunger and starvation and death? And what was it if not Faith—ennobling, uplifting, dangerous, manly faith—which Churchill infused into his embattled Island when he had promised its bleeding people "nothing but blood, toil, tears and sweat"? The non-spiritual man rejects the belief in a God by pointing to the fact of evil in this world. The spiritual man, by contrast, the man of faith that is, realizes not only that it is precisely this evil which makes faith relevant, by its lessening the power of evil, but that it is this faith through works which makes *God real*. The very same question, in other words, which stops the physical man from ever trying to cross the bridge that leads to what St. Augustine called "the City of God," causes the Knight of Infinite Contemplation to cross all bridges and stop short only at the last one which, with all other bridges crossed, appears to him more of a promise than a threat. That, it seems, was the state in which Rabbi Akiba found himself upon entering, and leaving, the Vineyard of Wisdom—a state which is faith's final goal and which is expressed in one word: "peace." It is conditioned upon the final realization that "the meaning of this world is of necessity beyond it." (Wittgenstein). And so it is: our inability to obtain the data for God in this world is the ignorant's excuse; the rationalist's conceit; the searcher's despair; the believer's heartbreak; and the saint's and hero's holy resignation!

To painfully, solemnly and resignedly accept the thought that there is something we can never know, something we must forever remain ignorant of, is precisely *not* to remain ignorant of all the other things—and they are as many as the stars and as vast as the seas—that *lead up* to this realization.

The story of Rabbi Akiba is the great Hebrew warning against ignorance. It is, at the same time, the dramatization of the credo that even people who, for many years and many reasons, were reduced to a state of total de-spiritualization—as was the case with Rabbi Akiba before he had met Rachel—even such people can reach out for wisdom, acquire it, master it, and become Princes in their house and in the house of their people. Rabbi Akiba—and we must not tire of mentioning it—was up to the age of forty a "convinced," aggressive ignorant—for ignorance, at a certain "mature" stage can be very aggressive. Then, when Rachel persuaded him to embark upon the long journey to the seas of God, he knew, for she must have told him, that this was not only a spiritual caprice, but a human must. He knew, moreover, for she must have told him, that according to Hebrew teachings, to acquire knowledge was not a right or a privilege, but a duty, and that this duty applied to everybody. Everybody must acquire knowledge as everybody must acquire freedom. If, as a result of the acquisition of knowledge, there is a desire to enter the Vineyard—let them; if, as the result of entering the Vineyard there is an urge to vandalize the plants—never mind. Rabbi Meir remained a pupil of the man, Elisha Ben Abuya, even after he had vandalized the plants. Of course, Rabbi Meir knew to "throw away the peeling" of the pomegranate and "eat its contents," and that is precisely what freedom of choice is all about: to know the difference between the peeling and the contents although they may look alike. But to reach this stage one must do away with ignorance. An ignorant is incapable of making choices for while he doesn't really know the alternatives he pretends that he knows them. That is why the ignorant was regarded by the sages as a villain. The real antithesis, the real answer to the Grand Inquisitor's painful plea for the continuous toleration of ignorant piety is contained in a brief Talmudic sentence which pronounces a clear, unalterable verdict: "No ignorant can ever *be* pious."

The Hebrew Sages rejected the piety of the ignorants as much as the impiety of the Epicureans. Wisdom, in their belief, equally eluded the ignorant and the epicurean. Wisdom is acquired through purity, and purity is neither contingent upon a denial of life nor is it limited to the few elect. It was Rabbi Akiba, again, who spoke to his people as a whole when he exclaimed: "How fortunate you are, children of Israel! . . . Before Whom do you purify yourself and Who purifies *you!* . . ."

For the children of Israel as a whole were those of whom the Prophet spoke in God's name and promised that "you will be unto me a nation of Priests, a holy people." And not only a nation of Priests, but, hopefully, of Prophets: "Would to God that all of the Lord's people were Prophets!" (Moses)

Survival for what?

For the sake of the Vineyard which the Hebrew Genius introduced into human thought and made relevant to a higher breed of men—be it as a hope, as a challenge, as a promise, as a ground or even as an abyss.

Chapter Four

A MIDWINTER-NIGHT'S DREAM

On a summer morning of 1938, the British in the Holy City of Jerusalem rounded up two scores or so of Jewish citizens, suspected of belonging to the "Irgun" underground movement, and threw them into prison.

This author was one of the detainees.

The "Kishle" prison was an old Turkish fortress whose walls, like those of the old city of Jerusalem, in the midst of which it was located, were as thick and as dark as rocks of eternity and whose bars—as heavy and rusty as unearthed underground water pipes. Its stone floors were uneven, low and damp, and they were covered, from wall to wall, with thatch mattresses which reeked like a cellar overstocked with rotten potatoes. The ceiling was high and rounded like a cupola, but its heavy paint, of a nondescript color, or whatever it was that covered it, was peeling in a morbidly repulsive way and it looked like human skin after boiling oil was poured on it. The smell inside was sickening—as sickening as the faces of the inmates who confronted us—murderers, rapists, arsonists, thieves, robbers—whose company, we knew, we were going to share for the duration of our detention, the length of which was unknown to us for we were detained under a special law for the *prevention* of political crimes. Those criminals, all Arabs as we were told, received us, the Jews, who, as they must have found out even before our arrival, were committed to Jewish statehood in a country which they regarded as theirs, with a chilling cry of hatred. For the entire first day they didn't stop laughing, shouting, cursing and threatening us, using a wildly obscene oriental language, accompanied by gestures lewd enough to make the gutter dry up in shame. Only with sunset there came an intermezzo in the noxious terror, when most of the criminals, on the loud urging of an old detainee, knelt to the ground in prayer, their foreheads touching the floor. It was the Moslem evening prayer faithfully executed by

79

the inmates as an intermission between the wild orgies of hatred which were as ugly as the face of the man who was in charge of it all—obscenities and prayers alike. He was an old, but powerfully built, blind Arab from Hebron who, as we found out later, was serving a ten-year sentence for having raped his twelve-year-old granddaughter. . . . Just to look at him and at his eyes—putrified wounds forced open—was enough to make one lose his desire to eat or sleep or even think orderly for days and nights in a stretch. We thought that the blind Arab—ugly horror personified—was also horror's climax, but we were wrong. As the lights went out in the prison, and the redheaded British sergeant ordered us to sleep, our Arab roommates, outnumbering us six to one, found a unique and inimitable way to increase the terror without running the danger of being caught in causing trouble. Suddenly, as if by a coordinated, well-rehearsed plan, they began to spit—yes, to spit —as we could tell or notice in the darkness—upwards! And what a spitting it was! It was a spitting that sounded like the staccato of machine gun fire from a distance, and it came from all over. The threat it presented to us, though not as deadly as bullets, was as numbing. The floors being covered from wall to wall with humans stretched out over mattresses, it seemed certain that no matter *where* the spit would fall it was bound to hit someone. Never having experienced anything of the kind before, we stretched the damp, smelly blankets over our heads, hoping that the nauseating barrage would inevitably subside when the reserves of saliva ran dry. But it was only close to midnight when the "attack" finally died down along with the mocking laughter which accompanied it—only to be replaced soon by an inhuman snoring. The entire atmosphere, even when our neighbors were fast asleep, was beastly. The utterly dehumanized nature of those unfortunates assumed a dreadfully concrete form even when completely divorced from consciousness and it seemed to be hanging in the air like the pieces of skinlike paint on the ceiling. The beast came out unashamedly from its flimsy human cavern and, hungrily feeding itself on the marrow of our sensitivities, had a ball. We saw and felt this beast and this ball as we did the nausea, the dread, the smell, the hatred, the evil. . . .

It goes without saying that we didn't sleep all night—but neither did we speak. Only when the first rays of light broke through the prison bars to announce to the Kishle dwellers the coming of day, did I carefully pull myself up against the wall in the corner and look astoundedly around. The first thing I noticed, not without relief, was the visible target of the liquid missiles that the criminals had unleashed in the invisibility of the now expired night: the ceiling! Our Arab neighbors, it seemed clear, were excellent high-altitude shots. . . . But no more of that.

As I leaned against the wall that morning hour at the Kishle, watching the faces of the sleeping criminals, more grotesquely inhuman asleep than when they were awake, contemplating the nature of man and what happens to him when he loses his Godly image, I was startled by the whispering voice of my venerable neighbor and old, good friend, Dr. Abraham Ben Adam: "What a lesson, eh?"

"A lesson in what?"

"In hope!"

I looked at him. He slowly drew up against the wall, his arm touching mine. He looked wistfully outside, toward the sunlit bars, and was silent for a while, immersed in deep thought. Dr. Ben Adam was a Russian-born, tall, bearded, deeply religious man in his middle sixties who was famous for his phenomenal memory and who combined the successful practice of law with a relentless study of what he would refer to as "the metaphysical sources of the Mosaic Law." At the same time he was an ardent follower and highly respected leader of the militant Zionist Revisionist movement which advocated the establishment of a Jewish State in Palestine without delay. Dr. Ben Adam, as all those who shared his views, regarded this statehood as a matter of life and death for the Jews. Hitler had already swallowed up Austria and was about to annex Czechoslovakia. Jews were escaping from Germany and from other threatened territories, but didn't have any place to go. A comparatively few were permitted by the British to enter Palestine while the number of the so-called "illegals" increased by the day—both those who were caught and sent back to Europe and those who managed to run the blockade and remain. The Arabs in Palestine, at the same time, were engaged in a little war of their own—attacking Jewish lines of communication on the highways and byways; opening fire at night on Jewish settlements and, very often, shooting at random Jewish men, women, and children. The "Irgun" underground organization retaliated, and the tension in the Holy Land was growing by the day. Some people among the Jews—there were less than five hundred thousand Jews in Palestine and about a million Arabs—spoke of revolt—a double revolt, that is: a revolt against the revolting Arabs, on the one hand, and against the British rule on the other.

Others—the majority—advocated resistance without bloodshed; others, still, spoke of self-restraint. The air in the land was explosive, so explosive, in fact, that even the outburst of hatred which welcomed us at the Kishle prison would have been regarded by us as normal under the circumstances if not for its outright abhorrence on esthetic—not political—grounds. Still, even the terror of our first day and night at the Kishle couldn't completely deaden the inner excitement that seized us at the relieving thought that while our neighbors were confined to these ugly walls because of evil deeds they had done, we were confined to them because of determination, for which one didn't necessarily have to be a "terrorist," to do away with an evil. . . . The evil, however, which manifested itself that night at the Kishle, was of such a totally *discouraging* nature that I was somehow startled by my much older friend's strange statement about a "lesson in hope."

"Yes," he went on after a while, "a lesson in hope. . . . There is a Talmudic story, whose exact wording I do not recall, about sages of Israel, among them Rabbi Akiba, who saw foxes roaming the ruins of the holy temple in Jerusalem. The sight made them cry, while Rabbi Akiba laughed.

" 'Why are you crying?' Rabbi Akiba asked. 'How shall we not cry,' they answered, 'when we see beasts roaming the ruins of God's house. But why do *you* laugh?' 'I laugh,' the Great Sage answered, 'because this destruction, as, indeed, the foxes grazing over it, were foretold by the prophets. So I feel confident that if the prophecy about the ruins and the foxes was fulfilled, the prophecy about the ultimate redemption of Israel will also be fulfilled.' "

"I see," I said.

"Not yet," Dr. Ben Adam went on in his own confidently patient manner which would often make me laugh, "for I am only at the beginning of my argument. What I am trying to say is that, contrary to the opinion of many thinking people, philosophers and laymen alike, I am convinced that the existence of evil actually *proves* the existence of an ultimate good."

"I don't know about that," I interjected sceptically. "To me it is as difficult to believe that God exists with all this evil in the world as it is difficult to believe that he doesn't exist with all this law and order in the universe."

"That is well put," Dr. Ben Adam commented, "but what I claim is that evil actually testifies to the existence of God, and the more unnatural the evil, the more valid the testimony."

"I wish I could see it that way."

"Look here," Dr. Ben Adam said animatedly. " 'Homo homini lupus est' ('man to man is a wolf') is a lie, as are many other proverbs, for wolves don't devour their own kind, nor do dogs, or lions or foxes. But men do. This in itself is unnatural, an unnaturalness which testifies to the lack of something that must be in man, that should be there, that could be there, but isn't for some good reason. Isn't it true that yesterday, when these miserable creatures unlashed that barrage of hatred against us here, more than they frightened us, we pitied them?"

"It is!"

"And we pitied them because we felt that they were lacking something without which they can neither endure nor triumph, and I don't mean 'they' as Arabs. It isn't their being Arabs that made them look evil in our eyes. I know Arab noblemen who, unfortunately, regard us as enemies and whom I desperately try to turn into friends. What I mean is that evil as such, precisely because it is so beastly and ugly, makes its opposite, which is God, look not only dreadfully necessary but marvelously real. Without God as its opposite, ugliness couldn't have been so ugly. And it is the very sight of ugliness—which fills us with horror—that also fills us with relief. I read somewhere about the reaction of a noble French lady during the revolution to a villainous judge who condemned her to die on the guillotine. As she looked at him when the death sentence was pronounced, she whispered: "Thank God he is so ugly!" There is something beautiful about these words. Beautiful! If the judge who condemned this innocent woman to death were not ugly—if he were a refined, well-mannered, scholarly, clean-cut gentleman—the pain of the evil judgement he pronounced would have been twice as great. Do you understand?"

"I do," I said. "I only wonder whether people about to be overcome by evil—consumed by it, I mean—can find consolation in this thought."

"Depends on the people," he answered. "When the spiritual in life *and* death is not grasped as an ultimate reality, evil is bound to look like a victor."

"But it depends on what you call 'spiritual,' " I remarked. "Yesterday, for example, with sunset, the criminals here knelt down in prayer. Some people may call that spiritual, too."

Dr. Ben Adam regarded me sullenly. *"That,"* he said, "was the *ultimate* in ugliness, for it was the ultimate in blasphemy. Iniquity may irritate God, but vulgarity curses Him. And there is a law, a Jewish law, coined by our sages, which says that 'the ignoramus

cannot be pious, nor can the vulgarian fear sin.' Vulgarity, ignorance and evil go inseparably together. I have never seen yet a wise
man who is evil."

"How about the Germans?" I asked.

"The Germans," he answered, "with a few great exceptions,
were never wise. Clever—yes; knowledgeable—definitely; intelligent
—of course. Even mystical, very mystical, in fact. But never, never
wise. A truly wise man—and there are very few such men in
the world—is a man with a *transparent soul*. Do you know what I
mean? If transparent evil, which is soullessness, testifies to the
existence of its opposite—God—how much more so the transparent soul? There are human personalities in the world in which
God's countenance shines so brightly that all doubts as to the
existence of a *personal* God—and if God isn't personal, He isn't
God—disappear. These are men—and they are terribly few—
whose external appearance alone is enough to convince us of the
ultimate truth of their sayings. That's what the Psalmist meant
when he said 'and the wise will shine like the lustre of heaven.'
That's also why the faces we see here, like the words we hear, the
snoring, the laughing, are so dreadfully subhuman. At the basis of
all subhumanity and ugliness lies ignorance, spiritual ignorance,
that is. A man can be a college graduate and still be a spiritual ignorant. He can, moreover, be 'religious' and be a spiritual ignorant. A religion which is mechanical and thus disconnected
from the constant search in the depth of the mystery which is in
and around us and which alone is conducive to the transcendence
and transparence of one's soul, is a spiritually ignorant religion
and is as meaningless as a spiritually ignorant non-religion—if not
more." "Our sages, by the way," he added, "and this is as significant as it is typical, regarded ignorance as an evil, much more than
a misfortune."

"Where do you take *that* from?" I asked.

At this moment our neighbors began to awaken, and the evil
chorus was starting all over again. We kept quiet till we were led
out for a brief walk in the courtyard, and it was there and then that
we took the decision to inform the British sergeant that unless the
Arabs were made to shut up, we would declare a hunger strike
forthwith and would not stop it till we were removed to another
place. The warning helped, and the sergeant, through his interpre-
ter, and Arab policeman, soon warned aloud the Arab detainees that
any mischief whatsoever would be punished by solitary confinement.

The same afternoon, Dr. Ben Adam and myself continued the

84

discussion in a corner of the prison. "I spoke of ignorance," he began, "and I said that our sages treated ignorance as if it were an evil. It is remarkable—I almost said, wonderful—how harshly, indeed mercilessly, our sages treated the evil of ignorance. They went so far as to say that 'He who has no knowledge doesn't deserve any pity.' Just like that! There was pity for the sinner, even the evil doer, but no, not for the ignorant! Ignorance, and we speak, of course, of arrogant spiritual ignorance, was regarded as the thing which, when it prevails, makes the ascendance of evil almost consequential. Ignorance of the law, of the Torah, in other words, is not a byway to a vacuum, but a highway to lawlessness. Thus the great warning of the sages that ignorance is the reason of all the evils that befall men. Evil being an active part of man from his inception, it lies in wait to fill the vacuum left by its inactive counterpart. 'Others gain authority over you if you possess a will distinct from God's will,' says Rabbi Nachman of Bratzlav. The human soul, in other words, doesn't know voids. If it isn't filled with God, it is automatically filled with Satan, no matter what form he assumes—the form of hatred, of cruelty, of avarice, of pride, of ostentatiousness, of conceit. That is why I would say that the Hebrew thought regards the acquisition of spiritual training as a commandment aimed at compelling one to make choices out of knowledge. 'Thou must know!' is the unwritten eleventh commandment. And the wonderful thing about this knowledge is that when you put your heart to it, something happens to your heart which is distinctly supernatural and for which there is no other word but elevation. Not that you feel elevated when you study about matters concerning *elevation*—that would have been natural —but you feel elevated even when you study about matters relating to *defilements*. That's the marvellous thing about the study of the law which no outsider to it will ever understand. This to me is also the supernatural source of the Mosaic law; and the Mosaic law, my friend, unless one *feels* its supernatural source and force, is a dead, meaningless letter, attributable—as it is by some—to hygienic, social and other conditions that prevailed in those days."

There was a pause and then I said, "I have a question on my mind, Dr. Ben Adam. You are a student of the law—both the law of the land and the law of Moses, and, at the same time, a fighter for Jewish statehood. When you speak of the law of Moses you speak about it as if it were a foregone conclusion that when Israel will be a free nation in this promised land, the law of Moses will be the law of the land. Yet, you will agree, I am sure, that even for the sake of religion itself, we don't want Israel to be a theocracy, or do we?"

"No, we don't!" Dr. Ben Adam exclaimed. "But let's understand what we mean by the 'Law of Moses.' It consists as we know, of two parts: that which concerns the relationship between man and God, and that which concerns the relationship between man and man. Contrary to Christianity, which is totally lacking a social side, Judaism regards its social side as the basis of the *entire* law, even that which concerns the relationship between man and God. One cannot sin against a fellow man for example, and ask God for forgiveness—something which is an inherent trait in Christianity. Sin against man can only be forgiven by the man against whom you have sinned, you know that. Thus Yom Kippur is a day that atones for the sins between man and God, not between man and man. When the great Hillel declared that 'and thou shall love thy neighbor as thyself' is the whole law and that all the rest is commentary—he actually stated, in unmistakable terms, that spiritual man who reaches out for God, cannot reach Him but through a constant concern for man. Social Judaism, in other words, is the *basis* for spiritual Judaism, but it is utterly worthless unless it regards spirituality as its sole criterion."

"This," I said, "is hardly preached by the Rabbis from the pulpits."

"It surely isn't," Dr. Ben Aram replied. "That is why the spiritual crisis in Jewry is so grave and getting graver. Our spiritual leaders have become self-appointed intermediaries between man and God at a time when man, in order to reach out for God, needs badly someone who would enable him to first reach out for himself, to intermediate between himself and himself—that is, or between himself and another self who is also looking for his own self but in the wrong direction. Judaism came to tell man how to turn a social search into a spiritual venture; how to bestow upon matters of an immediate nature the grandeur of an ultimate meaning; how to use the 'acceptance of the discipline of the Kingdom of heaven' as a means to improve the kingdom of the earth—a kingdom, by the way, whose final aim is to bring the Kingdom of Heaven down to earth—not the other way around—which is the final messianic state of mankind. What I am trying to say," he went on "is that in Judaism everything is interconnected, encompassing and purposeful. Judaism, to quote Moshe Hess, never separated the individual from the family, the family from the nation, the nation from humanity, humanity from the organic creation, and the organic creation from the creator. According to Judaism, he who says he believes in God without believing in man and he who says he believes in man without believing in God—and I mean a conscious personal, all-knowing God—are equally lying—to themselves—and to others. If man, his evil urge notwithstanding, isn't rooted in the supernatural, he is a beast; if God isn't concerned with man, he is non-existent."

"You asked me about separation between Church and State in the free State of Israel, but this very question, my friend, the very term 'Church and State,' isn't Jewish. It is Christian. Since Christianity never had a social or political side, its encroachments into socio-political areas were bound to have an adverse affect on the progressive development of those vital areas for which she had never had a judicial yardstick of its own. With Judaism it's entirely different. Take away the 'State' from Jewishness, its socio-political side that is, and there *is* no Jewishness; maybe Christianity can live on faith alone, but in Judaism the 'State' is the test of our deeds and faith alike. Without this test of deeds, faith is sterile, stale and hypocritical."

"Are you saying," I asked, "that in the future State of Israel the law of the land should be that of the Torah?"

"If you speak of the social part of the Mosaic law, the answer is most definitely—yes!" Dr. Ben Adam replied. "But let's talk for a minute about the philosophy of this law. The ignorants among our fellow Jews, and their number is increasing at an alarming speed, don't distinguish between churches or between states. They invoke the hallowed term 'separation of Church and State' while the Zealots among us are happy with their sect-Jewishness—as separated from life as from the spirit of 'the law of life.' Both these groups will reject my interpretation with equal vehemence. But a day will come, with the inevitable emergence of a Jewish state in this promised land of ours, when an assembly of the most learned men in Israel—learned both in the Hebrew law and in the law of the world—will draft in this holy city the most advanced constitution in the world. This constitution will be based, to start with, on the Hebrew thought that freedom is not a right, but a duty."

"I am afraid I don't get you."

"I'll explain it to you. The most advanced constitution in the world, the American constitution, speaks of freedom as a right. 'Every man is born with inalienable *rights* for life, liberty and the pursuit of happiness.' Those fine words were typical to an age in which people believed that liberty, once won by man, by any man, anywhere, would never be given up by him voluntarily. The founders of America—great humanists that they were—could not visualize a situation in which man, civilized man, would purposely and relentlessly work for the destruction of his own freedom and for its deliberate sacrifice on the altar of a Moloch called 'state,' 'class' or 'race.' In Germany—we must not forget this—only a very few years ago, Hitler rose to power *democratically*. What it means is that a majority of Germans *chose* to give up freedom. They used their *right*—their inalienable right—for liberty in order to do away with their liberty. Nobody alienated those rights but those who possessed them. Man in that land, famous for cultural and technical progress, *chose not to be free*. But can he do so? If liberty is a right, even an inalienable right—which means inalienable by others—he can. But if liberty is a *duty*—if you *must be free* because freedom is the very basic and very elementary condition of man which sets him apart from the animal—if you give up that freedom, even out of free choice, you are committing the crime of animality. You cannot, in other words, choose a state in which choosing—the freedom of choice—becomes impossible. You cannot choose yourself into non-choosing."

"That sounds very good," I said, "but where do you find this thought in the Hebrew law?"

"Our sages have said," Dr. Ben Adam answered, "that you don't go after a majority for evil. This verdict defines democracy from a spiritual, not only a social or numerical angle. A democracy is the rule of a freely elected majority, of course; but if a freely elected majority freely chooses to deprive you of your duty to choose —it is your duty to overthrow it, no matter what the majority wants. You, yourself, once you are free to choose, are free to choose yourself into a *personal* state of choicelessness—for good or for bad—but there must always be a free state of affairs—objective conditions, that is—which is constantly conducive to choosing. That is why the thing which ultimately determines the nature, the value, of a state, or a person, is not his freedom of choice, *but what he does with it*. And when I say 'what he does with it'—I mean what he does with it in his soul, in his family, in his country, in his universe, and finally—in his faith. . . ."

I interrupted him. "Are you implying, Dr. Ben Adam, that freedom, the way it was conceived by the Torah, is a spiritual as well as a social concept? What I am trying to say is that whenever the term 'freedom' is used in Christian and even some kind of modern

Jewish theology, it is used as a purely spiritual concept—isn't that so?"

"It is," Dr. Ben Adam answered, "and that's precisely what I am talking about. The Hebrew thought, my friend, regards the spiritual and the social as inseparables. Let me prove it to you. A slave who is given freedom by his master—and I am talking to you of an explicit Mosaic law—and refuses to accept it, is a criminal. 'The ear,' our sages explain, 'which had heard on Mount Sinai the words: "I am the Lord thy God . . . Thou shalt not have any other gods before me . . ." words which mean, according to the same sages, that "unto me the children of Israel are servants and they cannnot, therefore, be servants to servants"—the ear that hearkened to this commandment and violated it by *choosing* to submit itself to slavery—should be branded forever with the shameful mark of perpetual slavery.' This is a remarkable law! And it is remarkable for it presents the spiritual and the social aspects of man as two sides of the same coin. Why should man's voluntary submission to social servitude mean disobedience to God? Cannot man serve God spiritually while committed to the exclusive social and political obedience to a dictator? The Torah's answer is—No. He cannot. You cannot distinguish the social from the spiritual, period."

"This concept," I remarked, "may have very far reaching consequences when applied to real life!"

"Absolutely!" Dr. Ben Adam agreed, "what it actually means is that you cannot say, even when a certain country, like Germany today, chooses slavery of its own free will, that it is 'her internal affair,' and that one nation must not meddle in the internal affairs of another nation. There is no such thing as an internal affair of another state when that state has become a haven for evil—and an evil by a majority rule at that! The man, the family, the state, the universe, God—all these are a one and indivisible entity. If evil, even freely chosen evil, is imposed, or self-imposed upon a part of the human family, it is your business to fight it, for if you don't, it will spread to your own courtyard, to your own self. The minute evil—dictatorship, oppression, ignorance—takes over anywhere in the world, even if the take-over is achieved through democratic means, it is your duty to help overthrow it. Man cannot be man if he isn't first *free*."

"But Dr. Ben Adam," I asked, "this concept of freedom is somehow confusing—at least in the social aspect. Look at those wretches around us here in this prison. The only hope to restrain them is through restraining their freedom or taking it away altogether. Freedom to them is freedom of murder, rape, arson. Isn't that so?"

"What you speak of," Dr. Ben Adam replied, "is not freedom, but slavery; of men enslaved to their evil urge—of men whose enslavement to their evil urge is enslavement *to* murder; their freedom of rape is enslavement *to* rape, etc. The freedom I am speaking of, however, the freedom we are all looking for, is that which would enable man, born with an evil urge, to free himself from this natural self-enslavement by developing in himself, against overwhelming odds, a free moral will. Do you understand what I mean?"

"I do," I answered. "What bothers me, however, is the thought, the fear, that man can hardly be trusted to do the right choosing. While I realize that free choice is a basic tenet in Judaism, I wonder whether the freedom of choice, when invoked by people with not enough knowledge and data to apply it properly, may not lead to its very opposite."

"It may," Dr. Ben Adam replied, "but that is a chance we must take. Freedom is certainly a dangerous game, but without it man is dead—as man. Ever heard of Nicolay Berdyayev?"

"I am afraid not."

"Nicolay Berdyayev is a Russian revolutionary and former communist turned mystic and religionist of sorts. He now lives in Paris, I believe. Berdyayev, along with Dostoyevsky, another Russian giant, realizes that freedom per se is not a moral achievement but a basic condition of human life. With freedom everything begins; that is why freedom cannot be identified with goodness, or truth, or perfection, for freedom is by nature autonomous and basic. Freedom may lead to truth and goodness, but it may also lead to ugliness and evil. Any identification or confusion of freedom with goodness and perfection, according to Berdyayev, involves a negation of freedom and a strengthening of methods of compulsion: obligatory goodness ceases to be goodness by the sheer fact of its constraint. But free goodness, which alone is true, implies, as it is bound to, the liberty of evil. Berdyayev underlines that this vital human dilemma contains the mystery of Christianity. But, of course, this is as true as assuming that Christianity discovered love. Free choice, and the freedom of evil resulting from it, is as basic in Judaism as the Oneness of God. But Judaism added to this concept of freedom a social side which alone makes it complete, relevant and, if I may say so, existential. Berdyayev's dialectic of spiritual freedom, however, is very exact and I wish we'd bear it in mind nowadays when evil is on the increase all over. Free goodness involves the freedom of evil, Berdyayev argues, but freedom of evil leads to the destruction of freedom itself and its degeneration into an evil necessity. On the other hand, the denial of freedom of evil in favor of an exclusive freedom of good, ends equally in a negation of freedom and its degeneration into a good necessity. But a good necessity is not good, because goodness resides in freedom *from* necessity. . . ." " 'To be able to understand this world,' " Dr. Ben Adam continued, quoting from Berdyayev, and adding: "This man, Berdyayev, is at times so impressive—but only at times—that it wasn't difficult to memorize some of his greater passages—'to be able to understand this world,' he says, 'to keep one's faith in its deep meaning, to reconcile in one's mind the existence of God with the existence of evil, it is absolutely necessary that each one of us should have this *irrational freedom* in himself, for it clearly shows us what is the primary source of evil. *The world is full of wickedness and misery precisely because it is based on freedom, yet that freedom constitutes the whole dignity and the whole meaning of man and of his world.* Of course, at the price of its repudiation, evil and suffering could be abolished, and the world forced to be "good" and "happy," but man, having lost his freedom of choice, would have lost his likeness to God.' "

"These are very profound thoughts," I said.

"Very Jewish thoughts," Dr. Ben Adam went on, "for it attributes to freedom a distinctly superrational quality; what it lacks, however, is freedom's equally *rational* quality. If you accept or tolerate a system of social or political evil in your midst while you launch at the same time a successful struggle against sin—even a struggle in which you regard yourself as the winner—you are a miserable loser. You cannot, no matter what you say, kneel before God and Caesar at the same time, especially if Caesar claims Godly powers. The choice between God and the devil exists not only in spiritual matters, but—equally so—in political, social and economic areas. Freedom is indivisible along the entire range of human endeavors—it is even indivisible from evil! The difference is only that while the evil urge—and the submission to it—is blind and freedomless, the submission to God through faith and deeds is the epitome of freedom. But the soul of man, and be it even a great soul, unless it is the battleground where, along with spiritual warfare, decisive attacks are launched against the divisive forces in human society, is in itself divisive. One real, disinterested moral deed, executed by the elevated individual who is animated by spiritual considerations and acting out of a creative free will is a far greater achievement than all the peaks climbed by all morally indifferent cultures of the world. This deed alone encompasses the whole individual along with the staggering range of his responsibilities which begin with himself and culminate in God. Indifferent cultures have reared indifferent men, at best—gayly indifferent; at worst—cruelly indifferent. But Judaism—and this, too, should be a pillar of its constitution—regards indifference as a moral crime."

"It sounds wonderful," I said, "but where do you take *that* from?"

"From the Mosaic law. 'And thou shall not stand on thy brother's blood.' What does that mean? It means, I am sure, that when your brother is in trouble—and by now we know that when the Bible speaks of your brother it means your brother—man anywhere—and you do nothing to save him, to help him, to encourage him—you violate a moral law, a violation for which only man can forgive you—the man toward whose bloodshed you were indifferent—not God. Indifference versus a crime committed by others is a crime committed by *you*. But, of course, in order to reach this state, man must develop in himself an abhorrence to lip service, and lip service to me is another word for the hypocritical expression of sympathy invoked for his fellow man who is drowning and pleading for help by the man who can swim, but refuses to take the saving plunge. Expressions of faith, and love, and compassion are lies unless you practice them. Theories about final goals, great ends, marvellous peaks whose infallibility is proven mathematically in advance are meaningless unless justified and sanctified by means. The Hebrews around Mount Sinai reacted to the divine revelation with the most astounding response in the history of human greatness: 'We shall *do* and we shall *hear!*' What kind of answer was this to their *hearing God's* voice? Were they not supposed to say: 'We shall *hear* and we *shall do?*' Isn't it true that *hearing* precedes doing? How on earth can you *do* without having *heard* the word before? Our sages pose this question and give the answer which is the heart and soul of Jewishness: *In order for you to hear God's voice you must first do Godly things that are conducive to it. First do and then you will hear the voice.* When somebody asks me 'how can I become a true believer?' my answer is: become a true *doer*. There is no other way."

The same afternoon Dr. Ben Adam had a chance to expound his views on the question of ends versus means before a wider circle of listeners. The theme was important and topical, and most of the political detainees had very strong convictions about it. Terror was after all used by some of our ideological friends as a means to achieve a desired political goal. Man had to kill in reprisal for killings and also in order to make a potentially new killer think twice before committing the crime. The question whether terror was justified as a means to a just end was therefore hotly discussed throughout the land. Dr. Ben Adam's opinions on the subject were not known. He was militant in his political views, but neither his views nor his arrest was any proof to his considered opinion on the question of political terror. But Dr. Ben Adam, who wasn't over-eager to discuss this question prior to his detention, was glad, for some reason, to discuss it in prison.

"You see," he began, "if the question is whether, according to the Torah, unjust means may be used to achieve a just end, the answer is definitely no. There is even a clear, unequivocal prophetic warning against it: 'Justice . . . justice thou shall seek.' The great holy Yehudi asks the question why twice the word 'justice'? And the answer he gives is unmistakable: 'justice you can seek only through just means.' You can seek justice only through using justice in seeking it. That is the law. And let there be no mistakes about it."

I interrupted him. "But Dr. Ben Adam," I asked, "suppose this law clashes with another law—suppose it clashes, for example, with the law of 'and thou shall not stand on thy brother's blood,' of which you had spoken to me before? Suppose your brother's blood is shed and the blood of other brothers is threatened, and the only thing you can do about it is to use terror in order to frighten the bloodshedders away from committing new acts of bloodshed?"

"In such cases, I would say," Dr. Ben Adam answered, "and this is my own opinion, that it may very well fall under the category of another law, namely 'he who comes to kill you, kill him first.' Let me elaborate on it, gentlemen." He went on. "I don't have to tell you that we, Jews, never believed in the offering of the second cheek, nor did we have a chance to, for we were slapped simultaneously on both cheeks. The Christians actually never believed in it either, but they kept on repeating it as if they did—they kept on, in other words, repeating it in vain. And against keeping on rendering lip service and nothing else to holy concepts, or to professions of holiness, there is also a Mosaic law: 'And thou shall not mention the Name of the Lord thy God *in vain.*' What does it mean 'in vain'? What it means is simply that you shall not mention His Name when all you intend to render to Him is lip service. That's what it means 'in vain' and this is also the Mosaic law against the supreme sin of hypocrisy . . . but that's another question. We were on the subject of terror. The question was whether at times, and under very special, intolerable circumstances, unjust means may be used to reach a just end. That, my friends, is a bitter question, and the only answer I have to it is based upon the quality of the man, not only the nature of the deed. What I am trying to say is that under very special, very bitter circumstances, when unjust means must be used to achieve a just end, an end whose achievement is a matter of life and death, then it all depends on the person who is to employ such means. But before I continue," Dr. Ben Adam went on, "let me relate to you a very wonderful, and very relevant, Mosaic law. 'If a man steals an ox or a sheep and kills it, or sells it, he shall pay five oxen for an ox and four sheep for a sheep.' This law, mentioned, if I am not mistaken, at the end of the twenty-first chapter of *Exodus,* is tantalizing, to say the least. Why should the punishment for stealing one kind of an animal be greater than that which is prescribed for stealing another? Why five oxen for an ox and only four sheep for a sheep? But the sages—listen to me well!—explain it in a manner that makes wonderful human sense. 'The Torah,' says Rabbi Yochanan Ben Zakai, 'is here concerned with the *dignity* of man.' In the very act of self-debasement involved in a man's carrying off *on his shoulders* an animal he had stolen—a sheep he can carry on his shoulders, but not an *ox*—there is *already* the beginning of punishment for the crime. He pays less for the sheep because he had already humiliated himself by carrying it off on his shoulders, something which he cannot do with an ox, of course. This wonderful law, so typical of many other Mosaic laws and to the way they are interpreted in the Talmud, may explain what I want to say in answer to your question. It all depends on the way in which the man involved in doing an unjust deed in the pursuit of a just end, is affected, or 'punished' by what he is doing. It is one thing if he who is chosen to commit an act of terror accepts his task as if it were something tragic, bitter, even painful; but it is entirely different when the so-called 'terrorist' jumps into action as if it were a joy, a sport, or an act of bravura and show-off. Let me tell you something, my friends: each and every one of our neighbors here is capable of what is called 'terrorism.' You know that. This alone is enough to make us approach this very delicate area with double misgivings. Dostoyevsky understood it better than any other author in the history of literature. Not that he justified Raskolnikov's act in killing a vile, noxious insect of a usuress. What he did, however, was to portray a 'social'—which is the same as 'political'—murderer, who went to kill in a state of great inner conflict and torment. Maybe what he wanted to say was that—only a Raskolnikov can afford to kill."

Very few agreed with Dr. Ben Adam. One of us, later a known underground leader, haltingly remarked that Dr. Ben Adam must have spoken of "officers, not of soldiers." Another, the youngest among us, a tough, fiery and bitter young man, said almost sneeringly: "If a soldier doesn't get a good goddamn thrill out of his kill he isn't worth the pair of his wet pants." Dr. Ben Adam's face, upon hearing these words, grew tense. He turned first toward the man of the milder opposition and he said, "We want an army, young man, composed of officers; do you understand? The prospect of a day in which we shall have soldiers like those we saw in Tsarist or Communist Russia—soldiers without hearts, without souls, without knowledge, without minds—soldiers who are drunkards, rapists, vandals, arsonists, savages—the prospect of such a day of 'normalization' makes me sick, physically sick. Do you hear me?"

"I do, Dr. Ben Adam." The man answered apologetically.

"And you, young man," Dr. Ben Adam turned a sullen face toward the youngest heckler, "your remark was vulgar. Absolutely vulgar. Did you ever study the Bible?"

"I surely did."

"You surely did, didn't you?" Dr. Ben Adam continued in an angry voice. "Well, let's see. If you studied the Bible, as you say, you must surely remember the story of Jacob and Esau?"

"I surely do!"

"If you remember the story, would you mind telling me what was Esau's sin that justified the injustice which his brother Jacob did against him? And you know the injustice I am referring to: his depriving his older brother, Esau, with their mother Rebecca's help, of his rights as a firstborn?"

There was silence.

"Well," Dr. Ben Adam went on after a while, addressing himself to all of us, "what *was* Esau's sin? Weren't you bothered by this question when you first read the story of Esau and Jacob? I was, Gentlemen. I was bothered by it for many years till I found the answer in the explanation of the great Rabbi Mendel of Kotzk, and let me tell you what he said. Esau, he said, committed only *one* sin, and that was the supreme sin of vulgarity. Where do we find it in the Bible? In one single sentence which for a description of sheer coarseness, on account of voraciousness, hasn't got its equal anywhere else in the Bible. And the sentence I am referring to is this, 'And Esau said to Jacob: 'pour that red stuff, I pray, down my gullet'. That's all. But on the very same day, so the Scriptures say, Jacob asked his brother to sell him his birthright. Why? Because a vulgar man disqualifies himself, through his vulgarity, from being a 'firstborn,' which is another word for a leader, an officer, a man to follow."

Dr. Ben Adam's words made a deep impression on us. A long silence followed during which the reprimanded young man sat motionlessly, his eyes fixed to the ground. Finally Dr. Ben Adam went on: "And now to return to our topic. One thing I am sure of, Gentlemen: If we are not going to be better than the others, we shall be worse."

"Why not just *like* the others?" one of us asked.

"Because it is impossible."

"But why?"

"Because if the final hope of Jewry, following twenty centuries of oppression imposed upon us by the 'others,' is just to be *like* the others—we don't deserve, Gentlemen, to be like them either. That's for one thing. The other reasons—all of a different order—of an order I'd call superrational—are to me very often the only reasons that count. As long as there is evil in the world—and there will be evil in the world till the day of messianic deliverance—the evil-doers themselves will see to it that we *are* different. Do you follow me? They—through their very deeds, and words—will constantly remind us that we *are* different. For what typified our entire history is not only that we were against evil, but that evil was always against us! That is also the secret of our martyrology: since we are in the first fire-line against evil, since we are evil's chosen target, we are bound to suffer the greatest casualties. Another irrational reason for our differentness is the constant test to which it puts us and which the cowards escape like a trap and the brave accept like a challenge."

"The Talmud expresses this thought, this holy thought, in the following comment: Why have our forefathers—they ask—according to the Bible, chosen to bless their children that they should be as many as 'the stars in the skies and as the sand on the seashore'? Why the juxtaposition of stars—the highest of the highest—with sand of the seashore which is the lowest place on earth? To this our sages answer: It is the destiny of this people to be either as high and exalted as the stars or as low as the sand on the seashore. Our prophets—starting with Moses—speak of a people of prophets or a nation of priests. We are the only people on earth who, three thousand years ago, when kings were regarded as gods, had prophets who would come to the kings, point at them an accusing finger and say: you have sinned! While in the temples of Nineveh, Babylon and Sidon bloody and lascivious orgies were celebrated, Israel sat piously under its fig trees and chanted the praises of the Lord. In the Biblical days there were schools for Prophets in Israel as there were schools for philosophers in Greece. When Israel will be reborn, we shall have, I hope, schools for the *study* of prophecy. And when I speak of the study of prophecy, I don't mean Bible lessons the way they give them in our schools. This is not the study of prophecy. It is, very often, the misrepresentation and distortion of prophecy. A teacher of the Bible who doesn't believe in the Divine inspiration that animated the Bible renders himself incapable of understanding it and thus disqualifies himself to teach it. Prophecy will be taught in the schools of the future Hebrew state by inspired teachers exactly as poetry and ethics were taught in Greek schools in the era of Pericles. And we shall teach prophecy in our schools, or we shall establish special schools for the teachings of our Prophets, not only because we shall, by doing so, help to give purpose to our history as well as to the history of man in general, but, which is as important, we shall give meaning to our lives. When the Prophet says 'remember thy creator in the days of thy youth, for days may come in which you will say: I have no use for them'—he has spoken an eternal truth—truer today than ever before. The wisdom of the Lord is not something which is acquired through reading a book, listening to a sermon, or invoking a prayer. Oh no! For the wisdom of the Lord you need a disposition—a disposition which often takes a life time to acquire. But when the disposition is acquired early, and you know, through constant exercise and effort of the mind, to make it relevant, you will not face the great ugly void of boredom, of tedium, of ennui, of alienation and of futility that now attack more and more people in the world, and you will not say about the days of your life that you have 'no use for them.' That's a prophetic warning, Gentlemen, and you, the younger generation, should heed this warning. There are a thousand other prophetic warnings against ills and evil of this very day as there are a thousand prophetic ways to remedy them.

I'll just mention to you two other timely examples of prophetic timelessness. The Biblical words 'and there is nothing but Him,' which follow the statement 'for the Lord is our God,' lend themselves, as the philosopher Herman Cohen rightly pointed out, to another translation: 'and there is *nothingness* (Efess) without Him. . . .' Modern man is plagued by the inner nothingness he is left with in a world in which materialism and materiality reduced him to a cipher, a tool, a number among other gray numbers. He is plagued, at the same time, by materialism's and materiality's elevating themselves to the ranks of deities. He himself may serve these deities, but he feels their deceptiveness almost intuitively. Against this state of affairs, too, there is a prophetic warning: 'Their idols are of silver and gold, *the production of the hands of man.*' Man, be it in a regime of materialism or materiality, has become a slave of the tools he produces, and when man is enslaved to the production of his hands, or when he attaches to tools of production an *ultimate* importance, he is spiritually and morally idolatrous."

"And how about the prophetic warning against 'graven images'?" Dr. Ben Adam went on. "Doesn't it go much further than denouncing paganism? I therefore say that the acquisition of spiritual knowledge as the basis of all education may not rear supermen, but it will rear superior *souls,* great 'Neshomes.' In this differentness, my friends, there is beauty, as there is beauty in the differentness of the poet or the artist. That is why the study of prophecy, I am sure, will be obligatory in the future state of Israel as was the study of poetry in old Greece. . . ."

I interrupted him. "Dr. Ben Adam," I asked, "to make the study of prophecy in schools obligatory isn't quite compatible with complete freedom of choice, or is it? Parents will claim, and not without reason, that you are exposing their children to religious compulsion—and religious compulsion is somehow incompatible with freedom of choice!"

Dr. Ben Adam smiled. It was the smile I knew only too well. When something was said which irritated him intellectually, this smile would express a kind of a painful annoyance. Finally he spoke: "Your question is typical, my friend, but dangerously misleading. You are making the same mistake as the vast majority of people who believe that the enhancement of spiritual quests—a much better word than 'the study of religion'—may upset the balance of power in the youngster's mind and lead him in one prescribed direction. In Germany, so I was told, some Jewish parents avoided altogether to tell their children *anything* about spiritual matters so as to enable them 'to find out the truth by themselves when they grew up, without any pressure or prejudice for or against.' But this is, excuse my frankness, the liberalism of the stupid—the most silly and biased liberalism of them all. It is the liberalism of the people who are obsessed with the thought of 'objectivity,' of 'universality,' of 'cosmopolitanism.' They are lovers of 'humanity'—they declare themselves in love with the thing they see least, hear least, and know least about. They always love the 'people,' the 'masses,' the 'multitudes,' the 'nations'—always some entity that has no address, no personality, no individuality. But what these 'liberals'—the liberals who believe that freedom of choice is incompatible with obligatory studies of a spiritual nature—what they forget is that the pressure exercised by the very opposite of the spiritual—by the material, the banal, the vulgar, the profane, the showy, the ostentatious—is exercised by *itself* in every walk, every corner and every facet of life. What I am trying to say is this: the non-spiritual, as a result of an onslaught of materiality in every sphere of life, exercises more influence on the pupil, or student, or any man, than anything good he could ever learn in schools, in the clubs or in the streets. The anti-spiritual is thus "taught" without being actually taught. It is taught in the streets, at home, among friends, in intervals between classes, in movie houses, in books, in magazines, in small talk, etc. The impact of the anti-spiritual is so enormous, in fact—I would almost say so automatic—that it would take infinitely more than the obligatory study of spiritual subjects to counteract the destructive impact of these dangerously active and advancing forces of disruption. Take literature for example, and see which character was easier to mould by its author—the good or the bad? Why, even such giants as Dostoyevsky or Tolstoy, who didn't find it hard to draw evil characters, were at their weakest when it came to the moulding of convincingly good natures.

"Thus when a father, for example, refuses to teach his child spiritual matters, he actually exposes him to only *one side of life's choice*—to its *darker* side! Now don't ask me how it has come to pass that evil flourishes with much greater ease than good; why evil is there almost naturally while good has to be taught. It wasn't always like that, I am sure. But humanity, as a result of a thousand self-imposed distortions of its own inner make-up, has lost its way in a jungle of its own making, and there is nothing it can do about it. Once, in its earlier years, we tried to show it a way, but we were made to shut up. We kept quiet for a very long time while continuing to go our own way. It was a way all our own, and it was always leading to the thought that, while something supernatural could happen any moment, it may not happen for a thousand years. What I mean is the belief in the final messianic stage of mankind and that everything and everybody leads toward it whether they know it or not. And what enabled us to carry this national and spiritual message and this consciousness of a universal mission, are the things which I know that one day will go into the making of the new Israel. These things are:

The belief in the Unity and Oneness of a *personal* God;

The belief that such a belief is acquired *painfully;*

The belief in an *improved* man—a man who is not yet fully created and who has to constantly create himself;

The belief that without a God there is no hope for an improved man or an improved World;

The belief that only *deeds lead to faith;*

The belief that Freedom is a duty—not just a right;

The belief that the submission to materiality is a form of idolatry;

The belief that *means* determine the nature of *ends;*

The belief that indifference toward a crime *is* a crime;

The belief that the social and the spiritual will either work *together* or will *not work;*

And, finally, the belief that history, man, the universe, are inexorably moving toward one final and ultimate purpose—the day of messianic deliverance.

"All this," Dr. Ben Adam concluded, "is *in* us, latent, or active in our hearts and minds, yearning for a chance to make it *work in real life.* All this, my friends—defined, refined, clearly expressed and made relevant—will one day represent the essence of the message and mission of a free Israel. I believe in that. *Ani ma'amin.*"

On the following afternoon, our prison ward witnessed, for the first time, a scene of violence, but the strange thing about it was that it wasn't at all directed against us, but against someone, an Arab, we assumed, at the other end of the ward, who seemed to have suddenly aroused the fury of his colleagues by something frenzied he must have said or done. It happened like this: a group of our men, five, six of them, separated themselves in a corner and began quietly to sing something which was—and is—one of Israel's most popular—and most spiritual—prayer-songs. . . .

> Our father our Lord,
> Be lenient with us,
> For we have no *deeds* to report . . .

As the singing began, the Arabs received it with their usual, though restrained, mockery—shouts, curses, laughs, etc. All this didn't prevent our small group from continuing to sing, but it seemingly provoked someone on the Arab side to do something violent. We didn't see what he did. What we could see, however, was that almost the entire enemy camp threw itself on that man, determined to devour him to pieces. They did it, however, with so much shrieking and screaming that it almost immediately brought inside the British sergeant, accompanied by a few policemen. His shrill whistle stopped the fight at once. Minutes later the policemen dragged out a wounded, bleeding detainee, whom we had never seen before and who seemed to be, as he was carried out, unconscious.

Only on the following day, Sergeant Hastings, one of those fine young British lads who was doing his colonial duty without much enthusiasm, told us what had actually happened:

"You see, nobody knew he was Jewish. . . ."

"Jewish!?"

"That's right. The rest I can only assume."

"Why don't you tell us?"

"When that poor chap found out that you were here for different reasons than his, he must have felt kind of ashamed. Do you know what I mean?"

"Not exactly."

"Well, after he had found out why you were here and who you were, he must have decided to take sides, no matter the danger. The funny thing is that he pleaded with me not to tell you he was Jewish. . . ."

"But why?"

"He was ashamed, I guess."

"Ashamed?"

"You see . . ." Hastings looked for words, "he is serving a two-year sentence for attempted robbery, and he didn't want you to know, I guess, that a fellow Jew was imprisoned for that sort of thing. . . . They've almost killed him, the poor devil. But he'll be all right."

Survival for what?

For the hope that the law will one day again come forth from Zion and the word of God from Jerusalem.

Chapter Five

THE IMMEDIATE, INTERMEDIATE, AND ULTIMATE CONCERN

It was Sören Kierkegaard, that "other Prince of Denmark," as Louis de Rougemont rightly refers to him, who coined the term "the immediate man"; the late Paul Tillich introduced into existential thought a term which represents the extreme opposite of what preoccupies the immediate man, namely "the Ultimate Concern." To take the liberty, as this author does, to bridge the above-mentioned two concepts with something like "the intermediate preoccupation," is to complete the gradation of three spiritual classes of man: the immediate, the intermediate and the ultimate man.

Do we have to introduce the immediate man? Friedrich Nietzsche, that terrible German genius who disliked the Germans with the same passion he admired and hailed the Jews, and whose teachings were as much distorted by the German racists as were the teachings of Jesus by the Apostles—defined the immediate man in a most merciless, and most accurate, manner.

"Alas!" he cried out in despair. "The day comes of the most contemptible man *who can no longer condemn himself.*"

"Then the earth will have grown small and upon it shall hop the man who makes all things small. His kind is unexterminable. . . . The last man lives the longest."

"The last man lives longest. . . ." With these words Nietzsche had uttered a prophecy the possible realization of which may one bright day drive the physical, the immediate man, out of his mind —or whatever will be left thereof. The immediate man will soon face a longer life and shorter working hours and he will not know what on earth to do with himself.

For we deal here with a self who is incurably hollow as he is hopelessly tiny. And hollowness and tininess combined render one incapable of "condemning himself." What exactly does it mean "condemn himself"? It means that the immediate man who makes all things small—and he makes them small because he is immediate—will render himself incapable of seeing himself in the mirror of his own soul—for there will be no soul left to speak of—but in the next fellow's gaze, a gaze of social appraisal, not of spiritual judgment. Sartre's *No Exit* is about this sort of man—a man who lost his capability to look into himself for his self-worth, and believes that it will be determined by the way the next fellow, with a similar inclination, looks at him. Three such adorable creatures are condemned, in Sartre's famous play, to "live" in all eternity—for it all takes place in the hereafter—in each other's gazes, in which they had seen themselves throughout their lives. . . .In such a state, spiritual self-evaluation is as dead as self-condemnation. Whatever thoughts of self-evaluation or self-condemnation come to the shrinking mind of such a man, concern only the things he does to impress externally, not to enhance his ability to *receive inner* impressions. For the ability to receive inner impressions is of a distinctly spiritual, or intellectual, order and this kind of thing never comes to a man whose impressions are determined either by his instincts or by his sight. The impressions that are received by our instincts and, or, sight, create reactions not thoughts. Reactions are immediacies, which is not the case with thoughts, whose very nature suggests a degree of lastingness. People capable only of reactions don't think. And if they do it is only with regard to the immediacy of the reaction and its consequences. People capable only of reactions don't feel deeply either, for one cannot feel deeply unless his feelings are deepened by thoughts. These are thoughts combined with feelings which enable man to think critically—of himself to start with. With the loss of one's ability to think critically, one loses his human personality and he is slowly reduced to an insufferably one dimensional creature. A man who is incapable of spiritually condemning himself is not only a despiritualized man, but, very often, alas, a dehumanized man!

And this process is inevitable under the circumstances. The reason why the immediate man, living, as he does, in a physical and material atmosphere and having neither time nor patience for matters of a speculative, non-provable, non-tangible, non-visible nature, has lost his ability to condemn himself, is simply because he has lost the self *in* him—he has lost *himself*. And he has lost himself in a most silly and insipid way, for not only doesn't he know where to look for the thing he has lost, but he doesn't even know that he has lost anything!

We said before that the immediate man doesn't think. We should explain what we mean. And what we mean is that as long as thoughts are concerned solely with matter—and matter is matter even when it deals with "making God a partner to your business"—they are not thoughts, only prolonged self-preservational reactions which remain immediate in nature even when they cause one to plan his life in *advance*. This kind of man lives on actions and reactions, not on thoughts. When it comes to thoughts he often resorts to the "cliche"—to something he has heard from someone else and it sounded "intelligent" enough to memorize it, like a joke. The cliché is the immediate man's last resort to what he believes to be an independent thought and which he utters not for its depth—if deep it is—but for its cleverness. The immediate man is very often clever, and he appreciates cleverness in others, but it is the kind of cleverness which has as little to do with wisdom as impertinence with courage. It's the cleverness that was typical to the famous Syrian trader—an institution as old as Damascus—who knew how to outsmart a whole world, but didn't know how to read or write. Cleverness is not only unrelated to wisdom but, since it places all the importance on the provably "successful," it often becomes wisdom's most dangerous enemy. And not only that cleverness, the immediate man's claim to greatness, doesn't contribute an iota to his non-immediateness, but it actually makes immediateness look wise. The same is true with the immediate man's "knowledge." An immediate man can remain hopelessly immediate even if he is the master of a specialized knowledge *as long as this knowledge deals exclusively with matter*. The world is full with knowledgeable men who know more and more about less and less and who, in the process of acquiring more knowledge about the something they deal with, become totally ignorant of the knowledge of the world, the knowledge of the thing that deals with themselves. It was the Countess of Blessington who once expressed herself that "there is no knowledge for which so great a price is paid as the knowledge of the world; and no one ever became an adept in it except at the expense of a hardened and wounded heart." But what does "knowledge of the world" mean to the immediate man? "Travel" will be the answer. But exactly as there is no greater provincial than the big-city provincial, there is nobody with less knowledge of the world than he who believes that knowing the world *physically*—for geographically is also physically—is knowledge.

The immediate man's knowledge is as barren of thought as his cleverness, but, which is even more disturbing, he has settled down with his thoughtlessness and is rather comfortable with it. When T.S. Eliot speaks of the "growing terror of nothing to think about," he speaks of a higher class of the immediate man. For his lower class hardly feels any terror at having nothing to think about. Even boredom is foreign to him, let alone the terror of nothingness. When one feels the terror of nothing to think about he is already on the verge—but only on the verge—of self-condemnation. Colin Wilson in "The Outsider" uses T. S. Eliot in a different and more relevant context. Speaking of the men we describe as "immediate," he writes:

"These men, traveling down to the city in the morning, reading their newspapers or staring at advertisements above the opposite seats, have no doubt of who they are. Inscribe on the placard, in place of the advertisement, Eliot's lines:

> We are the hollow men;
> We are the stuffed men;
> Leaning together—

and they would read it with the same mild interest they read the rhymed advertisement for razor blades, wondering what on earth the manufacturers will be up to next."

"They have aims, these people, some of them—very distant aims: a new car in three years, a house in suburbia in five. But an aim is not an ideal. . . . They are not play actors—they change their shirts every day, but never their conception of themselves."

This is the immediate man—he may or may not change his shirt every day, that depends on his means, but he certainly never changes his conception of himself, for if he could change his conception of himself he would be capable of self-condemnation and, hence, he would be no more immediate. Only the immediate man is capable of reading exact definitions of his own self and not recognize himself in these exact definitions. That's what happens to a man who doesn't know that he doesn't know, and who, through not knowing his not knowing, unconsciously reduces everything to his size except, of course, the measurable things of his material pursuit which he would love to see bigger than life. While completely blind to the meaning of greatness, he readily applies to material things a yardstick of bigness. This man, the immediate, may have hunger, even unsatiable hunger, but not "thirst." A physical shack he craves to turn into a skyscraper, but a

106

spiritual skyscraper that falls into his hands he instantly turns into a shack. And he doesn't have to make any special effort to achieve this instantaneous reduction; the reduction is made through contact. Whatever the immediate man touches turns small. That is why this sort of man has all the answers to questions which giants of the heart and mind spent a lifetime to find a clue to, and died without finding. The ease with which the immediate man disposes of ultimate questions, especially when he does so in the name of "reason"—another gigantic institution which he reduced to the lamentable measures of his tininess—qualifies him, more than anything else, to join that undistinguished crowd of reduced creatures for whom Nietzsche had no other name but "contemptible."

The immediate man is the man most known to us all, but least defined to himself, for self-definition would have been the beginning of self-condemnation and this is something of which he is totally incapable. We see him all over and we hear him everywhere. He lives in immediacies—be they the immediacies of time or of matter—and he doesn't consider anything outside their range as important enough to be bothered about. When Schopenhauer says that most men regard the range of their vision as the range of the universe, he undoubtedly had in mind the immediate man. This creature, man or woman, young or old, rich or poor, is imprisoned in immediacies. As such—and let us say this in his sole defense—he has *unconsciously*—not consciously—reduced himself to a state which is, spiritually speaking, only a little higher than the animals. The opposite of this state is, to quote the Psalmist, "a little lower than the Angels."

He is a man, this immediate man, whose concern consists of things that can either be felt by the body, sensed by the instincts, seen by the eyes, or appraised by the mind, and these things are: health, wealth, status, family, clothes, work, business, security, sex, ego, acceptance, fun, etc.

That doesn't mean, however, that the immediate man isn't compassionate and even charitable. He is. But while his compassion he cannot help, for it is inborn, his charity is at least partly aimed at the social mirror of the next fellow's gaze. He gives more not necessarily because of the spiritual and human worth of the object in question, but because someone else in whose gaze he sees himself and whom he has, therefore, to match, also gives more. . . . He is often quite concerned, about things which have no apparent bearing upon his immediacies, but this concern too is rooted in immediacies for it is rarely, if ever, based on the thought, "can I, in any way, affect the course of events?" but, rather, "how would the course of events affect *me?*"

The immediate man talks mostly of immediacies without being at all aware that these are only immediacies he talks about. He talks, first and foremost, of other men, then of things, or places, or topical events, or sport news of the day, or stock market prices of the day, or headlines concerning sensational events of the day, or daily family matters, job matters, business matters, etc. When you listen to the immediate man's social talk you are appalled by his predictability. He is predictable even when he promises originality. Thus when the immediate man tells you, as he so often does, "I'll be candid with you"; or "let me tell you how I see it"; or "to me it seems that. . ."; or: "I'll be honest with you. . ."—you can rest assured that his promised "candidness," or "the way he sees it" or "what seems to him," will produce nothing but stale variations on a general theme of an increasingly sickening sameness. This sameness, by the way, is nurtured by a society in which differentness is regarded with suspicion and in which conformity is the key to acceptance. The immediate man not only doesn't know how to differ, but he is also afraid to.

An opinion emerges out of an acquired ability to use thought as an instrument of digging beneath the surface of facts. Thought emerges out of an acquired ability to take into consideration not only the immediate fact itself, but its non-obvious causes and its possible, non-obvious results. Opinions based on thoughts are enriched and are sharpened in contradictoriness—in the exchange of intellectual swords, in the cross fire of the great discussion. But all this is foreign to the immediate man who dwells in the obvious and lives on the surface of things without realizing that underneath him oceans are raging and abysses are opening and closing. The range of one's immediacies may be materially wide, but one can spend a lifetime in the widest range of his material immediacies while getting spiritually tinier by the day. How can a life which consists of the accumulation and, or, adoration of the visible, the measurable, the appraisable, the tangible, the calculable, be conducive to anything else but to one's immunization to all things non-measurable, non-tangible, non-calculable—all those things without which life would have been deprived of the last vestiges of beauty and meaning? What place can God and love and music and sorrow and poetry and nostalgia play in the life of a man whose taste is limited to the provable and who believes that the provable and the reasonable are one and the same thing?

And I do not want to imply that God and love and beauty play no role in the life of the immediate man. They do. But the role they play is one in which He reduces *them* to *his* size instead of his trying to rise to *their* grandeur. *His* very touch, which may have an enlarging influence on matter, has a diminishing effect on spirit. "The thoughts that change the world," Nietzsche writes in *So Spake Zarathustra,* "come on dove's feet." How true! But who but a man of a spiritual concern has his ears attuned to these tender touches of the soul, to the voices of silence—often the most powerful voices known to man? The immediate man's thoughts, or the thoughts he appreciates, must arrive noisily, or showily, on large wheels, in shiny vehicles, on missiles or, at best, in flying saucers. A thought that isn't elegantly wrapped and immediately and cutely catchy, he rejects as off-beat, unimportant, or even silly.

The immediate man loves to dally around with the word "reason" and regards it as a certificate of progressiveness and enlightenment. When this immediate man is successful, reason becomes not only his deity, but he makes others listen to him as if *he* were the deity himself. Reason, once hallowed by the Greeks as the language of the Gods, has become the excuse of the fools. The immediate man has robbed reason of every vestige of spirituality and turned it into the handmaid of his "smartness." "We are not the bearers of consciousness," a disenchanted European cried out, "we are the whores of reason!"

And the immediate man not only reduces everything to his size, but sees to it that the things which he reduces to his size are also well within his reach. Love he reduces to sex; God to Church or Synagogue; piety to ritual; culture to condensed books; drama to soap opera; civilization to television sets; ethics to manners; morals to conformity; self-realization to acceptance; enjoyment to fun; happiness to security; security to comfort; fulfillment to belonging; honor to status; pride to conceit; courage to impertinence; passion to lust.

And since everything is reduced to measurable, visible immediacies, ostentatiousness and showing-off are the inevitable results. When one develops in himself a capacity for inwardness—a distinctly spiritual trait—everything in him is directed toward self-transcendence. It is, in other words, only through self-realization that self-transcendence is possible. But if the trend is exclusively toward the materialization of the self and of all he stands for, man's spiritual shrinkage is bound to make a mockery out of his Godly image and turn the hallowed phrase "the dignity of man" into a tragic lie. There can be no dignity without spirituality. Ostentatiousness with dignity cannot live together. Either you are ostentatious *or* dignified. There is no other choice.

The ostentatiousness of the immediate man, moreover, never stops at ostentatiousness. Exactly as spirituality leads to humility —which must never be confused with meekness—ostentatiousness almost invariably leads to arrogance. And the parallel goes even further: while spirituality leads to the refinement of the senses, the arrogance of ostentatiousness invariably leads to vulgarity. In the absence of any ability to arouse, and get aroused, by higher stimuli, the immediate man is bound to resort to stimuli of an increasingly lower order. And contrary to stimuli of an esthetic, artistic, spiritual and intellectual nature which grows on you as you are exposed to it, the stimuli aroused by the vulgarities of the immediate man are as immediate and as showy as the man who has aroused them.

The same is true of "thrills" and "action." The immediate man, (or woman), be he young or old, poor or rich, is all out for "thrills" and "action." Try to apply the yardstick of "thrills" and "action" to the news media, for example, and you will easily find out not only what the immediate man likes, but who caters to his taste. An immediate newspaper is one that gives front-page predominance to "thrills" and "action"—murders, rapes, crimes and horrors of all kinds; an intermediate newspaper, by contrast, tackles, first, issues, or, at least, reports the news in a manner that casts a thoughtful light at the issues at stake. An immediate newspaper, moreover, is one that presents the news in a way that doesn't leave anything, or very little, for the imagination. This again is contrary to the intermediate newsmedia which hints at certain situations and makes broad use of the understatement. The same is true of the books the immediate man reads, of the movies he sees, of the fun he seeks—everything must be directed not at making him think, but at making thought superfluous. This is achieved through a combination of effects—sometimes stupefying and numbing effects, and, sometimes, through effects of a hilariously silly—at best funny—nature. All this is aimed at making the secret of thought as well as the thought of a secret equally needless and useless. Thought, secret, and the feeling for the hidden in general, is foreign to the immediate man. Everything to him must be open, digested, uncomplicated, down to earth, "reasonable." He will never understand what Einstein meant when he said that "the most beautiful and the most profound in man's inner experiences is the feeling of the hidden. . . . This feeling lies in the foundations of religion and serves as a basis for all deeper strivings in art and science. . . . He who has never experienced this feeling seems to me, if not like dead, at least blind. To feel that beyond what is given to us to grasp through our experiences there exists the hidden and unfathomable whose beauty and majesty reach us like flickering ungraspable sparks—is religiosity. It is enough for me to imagine to myself the nature of some of these hidden secrets in order to accept with humility the marvellous makeup of Being."

Einstein called the immediate man "if not dead, then blind." And blind he is, if not dead, because while his immediacies are only an infinitesimal part of that marvellous "mysterium tremendum" of the universe, he isn't at all intrigued with this mysterium and he acts as if it doesn't exist. The only mysteries the immediate man is interested in are the mystery thrillers.

Ninety percent if not more of all books published, of all movies made, of all plays staged, of all TV and radio programs broadcast, of all newspaper and magazine articles printed, cater to the taste of the immediate man. All the thrillers, the chillers, the killers of any kind, be they sex or spy stories, murder or war stories, family or fun stories, are meant to appeal to the immediate man in a manner that would insure his immediate satisfaction with what he sees or hears without the slightest effort to make him rise a step higher than himself. That is why the level of entertainment is so low nowadays, and why it is the opinion of every man of better taste that the entertainment media caters to a twelve-year-old mentality. In a world in which thought, mature thought, is dying, man, incapable of resorting to the poetry of spiritual and intellectual enjoyment, and thus totally dependent for his enjoyment on outside factors, needs shocks, thrills, and action to keep him going. If these outside factors are removed, even for a while, he may face emotional collapse. Erich Fromm has this to say about modern man—the same man we define as immediate—and what would happen to him if the outside stimuli were silenced for a while:

"Suppose that our western culture—movies, radio, television, sport events, and newspapers—ceased to function for only four weeks. With these main avenues of escape closed, what would be the consequences for people thrown back upon their own resources? I have no doubt that even in this short time thousands of nervous breakdowns would occur, and many more thousands of people would be thrown into a state of acute anxiety, not different from the picture which is diagnosed clinically as 'neurosis'."

How true!

For the immediate man has a problem and he neither knows how to cope with it nor how to define it to himself. And the problem, reduced to basics, is one of time—time which is the composite of the immediate, intermediate *and* ultimate versus the man who lives *only* in the immediate. There is bound to be a clash here, and in this clash, which is the source of all frustration, alienation, and loneliness, the comfortable immediate man is trying to kill time. Not that the immediate man, even the prosperous one, has too much time at his disposal; oh no! He is, if anything, a very busy man. But the little time he has got is often a problem to him, and particularly, to *her*. Something is happening to the immediate man and woman on a certain social level, ten years or so after marriage. Most marriages nowadays, when romanticism, like poetry, is associated with "softness" begin with very little "heart service," so to speak, but they aim at rendering all the "eye service" they can to families, neighbors, and friends. Ten years or so after such externalized unions, the immediate men and their companions for life have little or nothing to say to each other. As the unadmitted fear grows of having less and less to say, the hypocrisy of pretense begins substituting for sincere interest, while constant company, cards, parties. etc.—hold out the only hope for doing away with the embarrassment of boredom. Boredom, moreover, the result of non-existing inner resources inevitably leading up to mutual disinterest, is the cause, in many, if not all instances, of mental cruelty. And we don't mean the kind of cruelty which is used as a pretext for divorce, but the one which is the natural consequence of unadmitted mutual—or one-sided—disinterest. For only thus does it happen that hopelessly immediate women, obsessed with an unsatiable need for material externality, mercilessly drive their spiritually and intellectually immature husbands to greater material efforts and, finally, to collapse, nervous breakdowns, and heart attacks. Oscar Wilde once defined the cynic as a man who knows the prices of things, not their value. But this description, so it seems to us, fits much more the immediate man, who is as far from cynicism as from scepticism. Cynicism connotes a kind of perverted sophistication, but the immediate man is an ignoramus, not a sophisticate. The cynic comes to the conclusion that prices are more important than values only after he has had some experience with values and, because of bad luck, bad judgment, or bad characters he came across, he bitterly or nonchalantly dismisses those values as meaningless or useless. The immediate man, however, never knew the meaning of values in the first place. Woefully unsophisticated and inexperienced, he thinks that prices *are* values. In such an atmosphere, a direct result of the terrifying onslaught of materiality in all spheres of life, the soul is dying of thirst with nobody noticing it, least of all the soul's complacent owner. There are now couples—immediate people—in a higher social bracket who are afraid to go on vacations—or even to travel—alone, without another couple that is, lest they face up to a boredom made even more acute when there are no children or a household around to dispel it even through routine. When there is nothing to conveniently divert their attention from each other, there is the subconscious fear of facing up to something for which there is only one word in spite of all the "dears" and "darlings" and "honeys" in the world: nothingness!

And there is an unadmitted and undefined nothingness which devours the souls of the millions of immediate men and women who look for their inner selves anywhere but in themselves. These people, to be sure, belong to many "non-immediate" organizations: they belong even to synagogues and to churches. But there, too, they face the nothingness of a God who is either totally irrelevant or, which is even worse, completely "immediate." This God, the immediate God of a Billy Graham or a Norman Vincent Peale; this goody-goody God made so ridiculously "tangible" and "visible" by immediate soul-savers that the theologians of the "Death of God" movement, for example, found it so easy to aim at this poor God's very heart and "kill" Him—this immediate God was made to order for the immediate man. It is a God who has been reduced to a state of commodity in the supermarket—something you can get just by stretching out your hand, or to the "Status" (yes, there is also a "Status" God!) of a "Chairman of the Board of Directors of Universe Inc." (in the words of Erich Fromm). The entire concept of suffering which lies at the gate of wisdom, of getting involved with the mystery of the unprovable, of attuning the ear to the voices of silence and to the music of the infinite, is dying along with the taste for the classical, for liberal arts and great literature in general.

The small man is taking over in every walk of life, and it isn't even mediocrity which he represents—that wouldn't have been so bad—but inferiority. And not an inferiority complex, mind you; it is not a *complex* of inferiority he necessarily suffers from, though his doctor may have told him that he does—the trouble is that he *is inferior!*

But there is another feature to inferiority—complex or no complex—which may prove disastrous to our society and to our world. If the immediate man, particularly the immediate youth, will one day, as it may very well happen, find himself in a state of an acute economic crisis and thus deprived of his ability to buy thrills or to enjoy gains of a material nature, he may resort, as he did in the not too far away past, to the immediate thrills of terror and bloodshed. All the street victories of the Communists or the Fascists anywhere in the world were made possible by the immediate young man— his kind is the majority—who was all out for hallowed crimes and found them in movements where immediate means, any means, were sanctified by ends he never bothered to understand. With the ascendance of the immediate man, and as he more and more loses his ability to condemn himself, the danger of totalitarianism, racism, and Communist or Fascist concentration camps becomes terrifyingly real.

But hasn't the immediate man got one redeeming feature, you will ask? Yes, he has, and it is that little hidden cord in his soul— or whatever there is left thereof—which responds to the touch of spiritual tenderness even when it is of a reprimanding nature. That cord, consciously or unconsciously eager for a higher touch, holds the promise of music, though only in very rare cases does it begin to play by itself. It is this hidden cord about which that magnificent Yankee, Oliver Wendell Holmes, coined one of his most magnificent aphorisms: "Alas for those who cannot sing, but die with all their music in them!"

The Intermediate Concern

The man of the intermediate preoccupation may have, as he does, all the normal concerns of the immediate man, but added to all his physical and material concerns, and often as a corollary to them all, is his preoccupation with non-immediacies, or with things of an intermediate nature.

What do we mean by "intermediate"? We mean by this a concern with things which have nothing to do materially or physically with the person in question, but with things which transcend his personal situation. We mean, in other words, a man who has got not only aims, but ideals which he takes *personally*.

Now, who exactly is this man of the intermediate preoccupation? His kind is, to start with, a small minority among the immediate men around him, but his minority, though small, is by no means negligible. We see this man in all walks of life, and if we don't see him often enough, we hear plenty about him and we feel his existence. He is an idealist, for one thing, and, consequently, he is a *concerned* man. It may very well be the other way round: he is a concerned man that's why he is an idealist. "Idealist" however, may be a misleading term nowadays, for it somehow suggests a *constancy* of occupation or, at least, preoccupation, which must not necessarily be the case with the intermediate man. By saying "idealist," we do not mean to connote impracticability, dreaminess, unreality. We are not afraid of those words. Not only that the heart of man was moulded by traits such as these, but we are aware that their opposite numbers—"practicability," "down-to-earthness," "reality," "cleverness" have been reduced by the immediate man to a dreadful state of prosaic emptiness. The idealist we talk about may be a very practical man, but his practicability is not of the kind that will induce him to say what the frog in that fable whispered to the eagle: "Small wonder that things in our world look crooked and strange to you. You are too high up in the clouds, my friend, and you see things from an utterly impractical perspective. With me it's different; I may live, as I do, in the swamps, but that enables me to see reality as it is and to know how to cope with it."

These words, so descriptive of the immediate man, will never be intoned by the intermediate. And they will not be intoned by him not because he is too eaglelike and too high up in the clouds, but because it doesn't take an eagle to be dissatisfied with the "realistic" swamp of life. He may be a university student—this man of intermediate concern—a professional, a business man, a teacher, an author, a worker, an artist, a scholar, but he is a man who is first and foremost dissatisfied with things as they are, irrespective of his personal state of affairs. This dissatisfaction is sometimes of a cultural nature, sometimes of a social or political nature, but it is a dissatisfaction which has little to do with his own situation, but with the situation of society in general. His concern, in other words, transcends the limits of his professional or social immediacies and reaches out for the vaster areas of his community, country and world at large. He has a strong interest in politics, of course, but, contrary to the immediate man, he knows to distinguish between the politics that aim to satisfy the immediate lust for power of some spiritually inferior individuals, and that which strives at putting at the top men whose refined, imaginative, and progressive intellect is a guarantee for refinement, imagination, and progress. Adlai Stevenson or John F. Kennedy are good examples. They would have been the ideal political candidates for men of the intermediate concern. That is why Stevenson never made it to the White House, while John F. Kennedy reached it by a constant effort to lower his standards and make himself understood by the immediate man. . . .

The man of the intermediate concern cannot draw a line in his mind between the home front and the world front and is thus constantly aware of a kind of interhuman responsibility, which he regards both as a political necessity and a moral prerogative. He is bothered by things that are far both in time and in space, and he cannot help his being bothered by those things. He is bothered, for example, by the thought that in a hundred years, if no new sources of food are discovered and the population of the world continues to grow at the present rate, half of humanity may die of hunger, as he is bothered by the fact that half of humanity is undernourished even today. He is alarmed by the thought that man, as he gets more advanced in science, is getting more cruel, too, and that moral progress has long ago given up hope of keeping pace with galloping science. He is appalled by man's insensitivity to his own destiny and he is concerned that, the way things are, he may not be able to control the atomic monster he has created. With this we don't want to imply that the immediate man is in any way less concerned about the bomb than the intermediate. But there is a difference between their concerns. While the concern of most men is of a distinctly physical nature—the fear of destruction, pollution, etc.—the man of the intermediate preoccupation adds to this basic fear a moral dimension: he regards the physical survival of mankind, living as it does in the shadow of the bomb, contingent upon its moral strength, but since he fears that this moral strength is lacking, he is preoccupied with this fear of physical destruction as with the thought of his helplessness in the face of moral disintegration. This disintegration, at the same time, is associated in his searching mind with man's insensitivity to social and political injustices everywhere. The man of the intermediate preoccupa-

116

tion is thus very preoccupied with questions of social justice. This preoccupation leads him, at times, to join revolutionary movements—all revolutionary leaders were men of intermediate concerns—which to him represent attempts to deal radically with social evils on an international scale. As a man of intelligence, sometimes even intellect, he is often an addict of the intellectually and scientifically formulated blueprints for the cure of the world's ills, and thus he may even tend to mistake a well-defined scientific thesis for a proven fulfillment. That is the reason why so many younger men, particularly university students—particularly but not necessarily—in lands whose sense for social justice is feeble, join revolutionary movements and even guerilla bands in the mountains. To those men, rebelling against the immediate man's smug complacency at home—and be these men even their own fathers—the urge for social justice, as we all know, is quite often philosophically associated with historic materialism or the materialistic interpretation of history. Yet, the intelligent young men dying for it, as they do, have somehow managed to attribute to this kind of naked materialism—which is nothing but a scientific attempt, as is the medical materialism of Freud, to rob man of the last vestiges of his spirituality—superrational, almost mystical qualities! . . .

But that's another question. The intermediate man thinks internationally. He may be a nationalist, of course, but he is rarely a chauvinist. Nationalism, in the immediate, limited sense revolts him, for to him it is synonymous with the arrogant ignorance of the patriotic mobster—an ignorance and an arrogance that thrives on the basest instincts of the animalistic herd-man. The patriotic mobster, be it of the Fascist or Communist type, the one who is always there to shout "Down!" and "Heil!" and "Kill!" and "Long Live!" is the immediate man at his most abhorrent because he tries to give to his immediate blood-thirst an aspect of national, or social, or political, holiness. This bloody melodrama—blood per se doesn't turn a melodrama into drama—far from impressing the intermediate man, acutely depresses him. The intermediate man is depressed at the sight of lowliness masquerading around with big words and holy phrases.

The intermediate man is a reader of better books and is utterly unimpressed by star names or bestseller lists. Contrary to the immediate man whose library, if he has one that is, consists of books dealing with immediate questions of a material, sensual, and visual nature—of condensed bestsellers, detective and murder stories

117

and, if he is a man of some means, of an exquisitely bound encyclopaedia to fit the color of the sofa—the books read by the intermediate man deal with problems of a more universal nature. But he not only reads about those problems, but thinks about them. That is why this kind of man is more capable of being with himself. Not that being intermediate per se is a short cut to a common language with one's self—it often makes the way even more arduous—but it at least enables one to realize that to keep up with one's own self is at least as important as to keep up with the Joneses. . . . Company as such doesn't interest him unless it is stimulating. And stimulating to him is something which has the air of originality, which holds a promise of creativity and which says something new intellectually. Originality, creativity and intellectual newness are the things which to him represent the vital antithesis not only to boredom, but also to niggardliness of the soul—the immediate man's most typical trait. "It isn't your sin that cries unto heaven," Nietzsche exclaims, "but your niggardliness; it's your niggardliness even in sin that cries unto heaven!" The intermediate man, in most if not all cases, will prefer sin to niggardliness. Niggardliness he treats with noble contempt. If he is an angry man, however, angry at the state of affairs in the world, that is—his contempt may not always be noble. Such a man is often outraged. But the degree of this rage and its moral depth depend a great deal on the stamina, strength and sincerity of the man. Some angry intermediate men often sound like enraged muttons; others like enraged skunks. To sound like an enraged lion one has to be already on the threshold of the ultimate concern.

The intermediate man is often impatient. This impatience, normal for a soul stirred by misery, cruelty, and injustice, is at times pure, but more often than not, bitter. And what we are referring to in particular is the young man of intermediate preoccupation, wildly agitated by the lack of evolutionary progress in the world, who resorts, in his bitterness, to the immediacy of violence. And we are not speaking about the immediacy of the violent political mobster whom we have already described as the ugliest kind of the immediate man, but the revolutionary political leader or intellectual follower, who unscrupulously uses the immediate man for his goals.

This is the instance in which the intermediate man, in his impatience, turns cynical. One cannot incite others to violence, nor commit acts of violence himself, without being absolutely certain of what he is doing. But how can an intelligent man, unless blinded not elucidated by an ideal, be certain about the objective need to shed blood—and actually call for its shedding—without *pretending* for the sake of vain bravura or, at least, without being cynical for the sake of vain ambition? The intermediate man, be he the idealist or the cynic—it doesn't make any difference—has led all the violent upheavals in the world in the name of a conviction which he presented as the final word of history, in the name of a finality, of a certainty. But certainty was never the trait of a soul aware of its finiteness and seeking roots in the infinite. Even faith, unshakable faith, is not the same as certainty. Faith, in fact, thrives on uncertainties. Faith is what it is because of the onslaught of "certainties," trying frantically to undermine its strength. Faith, in fact, is a supernatural, inner reaction to natural "certainties." That is why it is a paradox and, at times, even an "absurd", as Kierkegaard pointed out. But this "absurdity" is the friction that ignites the spark of all great, struggling souls. The smaller the man, the more numerous his certainties and the more final his answers. Vagueness is a trait of maturity.

The intermediate man has, of course, developed a taste for the more mature dispositions of the mind. However, since these dispositions are only rarely guided by the controlling power of a higher spirituality—which is the same as a higher morality—it often happens that the active social concern of the ambitious intermediate man can make a dangerous creature out of him. It can, in fact, make out of him a creature infinitely more dangerous than the ambitious immediate man can ever be. The streets of many cities, the campuses of many universities, the rostrums of many public halls, are now the arenas where the intermediate man, his idealism as fierce as his ambition, talks the dangerously immature language of certainties to incite his followers for "action." The intermediate man may very well be a sophisticate. Sophistication may even be the trait of the intellectual revolutionary. But the minute such a revolutionary becomes the leader of immediate men, or, even, less sophisticated, more excitable intermediate men, he is bound to lower himself to the level of their tastes and—which is much more dangerous—he must cater to their *certainties*. By abandoning, or by not acquiring, the sceptical note, the tone of doubt, the notion of vagueness, the intermediate man reduces himself to the low level of expedient immediacy. Certainty is often the lowest form of immediacy.

The man of the intermediate preoccupation is, therefore, at his best when he is at his least certain. He doesn't think he has a remedy to the world's ills, but he seeks remedies; he wishes he were certain about everything, but he is certain only about uncertainty. He is often devoured by doubts, but he regards the doubt as the wind which turns the vital wheels of man's great search. He is impressed with scientific advances, of course, but he will never point at them as to a guaranty for social, not to say moral, progress. He is fascinated with man's mastery over the physical universe, but he is appalled at the fact that he is losing the mastery over himself. If the mind of the immediate man is a camera—that of the intermediate man is a radar network capable of receiving impressions of objects and subjects that go beyond the range of the human eye. As such, the intermediate man is already "different."

This being different is one of the most important traits of the man of the intermediate concern. Not that he seeks differentness, but he is different by virtue of his enlarged power of receptivity. He and the immediate man just don't talk on the same wave length. They don't talk about the same thing when they seemingly do talk about the same thing. The intermediate man, talking to the self-assured immediate man, is often appalled by the unlimitedness of human stupidity and man's total unawareness of it. It was Konrad Adenauer who once expressed himself that in view of the fact that God has put a limit on man's intelligence, it is somehow unfair that He didn't limit his stupidity. Tell this fine aphorism to an average immediate man and ask him to interpret it. If he won't confuse "intelligence" with success, he will skip the first part altogether as too obscure, or "philosophical," but he will not have any doubts about the second. Stupidity, in his interpretation, would definitely mean something which is on the opposite end of smartness. . . . The intermediate man, by sharp contrast, and we speak of the mature intermediate man who has met many clever men and found them terribly stupid—would suggest that cleverness is no barrier to stupidity and that stupidity is something the opposite of which is *wisdom*. But here we have already reached the threshold of the ultimate.

The Ultimate Concern

Paul Tillich's definition of the "Ultimate Concern" as the search for the Ultimate Ground of Being, suits us perfectly, except, perhaps, for the dry vagueness which surrounds his theological speculations leading up to the meaning of this much discussed term. We shall, therefore, use the Ultimate Concern epistemologically—as a definition, that is, of a relevantly higher state of mind and a trend of deeper thought in which man, in desperate search for a meaning, for an unshakable ground of Being, stretches his knowledge to a point in which everything—absolutely everything—is taken into consideration.

If the imagination of the immediate man stops where his sight, or senses, or instincts, stop; if the imagination of the intermediate man stops where his rational intellect stops—the imagination of the man of the Ultimate Concern *doesn't stop anywhere,* for it covers an area that transcends the physical universe and reaches out into the beyond.

Cleverness is enough to cover the area where the immediate man operates; knowledge suffices to cope with the intellectual limits of the intermediate man. However, for the man of the Ultimate Concern *wisdom* is needed.

We don't have to explain again why cleverness has nothing to do with knowledge. But we must say something on the difference between knowledge and wisdom. Spurgeon defined this difference very exactly when he said: "Wisdom is the right use of knowledge. . . . To know is not to be wise. Many men know a great deal, and are all the greater fools for it. There is no fool so great as a knowing fool. But to know how to use knowledge is to have wisdom."

Here Spurgeon has rightly attributed to wisdom the moral dimension which knowledge per se—not to mention cleverness—hasn't got. That wisdom is bound to be animated by an overriding moral concern is derivative from its distinctly spiritual quality. Of course, there is a wisdom of a kind, a mini-wisdom so to speak, which is sometimes bestowed even upon the immediate man. But this wisdom, as Goldsmith has pointed out, resembles somehow the instincts in animals: it is diffused only in a very narrow sphere, though within its circle it acts with vigor, uniformity, and even success. We are not concerned here with this kind of backyard "wisdom," but with the one which is the aggregate of all human experiences, and is in a state of constant selection and accumulation. And this experience, the accumulation of which we call wisdom, is born and develops out of a growing concern with ultimate things. This concern begins with man's preoccupation with his inner self. It begins, to be more exact, with three simple questions which Paul Gauguin, the great French master, wrote down as the name of one of his most famous paintings: "Who are we? Where do we come from? Where do we go?"

These questions are basic to the Ultimate Concern. These questions *are* the Ultimate Concern. A man who is not bothered by them is hopelessly immediate. The Ultimate Concern, in other words, starts with "Who am I?" It starts with the mystery of man's inner self, and—since it starts with his inner self as with a slowly unfolding mystery—it is bound to seek an *existential* contact with nature, with the universe, with God. For a man to find a contact with his inner self on a spiritual level—the only level that *ultimately* counts—he must first have a feeling of *belonging,* other than social. The need for belonging is elementary in man. Even the immediate man experiences it. He experiences it socially as well as socio-psychologically. It is a need for roots. But while the roots of the immediate man, even the intermediate, stem from below, the earth, the world—the man of the Ultimate Concern, while he has his feet on the ground, sets his roots in "heaven"; he is in search for a reality which is Ultimate and, therefore, all-embracing. He feels, or strives to feel, a part not only of a family, a community, a nation, but also a universe and an infinity which transcend the physical and scientific limits of man's mind, and give purpose and meaning to life. The very need for such a contact, the very search for it, is a spiritual experience of an ultimate nature and it elevates man to a higher rung of being. The Israeli author S. Yizhar expresses this need in the words of one of his heroes (in *The Days of Ziklag*): "I do not desire a lovely home, nor lovely furniture, nor even lovely thoughts, or any kind of possessions or values. All I want is that life should not be one big waste, one big running away from something, one big running to something, one big feeling of guilt and despair that the whole damn thing the way it is just isn't it. Doesn't this bother you? Doesn't it choke you? Doesn't it choke you that everything is 'just like that'? That it starts out 'like that' and it ends 'like that,' and that this 'just like that' is just the thing you dislike and reject? Doesn't it choke you that life is devoid of worthiness, that there is nothing in it to suggest the great arrival which one is supposed to be grateful for? Doesn't it torment you that life goes on without that burning love we all crave or that burning affirmation we all need, and that we pass through it, from end to end, with nothing but that big, moronic 'just like that'? Doesn't your heart revolt against it? Tell me, please, the fact that you live 'just like that' doesn't it eat you up? I can't take it any longer. I may not have the strength to do a thousand other things, but I've still got left the strength to scream 'No! No!' I don't want all this! I don't want to be one of those who somehow manage to exist through life in the same manner we were deposited into it— the manner of managing somehow, somewhere till our day comes."

"If I had *only* one thing, namely that 'yea, though I go through the valley of the shadow I fear no evil' etc.—if I had *only* this I would have *everything*. What else does one need? This is the *ultimate* in all possessions. This is everything. Everything. But I haven't got it! I would have given up everything to have it. Or if I had at least the courage to exist without it, free from the need of it. If, in my most terrible hours, I had some kind of faith and confidence, without real faith or confidence. Do you know what I mean? If such a 'I fear no evil' were in existence by itself, as a separate entity, independent, complete and pure, full and firm, one and unifying! If there was such an inner place in me capable of accepting the world as it is, just like that, without batting an eye. If I could accept it just like that because everything, including you, including me, are just like that. . . . If I only could!. . ."

Is this egotism? No, it is not. It is a concern which, no matter how subjective, is rooted in "Weltschmertz". Is it fear? Not at all. Fear is a mental reaction to physical danger, real or imaginary, while what we are dealing with here is life's meaninglessness. So what *is* it? *It is the will to a meaning.*

There is the will to pleasure ("the pleasure principle"); there is the will to power, and there is, in the words of Dr. Victor Frankel, (in "The Doctor and the Soul"), *the will to a meaning.*

The will to pleasure is the lowest, the commonest, the most immediate, most instinctive drive in man. The will to power may be as low and as common, but it usually develops alongside a realization that in order to achieve power a degree of knowledge— at least of a specialized kind of knowledge—is needed. That is why the will to power is a higher form of the will to pleasure. This is also because one can hardly be expected to gain power over other men unless he has gained some kind of power over himself as well as some kind of intelligence to direct that power.

It doesn't take any intelligence to possess a will to pleasure, nor is any sensitivity required for the development of a will to power, but it takes a good deal of both intelligence and sensitivity to acquire a will to a meaning.

It takes a *meaningful* man to acquire the will to a meaning!

And once this will is acquired, the soul is possessed of a great, unquenchable thirst, and this thirst, in turn, feeds itself on *anxiety*. And we don't talk here of clinical anxiety, the anxiety which is to be traced to childhood problems or to social frustrations, but to problems rooted in our very existence, in life itself. Such problems arise, as Paul Tillich rightly observed, only when man realizes the existence of *non-being*. Man's existence, according to Tillich (as well as to Heidegger), is rooted in the dynamic relation between Being and non-being. Man becomes aware of this tension when he experiences non-being in life. Facing fate in general and death absolutely, he comes to know himself as a finite being and, consequently, to ask questions as to the real nature of this finiteness and to the meaning of life in general. This certainty of death, according to Tillich, is not only an interesting facet of life, but a vitally important one: it grips the whole human personality and forces it to face itself. To the Jew, let's add, in addition to the inevitability of death, which forced him to face himself, it was the innate reality of evil, of which he was particularly aware, since he was its main target, which forced him to face the world as a constant challenge, as well as a threat, to the self he faced. . . . Under such conditions, estrangement, of course, is inevitable. But it is an estrangement leading up to the realization that man's predicament is something to which no "rational" medicines can be effectively applied. Existential analysis is, therefore, an analysis of man's estrangement from something very vital, though very hidden, in him; from an essential structure of his inner self which cannot be discovered unless a total effort is made to dig in depth. And what we are referring to is "man's falling away from his image of God which he is potentially. . . . Accordingly, existential analysis always is directed toward, and motivated by the human predicament." (Ernest Breisach, "Introduction to Modern Existentialism.") Even the non-religious, or anti-religious Existentialists insist that reason alone is simply insufficient to cope with this predicament, and that the anxiety caused by man's finiteness points towards roots in something which is beyond him. Tillich takes existential anxiety as the experience immediately pointing to God.

But to what kind of God does it point? To Judaism, the God it points to is One who is no substitute for individual efforts. It is not a God who is what He is because He once "happened" to man, but because of what man makes happen to himself. "The truth is that the one thing man is afraid of is within himself, and the one thing he craves is within himself" (Rabbi Nachman of Bratzlav). Each man must thus build his own mountain to God. He may be told how to climb it, the precautions he must take against the dangers that are rampant on the way, but the climbing, even the proscribed portions of it, must never be a matter of routine. Routine, when applied to the search of an ultimate reality, an ultimate Ground of Being, (remarkably enough, one of the mystical names used by the sages for God, is *"Ground"—"Makom"*), not only atrophies the search, but desecrates God's name. "He who prays today because he had prayed yesterday," so goes a Hassidic saying, "mocks the honor of his Maker." To climb the mountain of God requires not only a total effort of the heart and soul, but the realization that the climbing is a very dangerous proposition. Buber was very exact when he described the search for an Ultimate reality as a *"narrow ridge"*. "I wanted," he writes in his "Life of Dialogue", "by this to express that I did not rest on the broad upland of a system that includes a series of sure statements about the absolute, but on a narrow, rocky ridge between the gulfs where there is no sureness of expressible knowledge, *but the certainty of meeting what remains undisclosed*." This holy insecurity,—not the unholy security,—is the most typical trait of the great search. "Man," Rabbi Nachman of Bratzlav says, "is in great danger in the world."

The pain accompanying the quest for truth, the search for an Ultimate reality, is a never ending process, and it often involves the need to "wrestle with God"—the agonizing moments of the soul when the craving for an opening in the clouds—a tiny little break in the clouds—turns into an outcry. . . . The man with an ultimate concern is a man of faith, of course, but it is a faith which is ignited by the fuel of doubts and is, therefore, distinguished not only by its tormenting, but also purifying and uplifting nature. These doubts lead to a higher state in which the imagination of the heart is in constant prayer not to be defeated by the reason of the mind. The man of the Ultimate Concern, moreover, realizes, together with Vinet, (in his study of Cousin's book on the *Pensees* by

Pascal), that "the very knowledge of the mind as such has need of the heart. . . . Without the desire to see there is no seeing; in a great materialization of life and of thought there is no believing in the things of the spirit." What distinguishes the man of the Ultimate Concern is not so much his belief, as his terrifying *desire* to believe. He is not shocked at people who have come to the painful *conclusion* that there is no God, but at those who have no *need* for a God. Miguel de Unamuno—that great man Unamuno—had something very beautiful to say in interpretation of a Biblical sentence dealing with the question of belief in God: " 'The wicked man hath said in his heart, There is no God.' And this is truth. For in his *head* the righteous man may say to himself, God does not exist! But only the wicked can say it in his *heart*. Not to believe that there is a God, or to believe that there is not a God, is one thing; to resign oneself to there not being a God is another thing, and it is a terrible and inhuman thing, but not to *wish* that there be a God exceeds every other moral monstrosity; although, as a matter of fact, those who deny God deny him because of their despair at not finding Him." (*The Tragic Sense of Life*)

We wholeheartedly agree with everything Unamuno has said in this passage except with his final words. We do not agree that those who deny God, deny Him because of their despair at not finding Him. It takes a man with an Ultimate Concern to *despair* at not finding God. Most people either don't look for Him, or, if they do, they do it so superficially and painlessly that when "Reason" launches its first little counterattack, they raise their hands and surrender.

But this kind of surrender—the surrender that characterizes so many immediate men—far from proving the strength of their reason, actually testifies to the weakness of their concern. For what is this Ultimate Concern if not an unquenchable desire for truth concerning human existence—a desire made even more unquenchable by the saltwaters of reasons, "certainties" which try to quench it? The man with the Ultimate Concern is well aware that to know the full truth concerning human existence is impossible here below, but he also knows, in the words of Unamuno again, that "unless a man aspires to the impossible, the possible he achieves will be scarcely worth the trouble of achieving." (*The Tragic Sense of Life*)

The man with the Ultimate Concern is concerned with the *whole* of man, not just part of him, be it the social, political or artistic part of him. And not only with the *whole* of man, but with the whole of him versus the *whole* of creation. He is a man whose mind is not a camera, but a radar network, and not a country or even world-wide radar network, typical, as aforementioned, of the intermediate man, but a Universal radar whose alarm system switches on automatically whenever something suspicious appears on its screen. The sound of this alarm is at its most frantic when the suspicious thing that appears on its screen is injustice, but what is most typical of this man in this high state of sensitivity is that he regards futility, even without injustice, as unjust. The man with the Ultimate Concern cannot bear the thought of futility in general, but the thought of futile suffering, which makes him cry out in pain, he often rejects as a sin. He is looking for a pattern of thought that would make suffering relevant, for something in him tells him that there is a spiritual connection between suffering, purity, beauty and wisdom. The search for such a thought, for such a pattern, requires, to begin with, a concern with man, with mankind, which is out of the ordinary. It requires a concern that strains every fiber in the body and soul and makes thought as painful, and as inevitable, as death. One such extreme case of concern with the Ultimate is the late Greek colossus Nikos Kazantzakis. Himself not a believer in a personal God, though, admittedly, in a terrible need for One—his crave for the Ultimate was doubly tragic and doubly heroic. In his *Report to Greco* he thus describes the scope of his Ultimate Concern: "All my life I struggled to stretch my mind to the breaking point, until it began to creak, in order to create a great thought which might be able to give a new meaning to life, a new meaning to death, and to console mankind." On another occasion, in a letter to his wife from Vienna, he explains his attempts to reach out for an ultimate thought as follows: "When will the search end? Or perhaps my purpose is only the search itself; that is, the progression from point to point? (Ego, Humanity, Earth, the Universe, God.) Perhaps this is the very progression of God? The search itself, upward and with coherence—perhaps this is the purpose of the universe. Purpose and means become identified. . . . Oh, undaunted, unhealable searcher!"

Can this search for an Ultimate reality ever be satisfied in this world? Only as flashes of joy inexpressible at discerning, at times, not only a marvellous break in the clouds, but an even more marvellous opening of the skies. . . . "There are two kinds of spirit," writes Rabbi Nachman of Bratzlav, "and they are like backward and forward. There is one spirit that man attains in the course of time. But there is another spirit that overwhelms man in great abundance, in great haste, swifter than a moment, for it is beyond time, and for this spirit no time is needed." It must have been about such a soul that Wordsworth has written his immortal lines:

> In such access of mind, in such high hour
> Of visitation from the Living God,
> Thought was not: in enjoyment it expired.
> No thanks he breathed, he proffered no request.
> Rapt into still communion that transcends
> The imperfect offices of prayer and praise,
> His mind was a thanksgiving to the power
> That made him; he was blessedness and love.

Victor Gollantz (in *The Devil's Repertoire*) is right when he remarks that Wordsworth, in those last two lines, is by no means saying that he was *giving* thanks, that he *knew* himself blessed, that he *felt* himself loving or loved. What he said was that his mind, namely, he, himself, his whole being, *was* a thanksgiving, *was* blessedness, *was* love. He was "rapt," he was merged. Subject and object had become one.

This is the deepest awareness of an Ultimate ground of being. The most complete experience of Oneness—of "Echad."

Chapter Six

THE JEW AND HIS "NESHOME"

The Jew was—he is less and less so, alas!—the man with an ultimate concern par excellence.

The Christian concern with the ultimate, a concern that was exclusive of anything else (in particularly great souls) was also exclusive of existence. It was a concern that grew inorganically out of a rejected life, like a flower from an earthquake. The ultimate ground of being was reached by the few elect at the price of totally rejecting the immediate and the intermediate alike. The kingdom that was not supposed to be of this world, became an *adversary* of this world.

Not so in Judaism. The ultimate concern of the Jew was an existential, much more than a theological, concept. The Jew, of course, resorted to the ultimate whenever the immediate and intermediate seemed unbearable, but he resorted to it so as to make the immediate and intermediate *bearable*. He developed in himself an ability, unknown to any other people, to almost automatically switch to the ultimate ground of being whenever the immediate ground was on fire. But it was the very switching-on the ultimate which helped extinguish the fires of his *immediate* ground of being!

The Jew was the man with an ultimate concern par excellence because this concern grew in him not only irrespective of reality but in accordance with it—in accordance with a reality that grew more meaningful and, even, beautiful, as the touch with the ultimate persisted by the means of his "Neshome," his soul. The greatness and uniqueness of the ultimate concern of the Jew consisted, in other words, in his ability not to regard this concern as a rejection of the immediate and intermediate, but as their existential corollary. The metaphysical didn't try to reject the physical but to make it dance to its tune. That was the reason why the Jew never regarded any crisis of the immediate or intermediate as pointless. Like the rivers that are flowing to the sea, the immediate and intermediate streams of life, even when polluted, can find their "Tikun" in their *identification* with the great sea even before they *merge* with it, and that sea in man was called "*Neshome.*" That was also why the ultimate to the Jew, the source of his sorrow and joy, of his fear and love, of his anguish and hope, was never in a state of crisis. Man was in a crisis in relation to the ultimate, but not the ultimate in relation to man. "Other races," Sir George Adam Smith writes in his essay "The Old Testament," "have achieved ethical progress at the expense of their religion. But Israel never found their God wanting in any crisis of their history or discredited by any fresh ethical experience or problem which their spirit encountered however much for a time their faith in His righteousness might be shaken by their suffering and by the injustice and cruelty that prevailed in the world about them."

The Jew, of course, constantly strove to improve the immediate and he had never lost his practical sense of life, but he knew, at the same time, that the immediate, just because of its being what it is, namely a perishable commodity, is a failure, as anything transitory is bound to be when judged from a spiritual angle, but only in as much as it is divorced from the ultimate. The ultimate, on the other hand, was almost synonymous in his mind with perfection, with justice, with love, with beauty and, most important of all— with wisdom! Paradise was portrayed as a place where the secrets of God, life and death, unknown to man in his lifetime, are finally revealed to him in a manner that makes this knowledge the very ultimate in spiritual enjoyment. The great souls go to the "Yeshiva shel Maalah"—to the *study*-house of heaven—for study doesn't even stop when life stops!—where they enjoy the bliss of the Holy Presence. The Jew, constantly bothered by the failure of man in this world—a failure to which he had always tried to find a "Tikun" —has never attributed, not even in his gravest hours of agony, any thought of failure or injustice to God. To this kind of Jew —for example, the Jew with the true ultimate concern—man, not God, died in Auschwitz, for Auschwitz has proven to him what man can become, what he is capable of, without a God, or with the wrong concept of God. Let's pause for a moment at this point and say a word about a new movement which now solemnly proclaims the "Death of God." According to the theologians of this peculiar Neshome-less trend, who know the place and date of God's death, the God who died in this enlightened age of ours is the Old Testament God—the Lord God Jehovah, the God of Abraham, Isaac,

Jacob, Moses, David, Isaiah, Job etc. Jesus by contrast, remains a God—an undying symbol of spiritual morality—but only to the extent, to which the Christian mind gets rid of the burden of the Old Testament God, which, of course, is another word for the God of the Jews.

Without at all entering into a theological discussion with these curious fellows who not only "kill" God, but, which is the most inexcusable part of it all, "kill" Him in cold blood, as behooves Neshome-less creatures—we must say this: the "Death of God" movement, ontologically speaking, aims at doing away with a dimension in man which, more than any other dimension, entitles him to the name "man," namely, his third, and most vital dimension: the "Neshome." By reducing God to the "human", even if it's called "Ethical," His reduction to the subhuman becomes consequential. The "Death of God" movement is, therefore, *a Death of Man affirmation,* for man without a concern with the ultimate in the Old Testament sense is, or is bound to become, nothing but a petty idolator, a despiritualized ignoramus or an ideological assassin. It is not true that the Death of God movement really began with Dietrich Bonhoeffer, the Christian theologian who was executed by the Nazis (and whom we have mentioned on another occasion). The urge to "de-judaize" Christianity—and that's what the "death of God" movement is all about—arose among Christians each time evil, masquerading as a new "morality," or as a new deity, craved a free hand to do away with the old one. There was even a "religious" movement of Professer Hauer in Germany during the Hitler era (Julius Streicher had praisingly mentioned his name in his famous conversation with Hitler, as related in the first chapter of this book), which claimed not only that the Old Testament God, to use an incredible expression borrowed from the theologians of the Death of God movement, "perished by self annihilation in Christ," but that Christ had himself annihilated the Jew in him and had someow managed to become an Aryan. . . . What Dietrich Bonhoeffer did, however, was to put his question in a new context. In a series of letters, written in a concentration camp, Bonhoeffer described the religious implications of man's "coming of age." It used to be, he said, that man needed the hypothesis of God in order to explain all sorts of phenomena. "With the astounding growth of human knowledge, however, these have been reduced to a handful of *ultimate* questions, such as the meaning of death and guilt." How will religion speak, he asked, "when these are answerable *without* the God hypothesis?"

Since I have first read the Bonhoeffer letters I couldn't quite free myself of the thought that there is something very sad about the fact that a man of Bonhoeffer's stature was impressed with the "astounding growth of human knowledge" rather than inconsolably depressed that this "astounding growth" goes hand in hand with an even more astounding growth in human evil and spiritual ignorance. It was even more sad, it seemed to me, that Bonhoeffer was not induced, in a concentration camp, where human knowledge was working full time for human extinction, to question the theory that the advance of knowledge alone entitles man to regard himself as "coming of age." Anyway, Bonhoeffer was convinced that with the growth of knowledge, all questions will be reduced to a "handful" such as "the meaning of death and guilt." This statement is astounding, to say the least, for it is precisely the growth of knowledge which has made the question of *life,* let alone of death, more acute than ever. Science, moreover, its astounding growth notwithstanding, has already tried, and failed, to answer the question of life's meaning without the hypothesis of God. To mention just two examples: one, Marx's utterly Neshome-less assertion that alienation of man is a purely *social* phenomenon, and that it will disappear as soon as man will no more be alienated from his tools of production. Two, Freud's equally Neshome-less assertion that neurosis is a purely *clinical* phenomenon.

These two claims, to start with, are *reductionist* in nature, with or without the God hypothesis. For what is it if not a reduction of man if an external factor like tools of production, *and nothing else,* is to be blamed for his inner feeling of alienation? (It is a matter of fact that alienation in Communist countries has assumed epidemic proportions.) And what is it if not a reduction of the stature of man to a state of immediacy or, at best, intermediacy, if the claim is maintained that neurosis is to be traced *only* to clinical, never to *existential* reasons? Does man really have to attribute his *inner* misery at what is going on around him to diaper-wetting? And aren't we tired, not to say embarrassed, by now, in the words of Eric Bentley, of being told that if Napoleon, for example, desired to conquer Russia it was because he hated his father?

The thought that religion, true religion that is, which is the highest expression of man's Ultimate Concern, will have nothing to say when the "handful of questions" such as guilt and death will be answered by knowledge, would have been justified only if knowledge, in an era of astounding technical growth, would have made man's problems, and we mean man's *existential* problems, *less*

132

acute, or would have found a moral substitute for the "Neshome."
But the fact of the matter is that the question of life's meaning—
the questions of death and guilt are results of it—is more acute
now than ever before. "But what if science creates a happier
man?" one may ask. The answer is simple: science can create a
happier man only through making him less of a man—through
reducing his spirituality, that is. He may be then a happier man, of
course, but he will be so only at the expense of his sensitivity, of
his creativity, of his *humanity,* of his poetry, of his "Neshome."
The man science will rear, suppose it rears one, will be a disposable man, free of fear of guilt or fear of death, but also free of
freedom of choice, of God's image, of love's passion and of the
soul's great nostalgia. This happy, animalistic man will be the
immediate man par excellence, or, though less likely, the intermediate, but the Ultimate in him will die along with his poetry, his
wisdom, his love, his thirst for immortality, and his "sweet taste of
sorrow." He may even know love, mechanical love that is, but he
will never know that mighty feeling of the ultimate and immortal
in love which Dante Alighieri expresses in one inimitable line:

"D'antigua amor la gran potenza. . . ."

When science will reduce man's problems to "guilt and death,"
and then find a scientific way to reduce even these questions to
naught, it will do so by first succeeding to reduce *man* to naught.
The Ultimate Concern will be totally and finally eliminated when
man will become totally and finally *immediate.* And the totally and
finally immediate man will be born without pains and will die
without tears. He will be, this Neshome-less, immediate man,
exactly as Russell Baker had once humorously and brilliantly described him in the *New York Times* (June 28, 1964) "a disposable
man." This man of the "Nothing Generation" or the "Non-Age"
will be a complete no-man man. "The essence of non-life is non-
involvement, more positively known as playing-it-safe. And so
literature (in the non-life age) has created the anti-hero, for the an-
ti-theatre and the anti-novel. The anti-hero sits around in garbage
cans doing nothing for hours, except saying 'no' to life and waiting
to be disposed of. He is a great favorite of the Nothing Generation
which can listen to him for hours even of caffeine-free coffee. . . .
When the anti-hero wants to carbonate his stomach, he takes a
non-caloric soft drink. It comes in disposable no-deposit, no return
bottles, or a throwaway can. For amusement he sits in dehumidi-

fied air watching non-actors perform non-dramas about non-people and absorbing advertisements that tell how to take the misery out of washday, the odors out of living and the challenge out of opening a milk can. . . . The beauty of the Non-Age is that it makes the Non-Life so easy and it creates so much leisure time to enjoy non-living. The disposable diaper, for example, not only takes half the agony out of parenthood, but also gives the parents time to drink more odorless booze without offending baby's delicate nose."

Here is Nietzsche's contemptible man of the future, as inexterminable as the ground fly, reduced to the absurd. Here is the non-soul—man seen through the magnifying glass of caricature. Miguel de Unamuno, quoting Pascal, writes in his *Tragic Sense of Life* that a man completely non-concerned with the immortality of his soul, is a monster. How much more of a monster will he become—of a *dwarfish* monster that is—when he will be able to scientifically dispose of his soul, or whatever is left thereof, while still alive?

For what is that thing people call soul and that soul to which Judaism refers to as "Neshome"?

As far as soul is concerned, Coleridge has defined it very simply and very clearly. "Either we have an immortal soul or we have not. If we have not, we are beasts; the first and wisest of beasts it may be, but still beasts. We only differ in degree, not in kind: just as the elephant differs from the slug. But by the concession of the materialists, we are not of the same kind of beasts; and this also we say from our own consciousness. Therefore, methinks, it must be the possession of a soul within us that makes the difference." If that is the case, life, as Thackeray has expressed himself, is the soul's nursery, its training ground for the destinies of eternity.

To the Jew, however, "*Neshome*" is much more than a soul, even when the soul is defined, as it usually is in any theology, as that indestructible part in us which, when the body goes back to dust, returns to its maker. Judaism distinguishes between three kinds of souls: "Nefesh," the lowest form of soul which is given to man as well as to animals; "Ruach," a higher form of soul, which is exclusively human; and, finally, "*Neshama*" or "*Neshome*" as it is usually referred to in the vernacular Yiddish and Hebrew alike. In our own terminology, we can safely say that the immediate man has a "Nefesh"; the intermediate—a "Ruach"; the ultimate—a "Neshome."

Everybody is born with a "Nefesh"; not everybody realizes that he is born with a "Ruach," but very few know that they can *acquire* a "Neshome."

On what does such an acquisition depend? On a realization, which is singularly Jewish, that *eternity starts here.*

The soul returns to its Maker after the body is gone, but there is an acquired part in us, called Neshome, to which the *Maker returns* while the body is still alive.

How is this possible? It is possible *only* when any thought of divisiveness is gone from the heart, and when life and death, past, present and future, are viewed as a proposition of *oneness.*

Franz Rosenzweig, that giant of a Jew, had this to say about our oneness as a concept of history: "The fact that we do not live within the laws of world history, or, to state it positively, the fact of our everlastingness, renders all the phases of our history *simultaneous.* In the history of other peoples, reaching back for what has been left behind is only necessary from time to time; for us it is a constant, vital necessity. And we must not forget that it is a *vital* necessity, for we must be able to *live* within our *everlastingness.*"

"To live within our Everlastingness" is another word for a realization of Oneness.

There is only one community which counts time "from creation" and believes that time will end—time as we know it—with the coming of a Messiah *who has never as yet revealed his countenance to man.* There is only one community of which their sages say that all their souls, the souls of every Jewish man, woman and child till the end of the days, were present at Mount Sinai when the law was given. There is only one community in the world which is told by its sages that not only its forefathers went out from bondage in Egypt to freedom, but along with them, every generation that followed the Exodus—for the law of freedom is eternal, everlasting and simultaneous. There is only one community which speaks of life eternal not only as something which belongs to another life, to a life after death, but to life in *this* world. "Blessed are Thou, our Lord God, King of the universe," we say in the benediction after the reading of a section of the Torah, "Who hast planted eternal life *in our midst.*" To this Rosenzweig remarks: "The rays go forth only from this fire; and flow unresisted only to the outside. The fire of the core must burn incessantly. Its flame must eternally feed upon itself. It requires no fuel from without. Time has no power over it and must roll past. It must produce its own time and reproduce itself forever. It must make its life everlasting in the succession of generations, each producing the generation to come, and bearing witness to those gone by. Bearing witness takes place in bearing—two meanings but one act, in which eternal life is realized. Elsewhere, past and future are divorced, the one sinking back, the other coming on; here they grow into one. The bearing of the future is a direct bearing witness to the past. The son is born so that he may bear witness to his father's father. The grandson renews the name of his forebear. The patriarchs of old call upon their last descendant by his name—which is theirs. Above the darkness of the future burns the star-strewn heaven of the promise: 'So shall thy seed be. . . .' " (*Star of Redemption*)

It is against *this* background that the Jewish "Neshome" must be seen.

It must be seen, in other words, in a light of its own—the light of a people who doesn't seek the warrant of its existence in the past, present or future, but in the *wholeness* of it all. It also means, in the words of Rosenzweig again, that "the one people, though it is only *one* people, claims to contain the *whole*." When the feeling for this *whole* is decried and the claim to it renounced—and it is decried and denounced *only* because of spiritual ignorance —the Jewish "Neshome" is renounced and decried with it. And when a Jew renounces and decries his "Neshome"—and there are many such Jews nowadays—he renounces and decries his *humanity* though he may claim that he renounced his "Neshome" *because* of his humanity. A Jew who renounces his "Neshome" is a very dangerous man. Much more dangerous than he who had never had a Neshome to renounce in the first place.

"The soul of man teaches him" is an ancient Hebrew saying. What it actually says is that once a soul—and we speak of the super-soul called Neshome—is well entrenched in man, it has not only a life of its own, but something so independent from life that it becomes man's supernatural teacher—it is as if man, desperately eager to be taught, has a living teacher within himself which is a part of the world that goes *beyond* himself.

The "Neshome" is the creator of the harmony between the world which is within oneself and that which goes beyond him. Such a creation is a very long and very painful process for it requires an ability to regard heartbreak—heartbreak not dejection —as an act of creativity. . . . The "Neshome" doesn't deal with the creation of thought-systems, but with the experience of creation as a *whole*. It is the kind of creation, however, which thrives on mystery. It is a creation, or creativity, which is in love with mystery. The "Neshome" doesn't lift man out of the realm of nature, but it adds to nature—yes, to *nature*—a supernatural dimension. The "Neshome" is longing, but it is a longing which redeems itself in joy and it is a joy which is purified in sorrow. The Neshome is, to quote Shakespeare, "the sweet taste of sorrow."

The "Neshome," the way the Jew conceived of it, experiences God as it experiences itself. The "Neshome" is not a media to reach out for an ultimate ground of being, *it is an ultimate ground*. The "Neshome" is not a way to a higher reality; *it is a higher reality*. Only the very great poets—for the "Neshome" is poetry in a state of fulfilment—*intuitively* understood it. That's what Wordsworth must have meant when he spoke of the soul "in the high hour of visitation," as quoted at the end of the previous chapter. He wasn't saying, as already mentioned, that man in such a state was *giving* thanks; that he *knew* himself blessed; that he *felt* himself loving or loved. What he said was that he *was* thanksgiving; that he *was* blessedness; that he *was* love etc. The only thing Wordsworth had overlooked in describing the great soul was sorrow. The sorrow of the great soul, of the "Neshome," is the other side of its joy. A Chassidic Rabbi once expressed himself that there is nothing more *whole* than a broken heart.

The Jewish "Neshome" is the highest expression of spiritual *rootedness*. When one has a "Neshome," he *belongs* somewhere—nay, he belongs everywhere; he is at home in a universe which he *knows* and which he knows *knows him*. And not only that he is at home in the universe, but he is at home in history, even when history is an ordeal; the "Neshome" sings better in ordeals.

The ordeal is the testing stone of the Jewish "Neshome"—and we speak, as mentioned, of the ordeal of heartbreak not of dejection, for dejection and "Neshome" don't house together—and it is then when its simultaneousness, as Rosenzweig calls it, is revealed. The "Six Days' War" is a good example. During that war the Jewish "Neshome" came to the fore in all its mystical grandeur. People went to an "Immediate" war with a faith that can be described as "Ultimate"; they went to fight for their own survival, but they felt that at stake was the survival of every Jew everywhere; they fought like young lions, but they discussed their victory like old sages; they went to fight an enemy who was committed to their destruction, but they couldn't forgive their enemy not only his commitment to destroy them, but his forcing them to destroy *him;* they hated war, but few, in any war, fought more bravely than they did; they loved life, but gave it up without hesitation; they stood before the Wailing Wall as before eternity, and as they advanced they felt they were advancing *in* eternity; prior to the war most of them called themselves *"Israelis,"* not *"Jews,"* but in the ordeal of the war the word "Jew" assumed a supernatural meaning; when they went to Sinai they saw Auschwitz before their eyes, and when they entered Bethlehem, our mother Rachel's image was there to greet them; in battle there was no retreat, as there could have been no pity, but once the battle was won, humanness was the cry of the hour; commanders went to battle with military maps, of course, but beside the maps they had Bibles—to show the routes of our history as an eternity—the routes of the *everlastingness* of Judaic Israel and of Israelitic Judaism.

For it is in the Bible that the "Neshome" of Israel comes to the fore, and the "Neshome" of Israel is best expressed in the prayer of the great King Solomon who asked for "wisdom of the heart." We regard wisdom as a quality of the mind, not of the heart. The heart we associate with feeling, with sentiment, with goodness, etc. The mind—with knowledge, with study, with wisdom. "Wisdom of the heart" sounds almost like a contradiction in terms, but it *isn't*. For these are the seemingly contradictions in terms which make the so-called "old" testament eternally new and eternally true.

But the greatest "contradictoriness" of them all—a contradictoriness which is a basic tenet of the Jewish "Neshome," is that which is between the Jewish consciousness of *universal* salvation, which is the heart of the Biblical and post-Biblical Messiah idea, and the idea that Judaism maintains itself by *subtraction*. On the one hand: "for my house shall be called the prayer house of all peoples" and, on the other hand, the idea of "the remnant of Israel." "In defiance of all temporal history," Franz Rosenzweig writes in his remarkable *Star of Redemption*, "Jewish history is the history of the remnant of whom the words of the prophet that it 'will remain,' hold now and forever. . . . Temporal history deals invariably with expansion. Might is the fundamental concept of history because, with the rise of Christianity, revelation began to spread over the world, and thus all will to expansion, even that which is consciously nothing but worldly, has unconsciously become the servant of this great movement of expansion. But Judaism, and only Judaism, maintains itself by subtraction. . . ."

And that, again, is the spirit of the "Old" Testament, and the very heart of the Jewish "Neshome": the being *alone* among nations, on the one hand, and the messianic ecstasy at the thought of building one day "a prayer house for *all* the nations," on the other.

This is the hope of the Jewish "Neshome" and the heart of the Jewish Bible alike!

The radical Christian theologians of today may trace, as they do, their atheism to Nietzsche whose famous "superman" is "beyond good or evil." But it was no other than Nietzsche who understood that "the taste for the Old Testament is the touchstone with respect to 'great' or 'small'." But let's quote the entire Nietzschean passage in full:

"In the Jewish Old Testament, the book of Divine justice, there are men, things and sayings on such an immense scale that Greek and Indian literature have nothing to compare with it. One stands with fear and reverence before those stupendous remains of what man was formerly and one has sad thoughts about old Asia and its little outpushed peninsula, Europe, which would like, by all means, to figure before Asia as the 'progress of mankind.' To be sure, he who is himself only a slender, tame house-animal, and knows only the wants of a house animal (like our cultured people of today, including the Christians of 'cultured Christianity'), need neither be amazed nor sad amid those ruins—*the taste for the Old Testament is a touchstone with respect to 'great' or 'small': perhaps he will* find that the New Testament, the book of grace, still appeals more to his heart (there is much of the odor of the genuine, tender, stupid beadsman and petty soul in it.) To have bound up the New Testament (a kind of a Rococo of taste in every respect) along with the Old Testament in to one book as the 'Bible', as the 'Book in itself' *is perhaps the greatest audacity and 'sin against the spirit' which literary Europe has upon its conscience." (The Religious Mood)*

Let's add one remark to those mighty words: the taste for the so-called "Old" Testament is not only a touchstone with respect to "Great" or "Small" but, in the long run, also with respect to "good" or "evil". Anti-Old-Testament words such as are uttered by radical Christian atheists are, in a deeper sense, *anti-Jewish words, words which are an insult to the Jewish "Neshome," and, as such, have an ominous ring after Auschwitz.* When they say, for example, that it is only by "the gift of freedom in Christ that we become aware of the terrible burden of the law" we cannot help but sense the repetition of a trend which isn't new, and which, instead of saying "freedom *from* Christ"—from the limited moral deterrent represented by Christianity—they say "Freedom *in* Christ." This suspicion is even more strengthened when we come across an even more ominous sounding statement: "The Christian is liberated from the ancient power of the moral imperative by virtue of his life in Christ." These high sounding, distressingly meaningless, totally discarded words, uttered in the century of Auschwitz, bear unmistakable testimony to a moral insensitivity bordering on potential accommodation with murder. How, on earth, can one talk nowadays of "a life in Christ" after *Christ in Life*—the *daily* Christianity of the Christian peoples—has proven such a miserable failure?!

We had to say all this in the chapter about the Jew and his "Neshome" because an attempt is being made in our day and age, and not only by the "Death of God" theologians, to rob even God of His "Neshome" and to reduce Him to the stature of an intermediate commodity presented in the wrappings of a moralistic sophistry which has as little bearing on life as on truth. It is *particularly* in contradistinction to this reduced God that Judaism reintroduces into a world crazed by immediacies the undying image of its "Neshome." Judaism now, more than ever, looks proudly back on its unblemished spiritual and moral record which tells the saga of people who were ready and willing to sacrifice the immediate for the Ultimate, which, to them, was "immediate" in some way, and, in doing so, launched the only spiritual *mass movements* known to man. There were periods in the history of the Jews, and of the Jews *alone,* when even the masses, even the ignorant masses, *fully aware of their ignorance,* were made to reach out for the Ultimate. They were not philosophers, these people, but they developed in their "Neshome" an ontology, a philosophy of life, which made even unlearned men think existentially. Jewish history and the Jewish "Neshome" had the same characteristics. What typified the entire Jewish history, some great Cabalistic and Scholastic speculators notwithstanding, was not the search for the nature of God, but for the inspired human laws through which He had revealed Himself. To be more exact: the search for an Ultimate Reality was a search of a thoroughly existential nature whose aim was to live a daily life illuminated by the rays of an eternal light. This is not the reduction of the Ultimate to the immediate, but the elevation of the immediate to a state in which the Ultimate, as conceived through the "Neshome," becomes *relevant.* God is what He is—"Eheye Asher Eheye"—"I am what I am," and it is not for us to guess His nature. All we, humans, can hope for is to *feel his presence through drawing closer to Him.* The philosophy of Jewish history, or, to be more exact, Jewish meta-history, may, there-

140

fore, be traced, in the words of Nima Adlerbloom (*Memories of Childhood*) to "the profound concern of lifting oneself and the universe to the level of the 'God Image' . . . The emotional content reflects the vital moral force at the bottom of its life and the conviction which creates it. Its philosophy engendered that emotion which, in turn, constitutes its philosophy. A firm belief in the close relationship between God and His creation is one of its fundamentals."

The closest any *movement* in history has ever come to create a more intimate relationship with the Ultimate, were the Hassidic and "Mussar" movements in Eastern Europe, movements which grasped their "Neshome" as their ultimate ground of being. Professer Abraham Joshua Heshel rightly says in his masterful little book *The Earth is the Lord's* that the Jew in Eastern Europe has reached the "highest degree of *inwardness*." What does "inwardness" mean? Inwardness is the very opposite of alienation and is another word for "Neshome." A man who has reached a high degree of inwardness—which must not be confused with introversion—may seem to be alienated from the whole world around him, but he is never alienated from himself. With himself he has come to grips so that he can live his life *inwardly*. The Jew did precisely that. In a state of estrangement from the outside world which neither understood nor tolerated him, he found his glory in the inversion of his spiritual practices. The inversion was so great in fact, the inwardness so total, that he paid no attention at all to his exteriors. His whole life, lived dangerously and uprootedly, radiated, nevertheless, what Professor Heshel rightly refers to as a "wistful charm." The great worry was not lest one has nothing to live *on,* but lest one has nothing to *die with*. The great fear was not lest one is physically attacked—that was a daily experience—but lest one is defeated in the chambers of his heart. The chambers of the heart, the depths of the "Neshome," was the holy place of the Jew, the Holy of Holies, where no thought of defeat was tolerated. There is an ancient Jewish prayer which is called the prayer of "Kidush Hashem"—of sanctifying God's name—which was to be invoked by the Jew before he was put to death by evil-doers. It begins with the words, "Thou knowest the depths of my heart. . . ."

That was all that counted: the depths of one's heart as related to the "Thou." It was there where the crave for an Ultimate Reality —the immediate reality being so unbearable—assumed the nature of a great nostalgia in a state of realization. This nostalgia, noticeable even in the *eyes* of the Jew, animated the poor and the downtrodden, the beaten and the humiliated, to regard their sorrow, as well as their joy in the midst of sorrow, as an *openness* to God. The Hassidic movement contributed widely to the diffusion of the wistful charm of the Jewish "Neshome" among the Jewish masses in Eastern Europe. It did not dismiss the immediate and the intermediate in the name of the Ultimate but, rather, it brought the entire impact of the Ultimate to bear upon the immediate in a manner that added to it not only meaning and purpose, but joy of life. God was not the thing that is "over there," but over here and all over. "Without lessening the strong obligation imposed by the Torah," Martin Buber writes in his preface to *The Early Masters,* "the movement suffused all the traditional commandments with joy-bringing significance, and even set aside the walls separating the sacred and the profane, by teaching that every profane act can be rendered sacred by the manner in which it is performed. It has nothing to do with Pantheism which destroys or stunts the greatest of all values: the reciprocal relationship between the human and the divine, the reality of the I and the You which does not cease at the rim of eternity. Hassidism did, however, make manifest the reflection of the Divine, the sparks of God that glimmer in all beings and all things, and taught how to approach them, how to 'lift' and redeem them, and reconnect them with their original root. The doctrine of the Shekinah, contained in the Talmud and expanded in the Kabbalah, of the Shekinah as the Divine Presence which resides in this world, receives a new and intimate significance and applicability. If you direct the undiminished power of your fervor to God's world-destiny, if you do what you must do at this moment—no matter what it may be!—with your whole strength and with kavvanah, with holy intent, you will bring about the union of God and the Shekinah, eternity and time. You need not be a scholar or a sage to accomplish this. All that is necessary is to have a soul united within itself and indivisibly directed to its Divine goal. The world in which you live, just as it is and not otherwise, affords you that association with God which will redeem you and whatever Divine aspect of the world you have been entrusted with. And your own character, the very qualities which make you what you are, constitutes your special approach to God, your special potential use for Him. Do not be vexed at your delight in creatures and things! But do not let it shackle itself to creatures and things; through these, press on to God. Do not rebel against your desires, but seize them and bind them to God. You shall not stifle your surging powers, but let them work at holy work, and rest

142

a holy rest in God. All the contradictions with which the world distresses you are only that you may discover their intrinsic significance, and all the contrary trends tormenting you within yourself, only wait to be exorcised by your word. All innate sorrow wants only to flow into the fervor of your joy."

Yes, that was Hassidism, a spiritual mass movement, a "Neshome" movement if there ever was one, which sought, and found, a harmony and a unity between the immediate and the ultimate and which, through its prototype, the Zadik, the great spiritual helper, the master of the great "Neshome," has achieved a degree of consolation *even* in this world. There was, moreover, consolation in the very fact that there was *no* consolation! The very hopelessness bespoke hope, and the vilest manifestations of man's unredemption were the signs of reedmption to come, even if it will come only "at the end of the days." Meantime, prior to the coming of that age of redemption, the Jewish child, along with the sage, the Jewish man as the Jewish woman, the rich as the poor, the ignoramus as the scholar, knew to respond at any time, any moment and under any circumstances to the rallying call of eternity, the great battle cry of the Jewish "Neshome": "*Shema* Israel". . . . "Hear, oh Israel, the Lord our God, the Lord is *one!*" Here, in this outcry, the immediate merged with the Ultimate and became one. Here the oneness and unity of God and his people was proclaimed for all eternity. The invoking of this Ultimate password was the ultimate in fervor even when things were seemingly "normal." Thus the great Zadik, Rabbi Shlomo of Karlin, when someone asked him to promise to visit him the next day, replied: "How can you ask me to make such a promise? This evening I must pray and recite 'Hear, O Israel. . . .' While I say these words, *my soul goes out to the utmost rim of life.*"

But there were times when the Jewish "Neshome," upon invoking these words, went beyond the rim of life, to its ultimate source of meaning. We have spoken before of "Kidush Hashem," self-sacrifice for the sanctification of God's name, but one cannot invoke the 'Hear, O Israel . . .' without realizing the real magnitude of "Kidush Hashem." When humanity is gasping with despair, as it does nowadays; when science and art, far from reducing man's problems to a "handful, such as death and guilt," have miserably failed to save man from a sense of utter futility, the need for a consecration of his soul becomes acute. And if this is so in "normal times," how much more so in days of death? Thus the saintly Rabbi Menahem Ziemba of Praga, revered spiritual leader of the

Warsaw Ghetto, had explained Kidush Hashem *existentially*. And what he said is essentially this: The ideal of Kidush Hashem is born anew with every act of supreme fulfillment. Our appreciation of its glory grows with our experience. It is an act of wedding the ephemeral to the enduring, the immediate to the Ultimate, the reaching out for the highest point of eternity in the flux of temporality. "Our sacred lore teaches us," he tells the leaders of a ghetto facing extinction, "that in the long run the *inward* attitude is more important than outward conditions. . . . It is the verdict of history that the world is built on moral foundations. In the long run it is ill with the evil doer and well with the just."

And these words—let's not forget!—were uttered in the midst of a starving, bleeding, dying ghetto. It was in the midst of this hell on earth that the great man spoke of "Divine Guidance," "loving Father in heaven" and "spiritual healing"!

And that, the ability to hear in the midst of total darkness the voice that discloses the ineffable in the "Neshome," is also, so it seems to us, the secret of the *"Kadish,"* the inimitable Jewish prayer for the dead.

There is not a single word about dying in this prayer, not one single word, and that is the secret of its Ultimateness. The Kadish, because of what it says and how it says it, must be recited with a raised head and a stout heart. It requires a spiritual fortitude, a manly stamina, a holy faith, a passionate disposition, a heroic fearlessness and, indeed, an infinite resignation such as only those who see in death a transfer to a higher life and in life—a glimpse of eternity—can ever hope to experience. The main purpose of the *Kadish* is total identification with the *ultimate* when the immediate seems to collapse before our very eyes. Its power is great enough to drown in the Ultimate seas of God's glory any personal pain, any sigh of mourning, any cry of anguish, any fear of death or any thought of loneliness. The intensity of the Kadish's power, the crescendo of its Divine exaltation, the scope of its cosmic involvement, the magnitude of its transcending majesty, are of such dimensions that he who soulfully and humbly follows its words cannot help but experience what the Oceanic Neshome of its mysterious author must have craved and achieved: that man in mourning rises above himself and his natural, immediate feelings by realizing that, at times, the revealed majesty of the supernatural pales the natural and immediate into insignificance. The Kadish cannot, and must not be translated. Its power lies in its original words as much as in the unparalleled, hymnlike music in which it is traditionally intoned on High Holidays. The words, as the music, speak of life, not of death, in a manner that makes one wonder whether death is not an illusion.

Yitgadal Veyitkadash Shmei Rabah. . . .

And this song of glory, and life, and love, and gratitude—impossible to translate even partly—is called "The Prayer for the Dead"! A soul that sees death in its most shattering immediate aspect, and rises, on the wings of a mighty nostalgia, to the brim of the Ultimate, is an Ultimate soul, is a "Neshome" in a state of Oneness. Such a "Neshome" is capable of conducting a *dialogue* with its Maker when it should normally be muted by tragedy, silenced by grief and immobilized by terror.

Survival for what?
For the sake of the Jewish "Neshome."

Chapter Seven

STRANGERS TO GLORY

Alienation is the sickness of a consciousness in search of a self. When Dostoyevsky says (in *Notes from the Underground*) that "Over-consciousness is a real thorough-going sickness," he meant the existential neurosis which attacks man once he has risen above the immediate. Clinical neurosis—the neurosis which Freud speaks of—can attack also the immediate man, but one has to be intermediate in order to experience the existential neurosis and the feeling of alienation it often brings with it. Alienation, in other words, is the sickness of the intermediate man. The immediate man, unless it's a matter of being "alienated from tools of production," to quote Marx, or unless we deal with plain self-hatred, knows little or nothing of it. The aroused, enlarged, sensitive consciousness of man, however, often split against itself, estranged from its surroundings, in constant search for deeper roots and a more meaningful identity, is bound to go through the painful stages of alienation.

That is why the alienation of the Jewish intellectual is, in most cases, graver than that of his non-Jewish counterpart: his alienation as a man is greatly enhanced by his alienation as a Jew. Franz Kafka is a typical example. Here was a man with a spirit as alienated as any in this century and with an ability to give to this alienation a stark, shatteringly powerful expression. But Kafka, in his double alienation, remained a Jewish intellectual, or, to be more exact, a tormented intellectual of his Jewishness. Whatever Kafka wrote is *desperately* Jewish. Take "The Trial," for example: like the hero of the novel, the Jew is, or, at least, was engaged in an endless trial. He did not know his judges, hardly even his lawyers; he did not know what wrong he had done or what he was charged with. The only thing he knew was that he was considered guilty for some crime he had never committed, and that, because

146

he was considered guilty, he was going to be tried for his life. Judgment, however, was continually delayed. He took advantage of these postponements to improve his position in a thousand ways. But to no avail. Every precaution taken at random pushed him a little deeper into guilt. His external situation may have appeared brilliant at times, but the interminable trial quietly wasted his strength away. Finally the thing which had always seemed inevitable to him happens: some men seize him and, on the pretense that he had lost his case, carry him off and murder him in the suburbs. Or take *The Castle* as another example. Only Kafka could have conceived of and portrayed a man who is slowly crushed under the agonizing weight of an inability to know the nature of the hoped for "Castle," and the mysterious Lord who dwells therein, or, even, to get close to the castle—a weight as unbearable as the endless and unfulfilled messianic expectancy of the Jews.

The modern Jewish intellectual, however, is alienated in a different way: his alienation being as despiritualized as it is de-Judaized, he regards spirituality and Judaism as too subjective and sentimental propositions for a man who considers the "universal" and "objective" as a certificate of intellectual prowess. As such he is making pathetic efforts to make his Jewishness as unnoticeable as, for instance, his neurosis. His psychoanalyst, most likely as alienated as his patient (if he is an intellectual psychoanalyst, that is, which is as rare as a religious one), must have told him that his neurosis is partly attributable to his Jewishness. That helped him, of course, to explain the neurosis, but it didn't help to explain the Jewishness. The Jewishness of the Jewish intellectual, the ineradicable traces of whatever is left thereof that is, bothers him, because while he cannot rationally explain his inner preoccupation with something which is not supposed to play any role in his life—that "something," whether he wants it or not, *does* play a role in his life! That is why this Jewish intellectual is often a very odd creature, and, as often, a very pitiable one, too, for what he knows of his Jewishness isn't enough to make him want to know more, and what he doesn't know about it is plenty to make him want to forget the little he knows. When such a specimen is asked about his Jewishness, his answer, in most cases, will be composed of two parts: the first part will declare his admiration for the Jewish craving for justice, and the second—if there is a second part, that is—will tell of his love for "gefilte fish" or "matzo balls." He will be very careful not to exaggerate his admiration for the Jewish craving for justice, lest he be suspected of underestimating this craving in others, or, God forbid, of "sentimentalism"; but when it comes to his admiration for "gefilte fish" or "matzo balls," his praise will be lavish. He will, moreover, express the thought that while the Jewish heritage may fade away, "chicken soup and matzo balls will tarry on for awhile," though the "history of the Jews from now on will be the history of everybody else." (*Commentary,* April, 1962)

Thank God for the chicken soup and the matzo balls! It will provide dying Judaism with a badly needed culinary post-mortem. Imagine if it were the other way around: if matzo balls and chicken soup were to fade away while the heritage tarried on to make sure that the history of the Jews continued to bear the marks of a distinct destiny! The "objectivity" of the alienated Jewish intellectual, his desire to be like everybody else as a Jew, but his readiness to defend to the bitter end his right to be different as an intellectual, would be scandalized. But there is no such danger, thank God, at least not theoretically. Theoretically, the alienated Jewish intellectual is on safe apologetic ground when he officializes his divorce from Jewish thinking by making love declarations to Jewish cooking, for example. (This, by the way, can hardly be said of the externalized, despiritualized Jewish snob who would rather choke on clams than order chopped liver in a fancy restaurant. But we shall deal with this type later.) What such an "intellectual" approach actually amounts to is a curious attempt made by this kind of Jew to get away from the teachings of his forefathers by paying homage to the cooking of his grandmothers, and it's a very consoling approach, too. For we were somehow worried —though we are not in the delicatessen business—lest this strange Jewish mind-shaper places even the *taste* for matzo balls on the same out-of-fashion level as the ritual of eating tasteless matzos on Passover, for example. Now that the celebrated Jewish delicacy— and we mean the matzo balls, not the matzos—God forbid—is so frequently given an intellectual OK, our mind is at peace.

But not entirely so. We are somehow afraid—and we mean it very seriously—that in the professed adoration of chicken soup and matzo balls there is hidden a complex of a special kind which is unknown even to the fantastic terminology of Freud. I would call it, its jocular connotation notwithstanding, "the matzo ball complex." This is, to be sure, a complex of a very unique and very subtle nature. It is, namely, a complex which induces one to love something particular out of a much larger whole which he greatly dislikes. This man doesn't feel entirely happy, or he may even feel a little guilty, with his disliking the larger, indefinable whole—a whole he knows nothing or little about—that is why he resorts to declaring his love for something very definable and provable, but utterly irrelevant, out of the whole he rejects. The anti-Semite who says that some of his best friends are Jews has actually said, as we all know, that Jewry as such he dislikes.

The alienated Jewish intellectual is not the same as the alienated Catholic intellectual, or the alienated intellectual of any other creed, race, or nation. And the reason is that the alienated Jewish intellectual is alienated from something he knows nothing about except that it has caused too many of his people for many years lots of suffering and humiliations. His consciousness, as an intellectual, as a creative man, as an intermediate man, being larger than the usual—his sensitivity and, consequently, his ability to receive impressions is, of course, enlarged too. But in his enlarged ability to receive impressions, the impressions he receives are singularly one-sided. He received, for example, the whole picture of the calamity that befell the Jewish body, but incapable to see the Jewish "Neshome"—something which requires much more time than it takes to acquire a taste for matzo balls—he believes that the whole Jewish *via dolorosa* is meaningless. The problem of the Jewish intellectual is, in other words, the problem of his attitude toward suffering. Not toward evil in general, but toward an evil which has singled out his people as its "favorite" target. In this respect he is a very unique case. For the Catholic intellectual, for example, tries to find in his Catholicism *shelter* from sin and evil, which is another word for the seeking of inner security; the Jewish intellectual, by contrast, a stranger to glory, is constantly aware of the fact that to be a *Jew* actually means to choose *insecurity*—an insecurity which is in addition to that he experiences as a man. In order to reach a state of security in Jewishness one has to be a man with a highly developed taste for the ultimate, and this is something which is as far from the average Jewish intellectual as spirituality, for example, is from Sigmund Freud. The average Jewish intellectual is a man with a strong intermediate concern—no doubt about that—and his craving for justice is as sincere as any, only that the Jewish intellectual, victimized by complexes arising from the conscious or subconscious suppression of his concern with the ultimate, which is a concern with the widest possible range of man, believes that he must somehow "prove" this craving for justice by objectifying it. And what we mean by "objectifying" is the fact that the alienated Jewish intellectual, to prove his objectivity and universality, will prefer to associate himself with causes of other peoples rather than his own and, at the same time, will derive a perverse delight, which he will again describe as a sign of artistic objectivity, out of concentrating on describing objectionable Jewish characters.

He is, in fact, so "objective," the alienated Jewish intellectual, that while he gladly concentrates on the best traits of others, when it comes to his own—his own people—he is morbidly delighted to single out the worst. He concentrates in particular on those traits which the anti-Semite described as "Jewish" and which he, the anti-Semite, as Sartre has already observed, has actually created in the Jew through anti-Semitism. The anti-Semite has poisoned the life of the Jew, the atmosphere around him, the food he ate, the air he breathed, and even, in some instances, the soul he precariously sustained. But the alienated Jewish intellectual delights in describing this atypical, maimed soul in detail and he calls it "objectivity." That's how he calls it—particularly when his description of the objectionable Jewish type is coupled with a declaration of love for matzo balls and, of course, the "Jewish craving for justice." Oh, that "Jewish craving for justice"! The admiration for this craving —let us say it openly—is a curse when it comes from the mouth of an alienated Jew to whom the craving for justice is primarily a craving to overlook or to forget injustices done to those who are distinguished, as he himself admits, precisely by possessing this craving—his own people! It is this "objectivity" which is so revolting, the "objectivity" which typifies those "lovers of humanity" whose love is in proportion to the remoteness of the object they are supposedly in love with. Dostoyevsky has known and described such "lovers" almost a century ago. It is Ivan Karamazov who says somewhere that you can love humanity while actually hating your neighbor. "I could never understand," he says, "how one can love one's neighbors. It's just one's neighbor's, to my mind, that one can't love, though one might love those at a distance." The elder Zosima, in the same great novel, tells of a doctor who said, "the more I love humanity in general, the less I love man in particular . . . the more I detest men individually, the more ardent becomes my love for humanity." [1]

---

[1] The same, let us add without hesitancy, is true of another kind of lovers: lovers of the Bible. And I don't mean the non-Jewish lover of the Bible. He is an entirely different case. The true non-Jewish lover of the Bible tries to make the Bible relevant in the way he understands it, while some Jewish Bible-lovers, particularly in Israel, thrive on belittling the interpretational literature—as Hebrew as the Bible itself—which alone can make the Bible *relevant* to the Jew. I am referring to a phenomenon which is Israeli in

But let's come back to the alienated Jewish intellectual. What distinguishes this split personality, particularly of the leftist, not to say new-leftist genre, is the *anonymous* nature of his love. Impersonal ideology has replaced in him personal compassion, and the abstract thought has reduced his social consciousness, of which he likes to boast, to a sheer verbalism. By some sick twist of his imagination, this consciousness, even in its verbalized expression, is more dormant in face of evil committed against his neighbor than that committed against "humanity." The alienated Jewish intellectual particularly of the Marxist school, thus finds some kind of morbid satisfaction in underplaying, or completely disregarding, the tragedy of his people and in over-emphasizing his involvement with the plight of other peoples. Is this altruism? No, it is the

---

nature and which expresses itself in a general love of the Bible that goes, in many cases, hand in hand with an intense dislike of the applied, Talmudically interpreted Biblical law. The love of the Bible, as the love of humanity, has thus become a convenient abstraction which doesn't commit one to anything but humanistic oratory. Mr. Ben-Gurion is one of the exponents of this Bible love—a love which, as we all know, flourishes, in his case, on a total disregard for the mighty pillars of Jewish wisdom—Talmud, Cabala, Hassidism, etc. Mr. Ben-Gurion believes that nothing great has been created in the Diaspora—that the two thousand years of Jewish history, starting with Babylon and ending with the "shtetel"—a history which was one enormous effort to make the Bible existentially relevant—is irrelevant for the continuation of Jewish life in Israel and abroad. The old statesman and warrior finds it difficult to like the "shtetel" almost as much as Ivan Karamazov found it difficult to love his neighbor. Thus Ivan Karamazov's love of humanity, in spite of his hatred of his neighbor, is the equivalent of Mr. Ben-Gurion's love of the Bible in spite of his intense dislike of the "shtetel." To love the prophets is as easy as to love humanity. It is the applied interpretation of this love which makes or breaks it *ontologically*. For there is a love which doesn't commit one to anything but big words, and there is a love which commits one even to small deeds, which are terribly important. The first may be adapted even by tyrants and may be even used as an excuse for murder. The second is predicated upon the practice of the law of the deterrent. When the great Hillel tells the man who desired to learn the entire law "on one foot" that " 'love thy neighbor as thyself' is the entire law and all the rest is commentary; go and study it"—he had made a prophetic pronunciation. By saying so he has not only made clear that it is man—the next fellow—who is the measure of all things, not an abstraction called mankind, but he had put the onus on what was going to become in the future the real test case of love, namely, the man most difficult to love—your neighbor! "All the rest is commentary." But without the commentary, this love is unrealizable. It is as unrealizable as the Bible without the Talmud. To love the prophets while rejecting the Talmud is the same thing as to love humanity while despising man. The same, of course, is true of the love of God practiced by some ultra-orthodox Jews in Israel and abroad—a love of God totally lacking a social dimension—the dimension that concerns one's neighbor. The sages must have had such people in mind when they intoned the extreme warning: "I wish they had abandoned me, (said the Lord) but kept my law."

151

meanest kind of egotism which caters to the insensitivity of self-denial. For the truth of the matter is that he who doesn't show understanding for his own, or his immediate neighbor's pain, can hardly be trusted with the pain of others. And what typifies the alienated Jewish intellectual, his preoccupation with "social justice" notwithstanding, is his total lack of understanding as well as total lack of interest, in the meaning of his own pain or that of his kith and kin. Many of these intellectuals, moreover, regard their Jewishness as an embarrassing affliction even if nobody bothers them on account of this Jewishness. For when nobody bothers them on account of their Jewishness, they bother themselves on the same account—and, as a result of this bothering, they become the champions of remote causes at the expense of their own cause. The most extreme case of the alienated Jewish intellectual is trying to escape the "affliction" of his Jewishness by identifying himself with remote afflictions of others, even if these others are enemies of his people and committed to his people's destruction.

But even those who do not treat their Jewishness as an affliction are still struck with an inability to understand the nature of Jewish martyrology—something which cannot be understood even within the range of an intermediate preoccupation, let alone an immediate. Thus an important, non-alienated Jewish intellectual in the U.S.A. can make the following statement: "I have often wondered whether survival as a distinct group was worth one hair on the head of a single infant. . . . Did the Jews have to survive so that six million innocent people should one day be burned in the ovens of Auschwitz? It is a terrible question and no one, not God Himself, could ever answer it to my satisfaction. I think I know why the Jews once wished to survive, (though I am less certain as to why they still do)." (*Commentary,* February, 1963.)

The question of whether the Jews had to survive so that six million innocent people would one day be burned in the gas ovens of Auschwitz, is not for us to answer. But it *is* for us to conclude that *since* six million innocent people *did* die in the Auschwitzes of twentieth century Europe, *the survival of the Jews as a distinct group is now a moral imperative.* Not to wish to survive *after* Auschwitz is to wish to say to Auschwitz (and to Hitler): you have won! This alone makes the question of whether the survival as a distinct group was worth one hair on the head of a single Jewish infant not only meaningless, but blasphemous. We are dealing now not with an *a priori* choice between the hair of one single infant and the survival of a distinct group, but with an *a posteriori* fact of the death of a *million* infants who couldn't help their belonging to a distinct group any more than they could help their birth. Does this death *commit* us to something? The question is Hamletic: to survive or not to survive! Is the spiritual self-extinction of the Jews the right answer to their physical elimination? For isn't this self-extinction through voluntary assimilation, for example, another word for annihilation? Klausevitz defined war as politics implemented by different means. Isn't voluntary assimilation, by the same token, a "final solution" implemented by peaceful means? That's one thing. But there is something else, too: in the ovens of Auschwitz were undoubtedly burned many Jews who did not want to survive as Jews even before Hitler, but they had no choice, for even being born as a Jew, not religiously, but racially, as we all know, was punishable by death. To this, as another Jewish intellectual remarked, "Pride somehow falls short of an effective antidote." And he is right. Unless the antidote to this immediate evil is a preoccupation with evil on an ultimate scale, which is another word for a search in depth for the ultimate meaning of Jewishness and its suggested panacea against evil—Auschwitz, which had poisoned our deaths, will forever poison our lives.

But let's go back for a moment to the Jewish intellectual who believes that Jewish survival as a distinct group isn't worth one hair on the head of a single Jewish child. Now we are as concerned as anybody else with the survival of the Jewish child, but we fear that the juxtaposition of the infant's hair versus the distinctness of the group is dangerously erroneous. The fact of the matter is that the choice is no more between the survival of the child and that of the distinctness of the group, but, in the worst case, between physical non-survival of the infant *in spite* of his non-distinctness and survival *in spite* of distinctness; or in the best case, spiritual survival because of distinctiveness versus (spiritual) non-survival because of non-distinctiveness. Auschwitz has once and for all abolished the dilemma between survival of the child and that of the heritage (a dilemma which was valid particularly during the Spanish inquisition). Any totalitarian anti-Semitism after Hitler is bound to be Auschwitz-oriented. Any swastika painted anywhere in the world on overturned Jewish gravestones or on the walls of Jewish prayer houses, as is now the case in Germany again, as well as in other lands, is a reminder that the Auschwitz mentality is alive and kicking. It will be even more alive or more kicking when the prejudiced minds in the Christian world will decide that what they call "the Jewish influence" is growing too fast and too strong. That is why the question that faces us right now is this: if pride is not the antidote to Auschwitz, and it certainly isn't—Auschwitz inflicted a more severe and more lasting injury to human pride than the atomic bomb to the hope of human survival—isn't it true that *contempt* is, or, at least, must be?

"What is the greatest thing you can experience?" Nietzsche asks in *So Spake Zarathustra,* and he answers, "It is the hour of great contempt—the hour in which even your happiness is loathsome to you, and your reason and your virtue likewise."

That is true, of course. But, let's add immediately, that what is most loathsome to the truly sensitive Jewish mind in the hour of the great contempt is spiritual ignorance.

For if the hour of the great contempt doesn't make ignorance loathsome and evil in our eyes, our contempt will be as sterile as our knowledge and as impotent as our anger.

Jewry's hour of great contempt is the hour in which it will rediscover its "Neshome"; the hour in which it will regard and declare spiritual ignorance—and be it its own—as a crime against God and man.

For it's not the ignorance of a history we are talking about; or the ignorance of a language; or of a prayer book, or of a civilization, or culture, but the ignorance of the "Neshome" of Judaism— the ignorance, in other words, of the thing which caused, and causes, whatever is evil in the world to be its enemy.

If the evil of anti-Semitism, more than any other evil, culminating in, but not ending with Auschwitz, is rooted in the terrifying ignorance of the Gentile about the Jew, what is it but a form of evil—the evil of self-destruction—for a Jew to be ignorant about his Jewishness?

The spiritual answer to Auschwitz is a universal Jewish contempt for ignorance about Jewishness. For a Jew to ignore Jewishness after Auschwitz is to ignore Auschwitz, period.

And we don't speak of the contempt that goes together with hatred, but with dismay; not that which curses, but that which reprimands; not the contempt that destroys bridges, but that which creates storms. We speak of the contempt that *is* a storm—a thunderstorm, to be exact. It terrifies people and cleanses the air. Anne Frank hoped for a day, which never came—a day on which she could write stories that would "shake people out of their senses." Only in the hour of the great contempt are such stories written.

"The hour of great contempt!" What more than this hour of holy anger, this mood of wise, purifying wrath, this elevation to a stage of learned dismay, would have been a befitting reaction to Auschwitz? Only the hour of great contempt—a contempt purged of the desire to avenge and of the temptation to forgive alike— could have focused human attention on evil as it is and could make its reappearance under a thousand different masks *loathsome in advance*. Only such an hour could provide the lightning whose fiery tongues would constantly lick man's putrifying wounds. Only such an hour could provide mankind with a preoccupation with evil on a global scale. Such a preoccupation would infect people with a holy restlessness that would make them see themselves and shudder in disgust at their failings. And who could give expression to this hour if not those who master the art of expression to a point of sometimes expressing the inexpressible? This people—and we are talking of the alienated Jewish intellectuals—have given expression to all the immediate and petty contempts in the world— be they in the realm of the social, political or psychopathological —but the hour of the great Jewish contempt eluded them, for no man is capable of mastering the strength to launch such an hour without having tasted from the deep wells of the Ultimate Concern. The gates of the great Vineyard of Wisdom, or the great *search* thereof—which is in itself wisdom—the wisdom which, contrary to knowledge "cannot be communicated unless experienced," (Herman Hesse) remained more closed than ever in the era following Auschwitz. Nobody, but nobody, in the wake of Auschwitz, has peered into the depth of the dark, hidden vineyards and died in a scream of despair as did Ben Azzai in the great Tanaic era, following the destruction of Jerusalem; nobody has lost his mind in the maddening contemplation of the "vineyard's" unyielding secret, as was the case with Ben Zoma; nobody even vandalized the plants in a manner typical to an enraged lion, as was the case with Elisha Ben Abuya—not an enraged mutton or enraged skunk, but an enraged lion! For in order to be able to vandalize the plants one has first to *enter* the vineyard! To enter it even forcefully, violently, defiantly, to crush the gates if needed, but to enter it! For who can hope in our day and age for a Rabbi Akiba who could enter and leave the vineyard peacefully?

But no vandalization from within of the vineyard's plants is going on in our day and age; in order to do so one must first have acquired a taste for the plants and a need to irrigate them and see them grow. Without it the plants are not vandalized from within the vineyard, only spat at from without. And the terrible thing that has happened before our very eyes is that the alienated Jewish intellectual, aware that the plants he spat at grow on pains, grew ashamed of these pains!

Along with a thousand other intellectuals of other peoples and other creeds he is not ashamed to dive head on into the swamps of dirt, darkness, and evil which are hidden in the psyche's hinterland, but he is ashamed, or afraid, or both, to explore the meaning of the dirt, darkness and evil which caused in the very midst of the twentieth century people to condemn other people to death just because they were born members of a certain race. The alienated Jewish intellectuals' embarrassment at Jewish suffering is so great, in fact, that he rejoices at the belief that Marx and Freud, for example, (whose Jewishness he likes to underline) have "scientifically" undermined the spiritual distinctness of the Jew, a distinctness which he, the alienated intellectual, equates with useless suffering. That is why the thought of an ultimate concern is anathema to him. A Job—even if he *is* a Job—who is ashamed of his pains, instead of being aroused, angered and awed by them, doesn't even curse God and die—he lives to mock Him.

That is why the Ultimate Concern, the concern with man's third dimension, the concern with the Logos as a corollary to the Bios and the Ethos, is so totally foreign to the alienated Jewish intellectual. He knows something about suffering, of course, and is concerned with evil, but his tendency to objectify it bears more testimony to insensitivity than to humanity and to inferiority than to generosity. He lives on the shores of a great ocean, but feels at home in rivers, particularly polluted rivers. His only redeeming feature is his aversion for the dwarfs around him who don't even see the river, but who regard their tiny little lakes, the size of swimming pools, as oceans. For there is a level which is infinitely lower than that of the alienated Jewish intellectual, and that's the one of the estranged Jewish ignoramus, particularly when he is successful!

If the alienated Jewish intellectual at least seeks answers to questions of an intermediate nature, the estranged Jewish ignoramus is bothered only by immediate questions, and the few which go beyond the immediate he regards as a pest, not a challenge. If the alienated Jewish intellectual is pitiable, the estranged Jewish ignoramus is contemptible; and he is contemptible because the result of his self-denial is not even self-satisfaction, but, in most, if not all cases, an ostentatious self-aggrandizment which comes to cover up an unadmitted but unyielding sense of insecurity. This insecurity, in turn, seeks, in some cases, refuge in snobbery and in others, in vulgarity. The insecurity which seeks refuge in snobbery is typical of the Jew—even intelligent Jew—who can never free himself of the nagging, often tortuous thought, that had he not been Jewish, he would have been more successful and more "accepted." By whom? It is the answer to this simple question which tells of the tragi-comedy inherent in this mentality. This type of Jew knows pretty well that those whose acceptance he seeks don't have to possess any intrinsic values in order for him to seek their acceptance, yet he seeks it as if his life depended on it. He knows, moreover, that when it comes to values of a moral and spiritual nature, his own "unaccepted" people were those who had originally taught those values to a world of Christians whose acceptance he seeks in spite of a vague inner feeling that they were not very good pupils. He seeks this acceptance, in other words, not because of moral and spiritual reasons, but because of reasons of social convenience which not only subdue in his mind all other considerations, but which make him angry at being reminded that any other considerations exist! The estranged Jewish assimilationist is, therefore, not only an anti-spiritual, but an immoral man. For only an immoral man is capable of seeking "acceptance" of people whom he respects not because they are right but because they are prejudiced. If anti-Semitism is, at least in France, "a poor man's snobbery," as Sartre calls it (in *Anti-Semite and Jew*), assimilation is the snobbery of a pour *soul*—of soullessness that is. The estranged Jewish assimilationist knows very well that the portrait of the Jew as envisaged by those whose total acceptance he so desperately seeks is not the right portrait. He, himself, may not know, in his pitiable self-ignorance, what the right portrait is, but he certainly knows that a couple of thousand years of Christian prejudice is enough to create the wrong portrait of the Jew even in minds which claim to have purged themselves from such prejudices. Yet he tries to assimilate himself with people whose portrait of the Jew he knows to be wrong. Does he try to change the portrait which the others have of him? But how can he do so if he doesn't know what real portrait of himself he should present in the first place? So what does he do? He presents a portrait of himself which is not himself, but of the himself as he wants it to be seen by others. A phantom personality is created which haunts its creator all his life. And it haunts him all his life because while he pretends to be what he wants to be, he has actually become what he believes that others want him to be.

While he pretends to measure values by one quality, he actually measures them by an entirely different one!

Arthur Koestler in a brilliant essay on the incurable social malady called "snobbery" has this to say about its anatomy: "The phenomenon is so general that a society free from the germ of snobbery is difficult to imagine. In such an aseptic society human beings would be judged purely by their intrinsic value, and not by rank, fame, wealth, or professional achievement. But at once the question arises: what exactly do we mean by intrinsic value? Courage or humility, wit or warmth, or saintliness? We cannot arrive at value judgment without a frame of reference. Appraisals can only be made by selecting a specific yardstick. We cannot even ask whether the yardstick is 'appropriate' as such. A boxing fan is not a snob because he sets a higher value on Joe Louis than on T. S. Eliot; nor is the music enthusiast to whom Yehudi Menuhin is more important than Winston Churchill. Yet, the social hostess with the musicality of a cow who raves about Yehudi and longs to have him for a cocktail party is a snob *because she pretends to measure value by one quality whereas, in fact, she measures it by another.*" And what is true of snobbery is true of assimilation. Yes, assimilation is the snobbery of the poor soul!

I cannot restrain myself from relating a factual story on the subject. A New York society lady who is very active in all kinds of charity, particularly Israeli charities, once related to me, not without excitement, how golf came to the aid of Israel in a very critical moment. The lady in question had been trying for quite some time to overcome the resistance or, at least indifference, to Israel displayed by a group of fellow members of one of the most fashionable country clubs in the New York area. So what did the good lady do? She invited the Ambassador of Israel to be her and her husband's guest for a Sunday luncheon at the club, to be followed by a game of golf "with the boys." The lady and her husband invited to their table some of those estranged club members who were distinguished precisely by their regarding golf as much more of a status symbol than Israel, for example. They were never associated with Israeli causes nor did they ever visit Israel. They belonged to those adorable creatures who, when visiting the Near East, never go further than the Greek Islands . . . Jerusalem, Athens and Rome may have created what we now call "Western Civilization," but there is a strange breed of estranged Jews who would go to Rome and Athens, but stop short of Jerusalem. . . . . Well, anyway—the highly intellectual Ambassador, a graduate of

Eton and Cambridge, but otherwise not much more enamoured of spiritual Jewishness than his new table companions, did not discuss Israel with them, certainly not Jewishness. But the things he did discuss—sports, politics, etc.—he discussed in a style and manner that soon began, in the lady's words, to "lend some kind of status to the country he represented." This status, moreover, assumed the nature of a full, rounded, almost admirable, symbol of importance when the Ambassador's eloquence on the golf course matched that which he had displayed at the table. When the party returned for dinner, the lady assured me, some of the "boys" who played with the Ambassador "were satisfied that Israel was something to be proud of." I asked the nice lady what caused this sudden outburst of admiration, particularly in view of the fact that the Ambassador, as she herself told me, did not discuss Israel at all prior to or during the game of golf? The lady was amazed at my lack of imagination. "He didn't have to—don't you see? Up to their meeting with the Ambassador, they thought Israel, well . . . you know . . . they thought Israel was old-fashioned—'Yeshivas' and the like. Don't you understand?"

I did. I didn't say anything to my excited lady friend, but I thought a great deal of the curse of snobbery when it combines forces with ignorance and false pretense. For what has actually happened here is a typical case of pretending to measure values by the yardstick of one quality while actually doing so with another. The estranged Jewish members of the fashionable country club knew very well that neither the Ambassador's English nor his golf was typical of the land of Israel which he represented. These were, if anything, typical of him personally. Yet the members of the club changed their minds about the land because of the man. Why? Because the man suddenly appeared to them as a *social challenge* —as a "Jones" to keep up with at least for a while. That was enough to make them create the false impression, maybe even in their own shallow selves, that it was the land of Israel, not the man of Eton, that they have suddenly become proud of!

That is as far as snobbery is concerned. But snobbery in most, if not all cases, thrives on ignorance. The person who, in Koestler's words, "attaches more importance to Joe Louis than to T. S. Eliot" is certainly not a snob, but an ignoramus he is! He would not have been an ignoramus had he attached to them *different* values, even equally important different values, whose different natures were equally known to him. But if the value he attaches to Joe Louis is so great as to pale T. S. Eliot into insignificance, he *is* an ignoramus! (And it goes without saying that when we use the names of "T. S. Eliot" or "Joe Louis", we don't mean the specific values represented by these two specific men, but the values we describe as "Immediate," as represented by a Joe Louis, versus the intermediate values or, maybe, even the crave for an ultimate value, as represented by a man like T. S. Eliot who, by the way, hated the immediate and mediocre.)

In the confrontation between the members of the New York country club and the golf-playing Israeli Ambassador, the "golf" was the immediate, the visible, the provable, the "fashionable," a kind of a "Joe Louis" value. Israel, on the other hand, as pictured in the minds of some of the club members, was the non-practical, the spiritual, the old-fashioned, the "Yeshivas," kind of an unfashionable and outdated "T. S. Eliot" (for the real T. S. Eliot was rather fashionable!). However, the same members have changed their minds about Israel, its "Yeshivas" notwithstanding, because its Ambassador was a good golf player. Suppose he was not. Suppose the Ambassador was a "T. S. Eliot"—a poet that is, who is not fond of golf, but say, of walking, which is the poor man's golf, as most poets are, what then? The answer is this: an ambassador who is a "Joe Louis" can make a "T. S. Eliot" respectable in the eyes of the estranged Jewish ignoramus, but an ambassador who is a "T. S. Eliot"—without Eliot's fame that is—should rather stay home. "T. S. Eliot," of course, may be a good golf player, but in that case it will be the golf, not the poetry, that will constitute his claim to fame in the eyes of the immediate men around him. The golf will make the poetry respectable, not that the poetry will make the golf lovable.

Small wonder, therefore, that Jewishness is on the decline. In a world that is crazed with the immediate, the values which Judaism can offer, and which Israel is supposed to represent, require a "T. S. Eliot" rather than a "Joe Louis" yardstick. Israel was supposed to be a "T. S. Eliot" proposition to start with, and its "Yeshivas" were supposed to contribute to it. That doesn't mean that Israel was supposed to be disinterested in "Joe Louis"; on the contrary: "T. S. Eliot" and "Joe Louis" had to present in Israel two sides of the same coin. But "Joe Louis" *alone* was not supposed to be Israel's claim to fame!

The trouble with any successful, estranged ignoramus, particularly with the Jewish ignoramus, is that he confuses immediacy with modernism and is thus convinced that a man *is* what he owns or shows: if he owns a couple of modern cars, a couple of TV sets, a modern house with modern furniture, and a modern abstract painting on the wall (which he doesn't even like), not to say a modern swimming pool—he is "modern." But the jungle of modern houses swarms with spiritual cave men, as the modern offices do with dwarfs in gray flannel suits. There is no provincial like the big-city provincial and nobody is more outdated that he who lives only by his instincts and his reactions to the visual and external in life.

We said a little earlier that the estranged successful Jewish ignoramus seeks refuge from his insecurity either in snobbery or in vulgarity (or in both). We have dealt briefly with snobbery and we ought to say something about vulgarity.

Vulgarity was as alien to the Jewish mind as idolatry. A faith which provided for laws to cover the entire man from the cradle to the grave, and which sought a unity between the holy and the profane, had to be concerned with every minute aspect of man's behavior—even his behavior in the toilet (yes, even in the toilet!). As such, it went to incredible lengths to describe what constitutes gossip, for example, and even what constitutes "the dust of gossip"—a gossip that was not intended to harm anybody, but is harmful just because it is in some devious way related to gossip. The sages of Israel describe as a sin not only the usage of improper language, but the toleration of an unesthetic appearance. The sages go so far as to say that "a man of wisdom who tolerates a stain on his garments condemns himself to death." Tastelessness, self-neglect, on the one hand, and showiness, loudness, ostentatiousness, impertinence, conceit, coveteousness, on the other, were regarded as desecrations of God's name and, consequently, as desecrations of the holy name—man. Anything that was self-demeaning was God-demeaning and vice versa. The "Hafetz Hayim," one of the great illuminaries of Judaism at the beginning of the century, dedicated the most massive work in the religious literature of any people to the question of what constitutes "bad tongue"; and bad tongue was closely related in his mind and works to bad taste, for the whole yardstick of the Jew's behavior was the question of whether what he does, says, wears, deals with, etc. brings honor to the name of his Maker. If a Jew in his deeds, dealings, manners, clothes, talk, doesn't arouse respect for his God, he desecrates His name. In Eastern Europe, in the "shtetel" where the Jew reached the highest degree of inwardness, he reached it, very often, at the expense of an outwardness which he neglected, in most cases, out of an abject poverty which was desperate enough to have driven other people to criminality, immorality, and, finally, extinction. But what has happened to many of the children and grandchildren of the "shtetel" Jews is that as a reaction to the deep inwardness of their poor fathers, which they never understood and, therefore, rejected, they fell prey to a cheap outwardness which has as much to do with "modernism" as the abstract painting on their wall with culture.

Edmund Wilson relates (in his "A Piece of My Mind") the interesting story about John J. Chapman's switch from the glorification of the Jews to neurotic anti-Semitism. "There is a depth of human feeling in the Jew," the prominent New Englander wrote in a memorandum of 1897, "that no other race ever possessed. We do no more than imitate it and follow it. David, for instance, and his conduct about Uriah's wife and the child that died—and Absalom—and Jonathan. Compare the Greek—the Chinese—the Romans. These Jews are more human than any other men. It is the cause of the spread of their religion—for we are all adopted into Judah. The heart of the world is Jewish. There is the same spirit in the Old Testament as in the New. What monstrous perversion—that we should worship their god and despise themselves! We admire the pyramids and the Egyptians, but the history of the Jews is the most remarkable, the most notable thing, on the globe. Their sacred books and chronicle and traditions and history make the annals of every other nation mere rubbish—and I feel this same power in the Jews I know. They are the most humane and the strongest people morally, mentally, and physically. They persist. I am glad I am a Jew. (Chapman looked rather Jewish, and he wore an impressive beard in a period when beards had ceased to be fashionable; but neither Chapman himself in his memoirs, nor his biographer, Mr. M. A. deWolfe Howe, records that he had Jewish blood) I believe that's the reason why this paper-faced civilization impresses me so little. Take Habbakuk," etc.

This pro-Semitism, according to Edmund Wilson, was to some extent due to Chapman's political dependence on a devoted Jewish friend, Mr. Isaac H. Klein of New York, who worked with him in his efforts at reform. "The Jews have in my experience," he writes in a letter dated from Wall Street, a little later than 1897, "more faith than the Christians. They have clever heads, better hearts and more belief in the power of good every way. They gave to the world all the religion it has got and are themselves the most religious people in it. I work with them day and night and most of the time is spent in prying up some Christian to do a half day's work."

But between the eighteen-nineties and the nineteen-twenties,

Chapman's attitude toward the Jews underwent an astonishing change. One gets the impression from a letter, written in Atlantic City in December, 1919, that his disillusion may have begun with the spectacle of crowds of vacationing Jews who did not strike him as being the equals of Habbakuk and Isaac Klein: "They are uncritical," he now writes. "Life is a simple matter to them: a bank account and the larder." "They are too easily deflected, absorbed and satisfied." "They have too much sense—and will go for the glittering garments." "These people don't know anything." "They have no religion, no customs except eating and drinking."

Edmund Wilson, commenting on Chapman's strange metamorphosis, asks, "Why should he be surprised that these Jewish citizens from New York and Philadelphia show an interest in their larders and their bank accounts? Do Americans of other stocks not give evidence of similar interest?"

And Wilson continues, "But there is something else, too, in the curious shift from a faith in the Jews to a fear of them. The basic thing there is, I believe, that the Jews have been all too successful in convincing the rest of the world of their privileged relations with God. They have made it all too easy for visionary people—that is people like themselves—to believe that there is something supernatural about them."

Leaving the supernatural aside for a moment, there is something curiously typical about the statement by the distinguished American intellectual that "the Jews were all too successful in convincing the rest of the world of their privileged relations with God." If this were really so, we shall not be wrong if we say that "the rest of the world" must have a very poor opinion about the state of its own relations with God if it believes that precisely those whom it has for centuries deprived of all privileges, have actually succeeded in establishing a privileged relationship with Him. . . . As unbelievable as it may sound, it is a matter of fact that the job of spreading the "gospel" about the Jews' privileged relationship with God was unwittingly done by the Christians much more than it was ever wittingly done by the Jews. This was achieved by two different, though related, means. One, the means of "suffering"—a sacred Christian concept, or sacred concept of Christianity which, strangely enough, whenever and wherever one reads about it in Christian literature one can't help thinking not about the Christians, who have long ago lost their taste of creative suffering, but about the Jews. . . . Two, the means of "salvation". The Christian belief that "there is no saving but through Christ" and that "nobody can

163

come to the Father but through the Son," has placed those who have rejected the "Son's" divinity in a situation of either-or: either the Jews can come to the Father without the intermediacy of the "son" and then they must have "a privileged relationship with God"; or the Jews, having rejected the "Son's" divinity, cannot reach out for the "Father" at all, and therefore are damned souls. But if that is so—and this is a question that must be uppermost in the mind of at least the more sensitive part of "the rest of the world"—how come that all the morally damned souls of the world we live in—the universally recognized evil-doers of humanity, the moral scum that is accumulated in the garbage cans of history— were and are those who hate the Jews the most?

This inevitable either-or has led "the rest of the world," and rightly so, to the thought that there was something inexplicable and, therefore, supernatural, about the Jews. John Jay Chapman, it seems, along with a thousand other fine Christians, shared this view, at least for a while. That is why "he was startled one day to realize," in Wilson's words, "on the boardwalk of Atlantic City, that German, or Russian, or Lithuanian Jewish Americans were human beings like everyone else."

The revulsion we experience at reading about Chapman's switch to pathological hatred of the Jews whom he had once glorified, must not blind us to the reality of the shock which this strange man must have experienced at witnessing certain things on that undistinguished boardwalk which he couldn't possibly reconcile with his cherished vision of the Jews. For what did Mr. Chapman see on that boardwalk that so infuriated him? He saw, we must assume, some manifestations of vulgarity, of showiness, of loudness, of tastelessness, of herdman behavior which Mr. Wilson would regard as unpleasantly normal, but which Mr. Chapman could associate in his mind with anybody but the Jews, whom he regarded, for some reason, as super-normal. And let us not hesitate to say that up to that point Mr. Chapman, in our opinion, was right. Chapman knew pretty well that vulgarity, tastelessness or showiness are a curse that plagues universally the more affluent societies—particularly those whose affluence grows together with their ignorance—yet he believed that the Jew—even the average Jew, even the low-average Jew—had to be different.

Why?

We cannot answer this question without dwelling for a while on the problem of "witnesses." There is a crucial sentence in Isaiah (43:10), which is more popular in Christian theology than with the Rabbis, and it reads as follows: "Ye are my witnesses, said the Lord, and my servant whom I have chosen; that ye may know and believe me, and understand that I am He; before me no God was formed neither shall any be after me."

Professor Ernest Simon of the Hebrew University in Jerusalem rightly remarks (in his essay "The Jews as God's Witnesses to the World") that "it is possible that the Christian emphasis on the idea of Israel as God's witness before the whole world, and especially to the Church, caused the Rabbis to subdue this meaning and to reduce it to the relationship between each individual Jew and his God rather than relating it to the people of Israel and the Gentile nations, though that later meaning is undoubtedly the plain sense of the prophet's words."

Now what does it mean to be a "witness"? How are we to understand, particularly in the post-Auschwitz era, a prophetic sentence like "ye are my witnesses, said the Lord"?

Gustave Thibon, the French priest and spiritual mentor of Simone Weil, gives an excellent definition of the term "witness" as opposed to "craftsman," (in his essay "Vertigo of the Absolute"). "In all work of genius it is important to distinguish between the product of creative skill, invention, etc., and the record of personal experience. Some authors are almost entirely craftsmen and some almost entirely witnesses. The study of 'Phèdre' or the 'Legende des siècles' throws but little light on the personality and the interior life of their authors; there is nothing to suggest that Racine or Victor Hugo experienced the sentiments they express; it may well be that their work bears as little resemblance to their souls as a house to the architect who designed it. Moreover, the material for such work comes largely from the outside—from the beauty of the world, tradition, history, or the moral or religious atmosphere of the period. But if, on the other hand, we read Pascal or Nietzsche, we feel at once that the author is speaking primarily of himself, that he is fully committed to all his writing and that it is from his own experience—from an anguish and hope that belong to him alone—that he evolves not only the form, but also the material of his work. The face of Racine himself is very vaguely discernible behind 'Phèdre' or 'Athanlie,' while the 'Pensées' are like an exact cast of Pascal's features."

Absolutely true! A witness is he whose deeds and faith, whose work and personality, whose inwardness and outwardness, throw upon each other the full light of reciprocal harmony. The notion of thought detached from man is as foreign to the true witness as that

165

of man detached from God. The words of the witness are in harmony with his life, and his life in harmony even with death for even death is regarded as a part of a higher scheme of which the witness is consciously part of. Such a life, the life of a witness, must in some way be associated with sorrow, for without sorrow, truth is beyond reach. Kierkegaard went so far as to believe that sorrow alone is not enough to entitle one to graduate as a witness to the truth, but that in order to reach that stage—persecution, mockery, humiliation, degradation, and finally, assassination for no cause and no reason (Kafka's "Trial"!) are needed before man can be called a "witness to the truth" which, it goes without saying, is the very same as "a witness of God." You read Kierkegaard's and Thibon's definitions of "witnesses" and you wonder whom they were talking about. Weren't they talking, by any chance, without realizing it, of course, about the Jews? Yes, they were! They may have been talking about the Christian the way *he was supposed to be,* but they talked about the Jew the way he was! Gustave Thibon's definition of "witness" depicts the entire philosophy, the ontology, of the real authentic Jew whose works and faith are in complete harmony from birth to death. Kierkegaard's description of the witness to the truth is, at the same time, the exact description of the Jew and the way he lived and died ever since the emergence of Christianity as a repressive force. But to Kierkegaard, contrary to the Church, this kind of suffering was not a witness to one's unpardonable sins, but to one's ineradicable greatness. Kierkegaard went so far as to believe that happiness and ignorance are brothers and, as such, are equally abhorrent to true religion. For true religion is not so much the ability to withstand temptations as to stand tests. And that is precisely what Judaism was all about: to become a witness to the truth of God by the ability to stand tests. The history of the Jews starts that way: it involves the *test* of sacrifice. "And it came to pass after all this, that God *tested* Abraham. . . ." etc. Abraham's obedience to God even when the sacrifice demanded was that of his beloved son, is the beginning of Israel as a witness to God; it becomes later—as an entire people—a witness to His revelation on Mount Sinai; it is constantly tempted and tested by all kinds of false promises of happiness and bliss in this world or the other—from the golden calf to the golden cross—and though it loses, from time to time, some of the weaker among its members to the Molochs of complacency, happiness and "acceptance," the hard core of Jewry remained indestructible down the ages. For how did the hard core of Jewry look in the Middle Ages for instance? It is important to mention it for that was a time when prejudice was at its strongest. Leopold Zunz, the founder of the modern "science of Judaism," gives the following exact description of the Jew amidst Christians in the Middle Ages: "The position of the Jew . . . with his old faith, with his culture not understood (by others), with his yearning for Jerusalem, living amongst barbarians, and . . . enemies, superior in spirit, subject to them in real life, compliant as individuals, stubborn as a community, wanted and shunned at the same time, suffering loyally in the certainty of a grand future, yet uncertain as to the day of the morrow—this tragic position produced that contrast between unchangeable perseverance and permanent changes. People who, when fire broke out, were not saved from it, people whose title of human beings was contested and therefore the sword was always suspended above them, people for whom no suffering was out of reach and who had daily cause for weeping for their fathers, for themselves, and for their children—such people must have had something which inspired them with courage, and this courage must have given them a meaning to their life. (And what was it?) It was (the courage) to be a pious Jew, in order to become purified through sufferings for the time of the Messiah, and the world to come. That was the task of existence, and that determined the contents of life. . . . Only that was given. All other things were nothing but passing and minor." (*Zur Geschichte und Literatur,* Berlin, 1845)

The formulations of this Jewish historian, published in Germany a hundred years before the end of Hitler's reign of terror, are both exact and prophetic. That's how we were known to the Gentiles in the Dark Ages when the cynicism of the omnipotent Church permitted it to persecute the Jews and at the very same time claim that these persecutions, for which the Church was chiefly responsible, were a witness to God's anger at the Jews! . . . We were known, in Professor Ernest Simon's words, "as polite individuals, as a rule—timid, occasionally submissive, anxious to please and not to appear as too conspicuous, to seem at our best, always conscious of the insecure situation characteristic of human beings who are nowhere totally at home, who can be deprived of their rights any day, driven from their homes any night. Even in wealth and power some Jews have displayed such behaviour. And out of all this intimidation and compliance, a community emerged which, in all inexorability, has stood, stands, and will stand on its continuance and its peculiarity, on its mission and on its future."

"How can this contrast be overcome?" asks Professor Simon, "this discrepancy between the many average individuals who make up the Jewish people, like every other people, and the mission of the continuity as a whole, always to stand the test as the bearer of God's witness? To bridge this chasm is one of the main tasks of Jewish law as a way of life—*Halacha* (the law). It enjoins on its beliefs a discipline from early childhood on. It is total because it does not exclude or set free any province of life, but forms all of them according to its patterns. That is the spirit of the Covenant. Individuals may break it; the people of Israel as such cannot get rid of it, provided it chooses life. . . . More often than not the price of keeping the covenant was suffering. But suffering is not its content. Its content is the joyful obedience to God's will." [1]

But how can one be *joyfully obedient* to God's will in a world devoured by suffering, and hatred, and ignorance, and injustice, and evil? The Jews, of all peoples, have, at times, achieved this highest degree of joyful obedience to God in the midst of hatred and evil and have thus become witnesses to the truth. For only a threatened soul at complete harmony with itself and its maker is capable of contemptuously smiling in the face of evil, in the face of hatred, and in the face of death, and make evil, hatred, and death, look ridiculous in its presence. The students of the great Yeshiva of Slobodka, in Lithuania, were led by the Germans to dig their own graves. Holding hands tightly together, the young "Cedars of Lebanon," pillars of the law, giants of the spirit, torches of eternity, immortal witnesses to the truths of God and to the God of truth, literally *went* to their graves with the mighty song of "Ani Maamin" ("I believe") on their lips. ("I believe in the coming of the Messiah. . . .")

---

[1] "The strongest impulse of the character of Moses appears to have been that of protective justice, more particularly with regard to the helpless and downtrodden classes. The laws of Moses, if carefully examined, are a perfect phenomenon; an exception to the laws of either ancient or modern nations in the care they exercised over women, widows, orphans, paupers, foreigners, servants, and dumb animals. No so called Christian nation but could advantageously take a lesson in legislation from the laws of Moses. There is a plaintive, pathetic spirit of compassion in the very language in which the laws in favour of the helpless and the suffering are expressed, that it seems must have been learned only of superhuman tenderness. Not the gentlest words of Jesus are more compassionate in their spirit than many of these laws of Moses."

Harriet Beecher Stowe

These were witnesses to the truth!

John Jay Chapman, aware for a very long time of the quality of "witness" which to him, as to so many other sensitive Jewish as well as Christian minds, was a typical, though supernatural, trait of the Jews, was thus doubly sensitive to Jewish insensitivity. He may have been dreadfully wrong in his conclusions (following Atlantic City) but he wasn't wrong in his expectations. He didn't know, poor Mr. Chapman, that whether or not it's true that the Jews succeeded in convincing the rest of the world of their privileged relationship with God—they have almost succeeded in convincing themselves that they are just like everybody else! And when a Jew *tries* to be like everybody else (others don't have to try—they are!) he is sometimes reduced to a state of being *less* than everybody else. By deserting his element he often makes a mockery not only of his Jewishness, but of himself as a human being.

The sights of vulgarity on display which had appalled John Jay Chapman in Atlantic City were, therefore, not Jewish, but, spiritually speaking, anti-Jewish sights. When the people whose prophet had first coined the marvelous admonition, "walk humbly before thy God," choose at certain times and in certain places a mannerism which is the very opposite of humility (and the Jews don't confuse prophetic humility with Christian meekness!)—they are strangers not to the good taste of others, but to their own glory, and to their own God. Chapman, in other words, didn't see typical, but flagrantly *atypical* Jews. He saw—let's face it—Jewish ignoramuses who, as a sharp reaction to the spiritually rich inner lives of their fathers in the "shtetel," resorted to the glorification of the outer life in the big, free city. By doing so they rose, spiritually speaking, against their Jewishness, which is, first and foremost, a proposition of inwardness—something the ignoramus, the "Am Ha'aretz," as he is referred to in the Talmud, will never understand.

And now we come to the alarming phenomenon of the emergence of the "Am Ha'aretz"—the spiritual ignoramus—in all walks of life. The ignorance that goes together with poverty and disease is as identifiable and recognizable as are poverty and disease. But there is an ignorance that often goes together with health, wealth, social acceptance, and, even, university degrees; and this ignorance is now conquering the world. It has a strong ally in what people call "success" and an even stronger ally in what they refer to as "cleverness." Cleverness not only excuses ignorance, but very often makes it appear as its very opposite—which is wisdom. Wisdom is the antithesis to cleverness in the same sense that impertinence is the antithesis to courage, and conceit the antithesis to pride. But these are precisely the subtleties of such differences which are lost on the "Am Ha'aretz". He confuses security with happiness, success with intelligence, and being lucky with being "smart."

But there are other kinds of "Amei Ha'aratzoth"—of spiritual ignorants that is: there is the religious Am Ha'aretz who wears his religion like a garment, whose faith is exhausted by its ritual and who takes his God for granted with the same hollow ease with which the non-religious Am Ha'aretz takes for granted the finality of his "reason." There is the scientific Am Ha'aretz who confuses knowledge with wisdom, efficiency with genius, and specialization with the ultimate in progress; there is the ideological Am Ha'aretz who regards the small area of man which is covered by his limited ideal as the *whole* area of man, and there is the socio-political Am Ha'aretz who believes that a revolutionary change in socio-political conditions will solve man's existential problems.

For what does the term "Am Ha'aretz" actually mean? This Talmudic name given to the spiritual ignoramus close to two millenniums ago, actually means, in its literal translation "a man of the earth," or "an earthly man," or, if you like, "a carnal man." In a period when the Christian teachers of contempt who, in the fourth century, took over Christianity lock, stock, and barrel, had hurled against Judaism the accusation of "carnality"—at the very same time the Talmud conducted the most concentrated and, indeed, violent attack known to theology *against* carnality, earthliness and materialism. "The earthly man," as described in the Talmud, was not always a plain ignorant but, quite often, an intelligently-specialized ignoramus who believed he knew enough about the earthly thing he believed in to hate and despise the super-earthly thing he was ignorant of. What it amounted to was that this kind of "Am Ha'aretz," of earthly man, had actually turned his "earthliness," his carnality and materiality, into a cult. He believed so vehemently in the finality of his material views that he regarded the "Talmid Hacham," the spiritual man—the sage, as a hateful creature. How else can we understand the statement by Rabbi Akiba (to whom we have dedicated another chapter) that in the years of his "Am Ha'aratzuth"—or his spiritual ignorance—he would say: "Give me a Talmid Hacham and I shall tear him to pieces!" Such a fighting ignorance must have had some powerful anti-spiritual convictions to rely upon!

Such non-spiritual, or anti-spiritual believers the sages call igno-rants. And it is easy now to understand why. The non-spiritual man, not to say the anti-spiritual, may be a convinced materialist, a convinced socialist, a convinced Marxist, or a convinced Fascist; he may even be a holder of degrees in history, medicine, economy, law, sociology, psychology, psychoanalysis, chemistry, etc., but that does not mean that he is not, that he cannot be, a *spiritual* ignoramus. Anybody who mistakes the immediate or the interme-diate for the ultimate—anybody, that is, who regards a part of man, no matter how important a part, as the *whole* of man, is a spiritual ignorant. The ultimate includes, as it is bound to by the very nature of the infinite area it covers—the immediate as well as the intermediate, but the immediate and intermediate thrive very often on the *denial* of the ultimate. "The relative with all its riches and its virtues, never gives us the absolute and it may always hide it from us, but the absolute can always give us back the relative" (Gustave Thibon). The ultimate is wisdom, the relative is knowl-edge. Knowledge can be communicated, wisdom must be *experi-enced*. That is why a man of knowledge *alone* wouldn't know what the man of wisdom is talking to him about. Dostoyevsky said it long ago. Prince Mishkin had often observed that when a real believer discusses God with an atheist, they are all the time talking about two different things.

The difficulty to make this truth understandable and acceptable to the rational mind is the chief reason why spiritual ignorance is growing side by side with the growth of physical knowledge. This is a universal calamity which is slowly turning human beings into competent barbarians with no sense of spiritual or ethical wisdom. This calamity has affected the whole world, but the damage it has caused to Judaism is particularly severe because Judaism was first and foremost a spiritual proposition. If Jewish youths rebel against their parents and teachers, more vehemently than their non-Jewish counterparts, it is because their spiritual need for a meaning is so much greater. To those who console themselves with a kingdom which is not of this world, the alarming despiritualization of man-kind cannot possibly be as alarming as to people who constantly dwelled in the Kingdom of the spirit and bore such powerful testi-mony to its existence that they were described by early great Gen-tiles, who knew them well, as "Imitatio Dei"—imitators of God. The emergence of spiritual ignorance dressed in the glittering gar-ments of progress, modernism, efficiency and even "Knowledge" presents a threat to the very life of Judaism, for without spiritual knowledge—which is another word for wisdom—and the need thereof, Judaism is dead. To this threat to Judaism's very life—and let's say it without any hesitation—the state of *Israel* as such has not yet proven to be an effective antidote.

And let's talk for a moment about Israel. Something has happened to and in Israel as a result of the six days' war for which there is no better description than the one applied by the student in the preface to this book: "It is the first time in history that victory —not defeat—arouses spiritual cravings." Zionism, as such, was never a spiritual proposition. Ahad Ha'am had sensed the danger of its non-spirituality, of its placing the entire stress on the political side of the solution of the Jewish problem, and he raised a mighty intellectual voice against this trend, at the turn of the century. This voice would have been much mightier, and much more enduring, had it not been blunted by the "rationalism" which was typical to his post-enlightenment way of thinking. The two ideals which had formed the cornerstones of modern Israel—Zionism and Socialism —were children of the "enlightenment." "Enlightenment," as we may realize by now, was that vital period in human history which, its great contribution to technical and social progress notwithstanding, had issued, through its deification of rationalistic, positivistic and naturalistic ideas, a certificate of respectability to spiritual ignorance or, if you wish, to the ignoring of the spiritual. Now and then some prophetic voices of warning were heard against the onslaught of material certainties in the entire environment—to mention just two: Nietzsche and Dostoyevsky—but their voices were drowned in the sea of adulation which the emergence of the new deity—"reason"—had made to swell to flood proportions. Zionism and Socialism joined reason's bandwagon. Zionism believed in the rational-political solution of the Jewish problem—a Jewish state in Palestine—while Socialism believed that the ills of mankind as a whole—much more so the Jewish problem—can be rationally treated and cured by social medicines. Modern Israel was built by both these elements and by both these theories: Zionism which was politically responsible for the creation of a Jewish state in Palestine; and Socialism—realizing that the political solution alone is not enough—which was responsible for creating in Israel, among other things, an idealistic social movement called "the Kibutz". The two theories were rationally sound and simple. The one regarded the political change—"normalization"—as the panacea for all the ills that befell the homeless Jews; the other spoke of the social plus the political change—"equalization"—as such an overall panacea. The two theories, however, inspired as they were by an urge to right wrongs and see social justice prevail, were, spiritually speaking, materialistic. They both aimed, of course, to affect man's inner make-up and help him come to grips with himself, realize himself, *be* himself, but this did not happen, nor could it have happened under the circumstances. It did not happen in Israel, nor did it happen anywhere else in the world where socio-political remedies were prescribed for problems of man's soul. Political and social "solutions" failed, in other words, to provide an answer to man's existential problems. This by now is a recognized socio-psychological fact, no matter what the professional dogmatists say. Man, even when no more alienated from his land and from the tools of production which he owns, remained a stranger in the house of his soul, deserted by its own inner identity. When Marxist intellectuals confess, as they did not too long ago at the first Catholic-Marxist dialogue in Czechoslovakia, that Marxism, overemphasizing economic factors in history, had totally neglected the question of man and his meaning—they had actually confessed not only to the sad triumph of a spiritual ignorance which their hallowed "science" and "rationalism" have helped to enhance, but also to the disastrous results of this triumph—results which made man more bestial, more brutish and more inhuman than ever. This fact is the prime cause behind the spiritual awakening in Communist lands where intellectuals have suddenly discovered the soul and its agonies in a world ruled by spiritual ignorants. ("All misfortunes that befell mankind are caused by ignorants,"—Talmud, "Baba-Batra".) The situation in Israel is different, of course, since Israel was never, nor can it ever be, a totalitarian state of the Marxist or the Fascist type. But that doesn't mean that Israel doesn't undergo a grave spiritual crisis. The spiritual crisis in Israel is, in fact, graver than in other lands, for the Jew, more than anybody else, is addicted to the search for a meaning. It was no other than the late Mr. Moshe Sharett, a former Prime Minister of Israel, and one of the prominent ideologists of Zionism-Socialism, who had spoken, just before his death, about the failure of socio-political remedies to provide an answer to the rising inner problems of the young Israeli, even the Kibutznik. "We thought," he wrote (in *Ramzor*) "that we had the answers [to questions of meaning], but we haven't found them where we hoped we would. New vital questions are being asked now, and the old social and political remedies on which we had pinned our fondest hopes proved inadequate. . . . This year [1964] my son,

173

along with other members of his Kibutz, went for the first time to fast and pray in a synagogue on Yom Kipur. . . ."

Why? What happened? What kind of inner crisis has caused the Socialist Kibutznik, son of a prominent ideologist of Zionism-Socialism, to resort to fasting and praying on the day of atonement? And what caused his father to describe this metamorphosis both as a typical and welcome phenomenon? Prior to the six days' war, such questions were as rare in Israel as were the incidents which had caused them. Prior to that war, spiritual questions, though they have always emerged on the surface like corks which one tries in vain to keep under water, were suppressed as unfashionable or irrelevant. From the war of independence till the six days' war Israel had failed completely to whet its own, and Jewry's, spiritual appetite. It has, if anything, enhanced the spread of spiritual ignorance by fostering the illusion that Israel per se, the very fact that it exists, proclaims the existence, and the nature, of its soul. But there is no evidence whatsoever to the validity of Mr. Ben-Gurion's old claim, for example, that "only in Israel can a Jew live a full Jewish life." If what is meant by a "full Jewish life" is a state, a language plus social reforms—Ben-Gurion was manifestly wrong if he thought that these changes, vitally important as they are, can provide Jewish life with a badly needed spiritual raison d'être. The fact of the matter is that if the spiritual crisis in Israel is as grave as anywhere, and maybe even graver, it is because there is no greater ignoramus than the Hebrew-speaking ignoramus, and nobody is more alienated from his Jewishness, from the Jew in him, from the God in him, from his Jewish "Neshome," than he who claims that "I am not a Jew but an Israeli." The man who is uncomfortable with his Jewishness in Israel has, in fact, a graver spiritual problem than the Jew who is uncomfortable with it in other lands. For if one who doesn't accept himself because he is not accepted by others, is a joke—he who refuses to accept himself because he is not accepted by himself, is a menace. The problem which the young Israeli faced up to in the six days' war, without admitting it, and which he is admittedly facing now is one of spiritual self-acceptance and, therefore, of a distinctly metaphysical order. There is now a metaphysical restlessness which haunts the thinking Jew from the hills of Jerusalem to the shores of the Hudson River, and this restlessness was greatly enhanced in Israel by the six days' war. Jean-Paul Sartre must have had the thoroughly unauthentic Jew in mind when he wrote (in *Antisemite and Jew*) that "the disquietude of the Jew is not metaphysical; it is

174

social. The ordinary object of his concern is not yet the place of man in the universe, but his place in society. He cannot perceive the loneliness of each man in the midst of a silent universe, because he has not yet emerged from society into the world. It is among men that he feels himself lonely; the racial problem limits his horizon. Nor is his uneasiness the kind that seeks perpetuation; he takes no pleasure in it—he seeks reassurance."

This is, if anything, the most authentic description of the *unauthentic* Jew, of the total stranger to the glory of his unknown soul. Sartre, by the way, never knew an authentic Jew.

The emergence of the authentic Jew goes hand in hand with the unfolding of his spirituality, and his spirituality is, to put it briefly, a concern with the unity, continuity, uniqueness and purposefulness of Jewish history.

The six days' war brought this concern to the fore as nothing else in Jewish history since the days of the great spiritual revelations of old.

Those who fought in the war of Israel's independence were, for the greater part, a generation of rebels against tradition. The war was interpreted in purely political and social terms. The conviction prevailed that the answer to all questions lay in the political or social realm. Feelings of identity with the past, with the "Galut," with the "Shtetel" were repressed. The *spiritual* impact of the war of independence was nil. The generation which grew up in Israel after that war was a generation of Israelis who sought estrangement from Jews and from Judaism. It was a generation which was not only a stranger to glory, but which saw glory in estrangement.

The six days' war put an end to this mentality. The fight for existence was a moment of truth—of real, revelatory spiritual truth—which gave the lie to other "truths." "Those who went through the ordeal came out with a feeling of having been, in a certain sense, purified. . . . The idea of a 'peculiar people,' long relegated to the background by intellectualism, by modern liberalism, by the striving after 'normalization'—after the holocaust especially—has risen again. Israel has appeared on the center of a world stage—a ray of light and hope against the cynicism of great powers. And so one commonly hears: 'I am not religious, but. . . .'" ("Petahim" I.)

The feeling of chosenness, which indubitably makes for a higher morality, manifested itself in the six days' war as in no other war in history. Jewish self-haters, that contemptible breed of intellectual outcasts whose number, following the six days' war rose precisely on account of Israel's victory, may say what they want, but it is a fact that rarely, if ever, have a people taken up arms more reluctantly, fought more bravely, defeated more roundly, behaved more humanly and talked of their victory less boastfully than the Israelis. The entire Israeli war literature is studded with gems of compassion for the enemy who had pledged, if he wins, to exterminate every Israeli man, woman and child. This charity in heroics was matched, all over the world, by heroics of charity. "Although nothing in all the political and military actions contravened physical laws, the concatenation of events and the absolute effort of the whole people cannot so easily be explained; there is felt to be something of the miraculous. The words 'repentance,' 'atonement,' require, for their full meaning, a belief in God; but even 'nonbelievers' have had a sense akin to atonement; people even spoke of 'redemption'." ("Petahim" I.)

Yes, that was the spiritual manifestation of a war which the antispiritual forces of humanity, led by the Communists, decried as "imperialistic"! When Kibutz boys wept at the Wailing Wall, they wept not only out of joy of victory, but, in many cases, out of happiness at self-discovery. "There are hearts," the great late Rabbi Kook once wrote, "which are stones, but there are stones which are hearts, like the stones of the Wailing Wall." And it was in those stones, which are hearts, that Kibutz boys and hardboiled, battle-wearied paratroopers discovered the secret of their own hearts and the heart of their people, and not of the natural, but the supernatural heart! "This war has added some beautiful pages not only to the Jewish history, but to the history of mankind. . . . Though we know that the victory is a result of an exact planning and long preparations, of thorough military schooling and an excellent intelligence service, of the acquisition of the necessary hardware, and many other things, yet there is the feeling that higher forces have intervened in this battle. When our air force fought in the air, it wasn't the air force *alone* which has fought there; When our land forces fought on the ground, it wasn't the army *alone* that has fought there. The events, racing one after another, had about them something of the miraculous. Words are powerless to express this feeling. In the air of Israel there whispers now a quiet symphony of Biblical sentences, of prophetic words, of Kaballah, of mystery.—It is the realization of a promise, the concretization of a dream, an earthly silhouette of an unearthly reality. It is the mingling of the natural with what is supernatural." (Aaron Meghed)

The six days' war was a war with immense spiritual connotations, and, as such, a denial of the Marxist view that history is created by economic processes. The wrath of the Communists at Israel's victory in the six days' war is ideological as much as it is political. Ideologically—from the angle of Marxist philosophy that is—the Israelis were not supposed to win that war. Ideologically, or Leninistically speaking, the Arabs are the "progressive, anti-imperialist" peoples while the Israelis are "tools of imperialism." As such, the "exploiting" Israelis had to be crushed under the impact of the social wrath of the Arab masses. The fact that the Israelis, few and alone as they were, won one of the most decisive victories in history against the many who were, at the same time, the allies of the Communists, was an ideological blow to Communism as much as it was a military blow to the Arabs. The six days' war has proven that human history, if anything, is shaped by spiritual much more than by economic processes. This the Communists will never forgive Israel. In their mad fury they compared the army of Israel, unequalled for restraint and humanity, to the Nazis. If only the Israelis had lost—what nice guys they would have been!

But this is precisely Israel's newest, and finest, contribution to the suppressed, and confused spirit of Jewry and mankind at large: the denial, through its own self-discovery in war, that history is determined by materialistic factors to which everything else is subservient. Exactly as the Jews, in their frenzy of despair—a despair for which the Christian world was totally responsible—were the first and most vehement Marxists, they are now, in their reflection, (Wordsworth defined poetry as "emotion recollected in tranquility") the most vigorous carriers of anti-Marxist banners behind the Iron Curtain. When the Communists hurl the label "Zionist!" in the faces of the rebellious intellectuals in their midst, they are unwittingly telling a truth which is unfortunately unknown either to the Zionists or the intellectuals: the truth that Zionism, in its prophetic or messianic sense, is a proposition of spiritual Oneness which is the denial of materialism. In it the temporary and the eternal, the individual and the community, the past and the present merge together in order to create a new type of man. One of the most amazing, and most typical, not to say most moving little stories—little *factual* stories that is—to come out of the six days' war is the one about looting. In a world in which misguided people, young people, believe that revolutionary work and warlike activities begin with looting, the following account has a distinctly prophetic sound: "This happened after the battle. The unit was preparing to descend from the heights. The soldiers were rushing and were still collecting from here and there all sorts of things for souvenirs. The troop leader did not pay any attention.

"But a small clay jar, really miniature, stuck in the ground, caught my eye. All the soldiers kicked it in passing and for some reason it did not break. I picked it up and thought I would bring it to my girl friend as a souvenir.

"We descended from the Golan Heights and drove away. When we reached Jericho, we stopped to rest. There the troop leader took out the Bible from his pocket and read to us the chapter on looting from the book of Joshua. *When he finished, all the soldiers in silence pulled out all the things they had collected, made one pile, poured petrol on it and burned it.*" ("Story of a Warrior," "A Kibutz Bulletin," 7,67)

There is not, there can not possibly be, such a case in the history of any other army, of any other victory, anywhere in the world! It is a manifestation of moral chosenness of the highest order.[1]

The prohibition on looting, issued by Joshua 3500 years ago, became spiritually binding *today*. And it became so without questioning, without doubt, without hesitation. And that was not the only spiritual law—the law that aimed at curbing man's greed, the

---

[1] In a symposium on the question of "Chosenness," organized by and published in the Israeli daily "Maariv," (June 18th, 1965) Simon Peress, a former deputy minister of defense under David Ben-Gurion, had this to say on the subject: "When I say 'Thou hast chosen us' I experience a clash between politeness and historic truth. . . . It isn't polite to speak of 'chosenness' for the term carries Chauvinistic undertones. But when I remind myself of the words of the famous American architect Frank Lloyd Wright that 'I am not polite enough to be insincere,'—'chosenness' assumes a very legitimate sound. It is perfectly legitimate for a man to experience in himself sources of strength even when others don't admit to their existence. . . . Of course it is non democratic to conquer the world by force, but isn't it democratic if you publish a Bible and you conquer the world with it? In Judaism there is the 'Thou shall not kill!', but there is also the 'Kill him who comes to kill you!' Judaism may not be all perfection, but it is the only faith which doesn't lie to itself. If there is one single trait which typifies Judaism through all its interpretations, a trait to be truly proud of, it is its total lack of hypocrisy. . . . I haven't met a Jewish Millionaire who enjoys a week-end as fully as his Gentile counterpart, but I saw how the most simple Jew can be truly happy on 'Simhat Torah' ('the Feast of the Torah'). . . . In my work, I came across many peoples and many cultures; some of them are distinguished by their renunciational morality and others by their joy of life, but I am yet to meet a people, like ours, whose attitude toward the joy of life is typified by a moral seriousness, and who are capable, at the same time, of displaying a unique ability to resort to the moral deed with a sense of real joy and satisfaction."

law that aimed at implanting a spiritual deterrent in man—which was practiced during and after the six days' war. Of course the Israelis can be terrible in war—as they should be—but once victory is won, humanity is practiced. To kill an enemy in cold blood just because he is an enemy; to rape a woman just because she belongs to a people that is at war with you; to boast of heartlessness; to enjoy the misery of the defeated—these are not Jewish traits, these are not the traits of a people which, for centuries, practiced the law of the deterrent, the law of Sinai. A little book was published in Israel after the six days' war, and the name of the book is *Warriors' Talk*. It is a collection of talks and meditations of those who participated in the war, of those who fought and won it. If there was any additional proof needed that the Jew has developed in himself, as a result of his conscious or subconscious feeling of oneness with eternity, an inner deterrent against evil, this incredible book proves it beyond any shadow of a doubt. For it is a book in which soldiers talk—soldiers of a people who were threatened with total annihilation, mind you—of the *pains* of victory, of the *heartbreak* of *defeating,* not of *being* defeated, of the *sorrow* of destroying, not of *being* destroyed. The subdued compassion of this book, the wrath at being *forced* to kill; at being *compelled* to shed blood; at being *constrained* to be cruel, bestow upon it a halo of spiritual grandeur unknown in the literature of wars. That book, mostly written by members of the Kibutzim, bears witness to the highest manifestations of the Jewish soul, a soul that was moulded by an abhorrence for the shedding of blood. You read that book and you cannot help but think of a famous sculpture by Michelangelo—"Victory." The sculpture, which stands for the last four centuries at the Palazzo Vecchio in Florence, depicts the face of a victor as he holds his foot on the back of the vanquished. What is so extraordinary about that statue, however, is that the victor's face is averted. It doesn't look *down* on its victim, nor does it express any vindictiveness or joy of destruction; instead, it conveys the distinct impression that the victor, while holding on to his victory, finds it somehow difficult, almost painful, to *enjoy* the sight of his victim under his feet. And that's precisely how the young officers of the army of Israel, their quest for social justice as powerful as their love of freedom, looked upon their victory in the six days' war. For it is the attitude of these victors toward their victory, much more than the victory itself, which is so Sinai-inspired and of which very few, if any, armies in the world can boast. It speaks not only of the eternity, but also of the re-

179

sponsibility and, above all, of the sensitivity of the Jewish soul. A twenty-one-year-old soldier-Kibutznik sums it all up in a remarkable article called "Something Happened to Us" and published in *The Jerusalem Post* of June 14, 1967: "Solidarity stems from a moral feeling for justice, from historical uneasiness, from admiration for the enormous achievement. These sources belong to the rational sphere of human existence, or correspond to it.

"But identity is the nucleus, the center of us all, that from which we came to be what we are, *the law by which we started.*

"Identity is an origin, an origin of existence which hence shall bear the title 'Jewish.'

"We heard that Jerusalem was liberated and I saw the eyes of the Kibutzniks as they spoke about it. They are not religious in my kibutz, and for them the Wailing Wall is not a symbol of our belief; still their eyes were shining. Their happiness derived from the same source that had once given them the strength to go into the desert and to build a new existence.

"It is, perhaps, symbolic that Yitzhak Rabin is the victorious general of this war. In his speeches he could have shouted fiery words, as other generals have done before him in similar situations, but he spoke always with unprecedented modesty and simplicity, and also without hate or rancour.

"That is it—the background of our war is too great even for the greatest men of our nation. . . . It is the illumination of our innermost being, and it leaps at us from a thousand mirrors.

"Perhaps it is a feeling which Franz Kafka once described—a deep suffering, a pain that takes complete possession of him—and is nevertheless the greatest truth he can discover. 'Today I constantly felt my depth,' he says." (Jacob Hessing)

"Today I constantly felt my depth." What a marvellous definition! For the beauty of Judaism lies in its depths. There is no such thing as surface Judaism, (an exclusively ritualistic Judaism *is* surface Judaism;) and if there is, it is not going to last long. Judaism may be a culture, a civilization, a peoplehood, a religion —call it anything you like—but it is, above all, a call, an eternal call to a living in depth. "The thing is not even experienced. It is simply *lived*. It is what one *is*" (Franz Rosenzweig). Judaism, like an iceberg, is seven-eighths submerged. From the meditation on primary causes to the vision of the end of the days, the Jewish inner urge is to look beyond the visible, the easy, the provable, the surface, toward a general pattern that consciously leads somewhere. Only a Judaism lived in depth is capable of realizing how indispensable a part it is of that pattern. This realization is the glory of Judaism.

The glory of Judaism lies in its *unity*. The beginning and the end, the Godly and the worldly, the spiritual and the material, are all interwoven in one great craving for a final universal harmony. This craving is so total that it invests with consciousness areas of life which, seemingly, lack that virtue. Thus the ultimate state of perfection of the truly great soul is one in which he is not only at home in the universe, but he is constantly aware of the universe's awareness of him. Of such souls it is said that they understood the language of beasts and birds and could hearken to the voices of leaves of grass.

The glory of Judaism lies in the totality of its experience. One cannot arrive at the true meaning of Judaism unless he has made the whole long journey that precedes the arrival. The difference between saying, or defining, what Judaism stands for and actually experiencing it is as great as between the craftsman and the witness. One can become a Christian by "embracing" Jesus, but to become a real Jew one has to "embrace" the universe, for the whole of the world, the whole of man is covered by the law, by the prophecy and the wisdom of Judaism. This, indeed, is the secret of *"Shema."*

The glory of Judaism lies in its *unity of ends and means*. Means, to Judaism are ends, and ends are means to greater ends till history fulfills itself in the messianic age. They asked the "holy Yehudi," as mentioned earlier. "Why is it written: 'Justice, justice shalt thou follow' (Deut. 16:20)? Why is the word 'justice' repeated?"

He answered: "We ought to follow justice with justice, and not with unrighteousness." "That means," Buber explains, "that the use of unrighteousness as a means to a righteous end makes the end itself unrighteous; injustice as a means to justice renders justice unjust. . . . What knowledge could be of greater importance to the men of our age, and to the various communities of our time? The saying sounds as if it were derived from the experiences of contemporaries. And yet it stems from the Napoleonic Era, and was not spoken at the hub of events, but in a Polish ghetto, and by a Zaddik. . . ." (*Ten Rungs: Hassidic Sayings*)

The glory of Judaism lies in its spiritual inability to think in the secular terms of separation between "Church and State," and thus to relegate God to a special, "harmless" area of existence. "The men of the Bible are sinners like ourselves, but there is one sin they do not commit, our arch-sin: they do not dare to confine God to a circumscribed space or division of life, to 'religion.' They have not the insolence to draw boundaries around God's commandments and say to Him: up to this point You are sovereign, but beyond this point begins the sovereignty of science, or society, or the state." (Buber in *Israel and the World*)

The glory of Judaism lies in its eternal repudiation of *idolatry*. The adoration of "the works of our hands," the idolization of "the tools of production" is idolatry as is the worship of matter and of anything that is visible, tangible, measurable or estimable. When we think of Rome we think of Caesar; when we think of Athens we think of Apollo; when we think of Jerusalem we think of God!

The glory of Judaism lies in its abhorrence of ignorance as the root of all evil. The fact that man is born to be free doesn't yet make a better man out of him. Freedom alone—the freedom to choose—may even lead man, as it did so often in the past and present, to choose evil. But man was born to *know*! Only knowledge—and we mean *spiritual* knowledge—can make man's freedom conducive to self-realization and to the realization of an ultimate reality. The triumph of technical efficiency that lost its sense of wisdom, is not only the triumph of ignorance, but also the triumph of idolatry.

The glory of Israel lies in its *oneness* with God. The Roman historian Tacitus summed up the creed of the Jews (prior to the destruction of the Temple) as follows: "Mente sola unumque numen inteligunt." ("They understand the Divine to be *one* and grasped by the mind alone.") What follows is a concept of oneness which embraces body and soul, spirit and matter, life and after life. What follows, in other words, is that since God's kingdom is of *this* world, too, and the "earth is the Lord's," no title to land, for example, can be given in perpetuity. This is the law as it was laid down in Leviticus 25:23. "For the modern man the premise is as breathtaking as the consequence is revolutionary. Yet for the Hebrew Bible the premise is obvious, and the consequence a simple deduction. Agrarian reform flows immediately from theology, a theory of property from the nature of God. (There is a connection, by the same token, between what you eat and what you think and between the tenor of your voice and the moral state of your soul.) Moral living rests on similar basis: it is uncompromisingly God-derived. When we are told not to reap the corners of the field or not to put a stumbling block in the way of the blind; when we are to love our neighbor as ourselves and to honor the old, it is not in the interest of private advantage or of the smooth running of society, but because 'I am the Lord your God.' " (Professor L. Roth)

That's the glory of Judaism!

The glory of Judaism lies in the astounding fact that, contrary to Christianity, its fundamental character emerged and became recognized not through the victory of its worshippers, but through their "defeat." (Professor Leon Roth)

The glory of Judaism lies in its belief that the study of the law is a form of worship, at times the highest form of worship. To commemorate the anniversary of the passing of a dear soul, the sages commend the study of "Mishna"—the basic code of the law—as more important than any form of prayer!

The glory of Judaism doesn't lie in the worship of reason, but in its belief that it is reason properly developed which can lead us to the conclusion that there are things in the world—and these are the things that count most—which are beyond reason.

The glory of Judaism—inexcusably disregarded by some of its strictest spokesmen—lies in its *uncompromising, Sinai-derived social consciousness*. The entire law, according to Hillel, is only a commentary on "Don't do to thy neighbor what you wouldn't want to be done to you."

The glory of Judaism lies in its regarding social and political freedom as a *prerequisite* for spiritual realization. The exodus from Egypt had to precede the revelation on Sinai. Freedom precedes the law, and the law was given to Israel as a *whole*.

The glory of Israel lies in the belief that while God had revealed His countenance to the chosen ones of other peoples—he had revealed his countenance on Sinai to the *entire* people of Israel. This is a chosenness, however, for a constantly renewed universal responsibility—not the chosenness of an inherited fortune or of an unearned privilege.

The glory of Judaism lies in its declared aim to meet a new conception of human ends through the implementation of means which alone are leading up to it. These ends consist of the *creation of a human being who is unable to shed blood*. "Forgive thy people Israel who thou hast redeemed and suffer not innocent blood to remain in the midst of thy people." (Deuteronomy 31:8) To this the Rabbis comment: " 'Whom thou hast redeemed,' it was for this that thou didst redeem us *that there should not be among us men who spill blood*."

The glory of Judaism lies in the intimate nature of the dialogue it has conducted with God since its emergence. From our father, Abraham, who lovingly quarrels with his maker, asking Him to spare the wicked cities of Sodom and Gomorrah, through Rabbi Levi Yitzhak of Berditchev who demands—yes, demands—an end to God's patience with evil, and down to the not-so-fictitious character of "Tevye" in the famous story by Sholem Aleichem—there is a dialogue on an "I-Thou" basis between the Jew and his maker which is the lot only of those who can dwell in His house not as strangers.

The glory of Judaism, contrary to that of Hellenism, lies not in the consciousness of that wherein human nature excels, but where it requires correction. (Roth)

The glory of Judaism and the main difference between Judaism and any other "weltanschauung"—for Judaism *is* a "weltanschauung" —is this: while all the others hope to bring about a change in man through a change in the world, Judaism aspires to cause a change in the world through a change in man.

> The *glory* of Israel was *not* slain
> In the *low* places
> Where the mighty fell along with the weak:
> *Tell it* in Gath,
> *Say it* in the streets of Ashkalon,
> Lest the daughters of the Philistines rejoice,
> Lest the daughters of the uncircumcised jubilate. . . .

Survival for what?

For the *unknown* ointment of Judaism yearning to be applied to our wounds as well as to the wounds of mankind in general.

Chapter Eight

SURVIVAL FOR WHAT? *

In the fall of 1943, the Gauleiter of Cracow, in Nazi-occupied Poland, summoned to his office the President of what was left of the once great Jewish community in that historic city, Dr. Roman Landau, and put to him the following question: "Dr. Landau," he asked, "why don't you commit suicide? And I don't mean you only personally. I mean all of you here. Why don't you take an example of your brethren in Germany and in Austria? Not all of them waited for us to kill them. A good many of them have killed themselves and thus saved themselves lots of trouble."

History doesn't record what Dr. Landau replied to the Nazi Gauleiter, but ever since I first read about this encounter it seemed to me that the Gauleiter of Cracow, if his words were to be purged for a moment of their diabolic cynicism, had actually asked a question of historic importance. Why is it that in Germany and in Austria many thousands of Jews committed suicide following Hitler's rise to power, while in the ghetto of Kaunas, for instance, where the remnants of Lithuania's great Jewry were concentrated for systematic elimination, there were only *two* cases of suicide recorded in almost four years?

In order to answer this question we must, for a change, talk freely, not only about the righteous ways of our predecessors, as we are used to, but also about their transgressions. A hundred and fifty years ago, a great Jewish philosopher in Germany foresaw a hoped-for day when the stream of Judaism will fall into the sea of universality—which, to him, was another word for assimilation, like the waters of the Jordan that fall into the sea of Galilee. Only the very experienced fisherman, he said, will be able to distinguish the river's hardly noticeable separate stream in the deep waters of the universal "Kinereth," and the less other people will distinguish it, he concluded, the better for all concerned. The chil-

---

* Address delivered at the National Conference of the Young Leadership of The United Jewish Appeal, Hilton Hotel, N. Y., September 1965.

dren of that great German Jew, however, didn't bother for long to keep even the imperceptible stream of their Jewishness flowing in the seas of German culture. They converted themselves. But they, of course, were an exception. Most of the German Jews kept a vestige of their River Jordan alive in the big sea of Germanism that was roaring around them, but they tried hard to completely reconcile it with that sea—to prove, that is, that the river is so totally committed to the sea that without it, it would lose its reason for being.

And so it came to pass that when the big sea was suddenly stirred up by the Brown Dragon, and the total commitment proved meaningless, it was also bound to prove fatal. The spiritual Jordan can chart its separate course only in a benevolent sea; but in a sea of turbulence—not to say, blood—the Jordan is either to become perceptible or to disappear altogether.

When the Jews of Germany and Austria were told they were no longer Germans or Austrians, there was nothing for them to fall back to. An imperceptible Jewishness is an affliction instead of a solace, and when the affliction became unbearable, they killed themselves en masse. But in Lithuania, or in Poland, or in certain parts of Russia, or Slovakia, things were different. The river of Judaism was stronger there than the sea in the midst of which it ran its separate course and, consequently, the river refused to disappear voluntarily even in a sea of blood. And the river refused to disappear not only because no river wants to die, least of all one on which depends the fullness of the sea, but also because that river believed in the ultimate meaningfulness of its separateness. It's not for us to say—we who weren't there—why so many Jews let themselves be killed, but it is for us to know why, in certain places, and under circumstances which were as conducive to suicide as they were to murder, they didn't kill themselves.

This question is important today because we live in a world in which people know more and more about less and less, a world which has substituted comfort for meaning and entertainment for enjoyment of the mind. It is even more important because people nowadays, more than they strive to know, they try to forget, and they are as uninclined to be bothered by unpleasant things as they are disinterested in stories with a message.

But right now, for example, a great message of an ancient story is being strangled in Communist Russia. The great River Jordan of Russia's Jewry refuses to be swallowed by the Soviet version of the Red Sea, and the Communists, in retaliation, are shedding the blood of our souls before the very eyes of a world which is as indifferent to this act of soul-assassination as it was to the act of our physical extermination under Hitler. For in the blood of our souls, which is being shed now in Russia, there is the message of our uniqueness. It was this message that gave a God and morals and a code of ethics to a pagan world and which, in its prophetic expression, was, and still is, the magna carta of the poor and the oppressed, as Thomas Huxley called it—the greatest instigator of revolt against all forms of despotism.

And this message—suppressed, ignored, misunderstood—is needed today more than ever, for we live in a world in which the gap between the achievements of science and the yearnings of the heart is getting wider by the day, and in which the quality of life has fallen prey to an obsession with standard of living. We know what contributed to this situation: the two world wars; the decay of traditional religion in spite of the ascendance of religious institutionalism; the discovery of nuclear fission; the incredibly fast mastery by science of the physical universe. All this caused an alarming increase of materialist influences in the whole environment. Among large segments of young people—who think that they have an answer to everything—hope, the handmaid of spirit, is dying, to be replaced by cynicism, indifference or juvenile delinquency. Among the more mature people—mature in years, I mean—a lack of sophistication has created a natural disposition toward vulgarity. The ideals we serve—there are only a very few left to cherish —are mostly external. External glitter and quantitative colossalism are the cry of the hour. "Not being able to make our values beautiful," Pliny says, "we make them huge."

Quantitative colossalism tends to become the criterion of all values, for every value—including those considered priceless—has a price tag attached to it. The best business firms are those that are the largest. The society leaders are those that are richest. The largest theatres are the best. The best show is that which attracts most people. The greatest scholar is he who is paid the largest salary and attracts the largest audience. "The biggest firm"; "The largest store"; "The widest circulation"; "The tallest buildings"; "The highest paid star"; "The supermarket"; "The superspectacular" etc. And while in external colossalism, size is the measure, in the inner portrayal of man—the way he is depicted in modern art and literature—lowliness is the subject.

"There is a morbid fascination," to quote Professor Sorokin's powerful little book *The Crisis of Our Age*— "in our period of sensate art with pathological types of persons and events. Contemporary art is primarily a museum of social and cultural pathology. It centers in the police morgue, the criminals' hideouts, and the sex organs, operating mainly on the level of the social sewers and labeling it 'artistic truth' just because such levels exist and are sensory. Anything that is above the senses and beyond them—from the conception of God to the Spirit of Man—anything that is non-material, non-tangible, non-sizable,—anything, in brief, that could not be seen in the way of daily experience, nor heard, tasted, touched or smelled—is regarded as unreal, non-existent and of no value." That's exactly what is happening in the world we live in.

But in the world we died in, in the world that Hitler had annihilated, other things happened. Long before the emergence of the tyrant, the Jews in Europe lived a life devoid of any external glitter and any vestige of what we referred to as "quantitative colossalism." They lived in small villages; they dwelled in humble abodes; they existed on humble means; but they were concerned with *ultimate* questions and, as such, were the carriers of that inner spark which bore constant testimony to the glory of the Ever-living God. They didn't build magnificent structures, visible to the eye; they didn't raise statues or erect monuments. Anything that was too external, too glittering, too showy, was abhorrent and, consequently, classified as something forbidden, like graven images. These people, who were killed, but refused to kill themselves, lived an inward life. It was a life which was inwardly illuminated by a total adherence to a great tradition and, at the same time, by a total commitment to great hope—the hope for a drastic change in human nature—and a final improvement in the human condition—through the coming of the Messiah. Deep within the consciousness of the Jew in the diaspora there burned a recognition of a unique spiritual destiny, and his entire existence was bound up with the fulfillment of this mission, which was, in the long run, a mission to all men. For a hundred generations, Judaism was motivated by a constant urge toward a specific spiritual norm which was the highest expression of Jewish selfhood. This norm was a puzzle to the world as it was a burden to the Jews who didn't grasp its meaning. The world, the non-Jewish world that is—and I am referring to a minority of the intellectual illuminaries of Christianity—had always felt, and still does—that there was something about our existence which, being a denial that matter alone determines the destiny of peoples, was an ode to the spirituality of life. But while the ignorance of the Christian world in general about the

Jew grew side by side with the deepening of the Jew's inwardness —the ignorance of many so-called enlightened Jews about the ultimate meaning of our inwardness—stood out, and still does, as an example of self-denial which, in many cases, degenerated into self-hatred. Judaism, forbidden as it is to make proselytes, and, hence, to advertise itself as others do, is the least-known religion in the world, and the Jew—as long as there is left a vestige of his inwardness—the least known human specimen. Those who gained a glimpse of this inwardness, perceived eternity. Those who were incapable of perceiving it, however, besmirched it with their ink, their tongue or their deed. At the same time when a Matthew Arnold or a Renan, a Tolstoy or a Huxley, a Victor Hugo or a Longfellow, a Mark Twain or an Oliver Wendell Holmes—to mention just a few—beheld the vineyard of Judaism and marvelled at its beauty, the spiritual ignorants of Jewry—spiritual ignorants even if they call themselves "intellectuals"—their ignorance conducive to aggressive self-hatred, derived special joy out of spitting at the vineyard from without. For what those non-Jewish illuminaries have said about Judaism, Jews often hesitated to say. For it was they who defined the Jews as the "Swiss Guard of Deity"; as "the conscience of humanity"; as "that chosen breed which has brought down from heaven the eternal fire"; as "the first to brave the seas of God and emerge with the pearl of wisdom"; "as the founders of whatever is spiritually great and morally beautiful in western culture". Yes, at the very same time when humanity's most enlightened minds have seen in us—in our finite existences— intimations of the infinite, so called "Jewish intellectuals" found a morbid fascination in concentrating not only on the finite in us, but on whatever was deplorable in the finite. The fact of the matter is that the Jew, like the Bible which he had given to the world, and in whose accent, as Heine put it, "Freedom spoke since the Exodus from Egypt,"—the Old Testament that is—is an enigma to himself as to others. He is, however, an enigma, and often a bothersome one, as long as he doesn't make an effort to reach his own depths. When he does he is like the Bible—a book of books which can truly be understood only in its original. The Bible nowadays is as much, or as little, understood as the Jew—and the Jew as the Bible. It was of the Bible that Goethe expressed himself as follows: "I am convinced that the more you understand it, the more beautiful it becomes."

We like to talk about our Jewish heritage, and that is very nice, of course. But if Judaism is only a heritage, no matter how noble, its decline is unavoidable. It's in the nature of a heritage, if it isn't squandered away by unappreciative heirs, to degenerate into a museum piece, a fossil. But if we regard Judaism not only as a heritage but also as a mission; if an accident of birth grows into an assignment of fate; if Judaism is, as Professor Heshel puts it, "God's stake in human history"; if it's true what Matthew Arnold said, that as long as the world lasts, all who want to make progress in righteousness will come to Israel for inspiration; if Renan was right when he said that the pure religion which we dream of as the bond that shall in days to come hold together the whole of mankind, will be the realization of the religion of Isaiah, the ideal Jewish religion,—if all this be true—and heaven and earth and seas of innocent blood bear witness to this truth—then let's make the Jewish mission clear before God and men. Let's make it clear that if we are the ancients of the earth, we are also the morning of the times; that if we were the challenge, we are also the test; that if ours was the Via Dolorosa, ours is also the Arch of Triumph. But, above all, let's put the question clearly to ourselves and the world that if our enemies are so evil, so dark—what are we, if not the bearers of a great light?

Something went wrong with us, and we know what it is basically: the desire to conform, to be like the others, the fear of being different. But is there anything great in the history of mankind which was created by those who were *not* different? When D. H. Lawrence cried out, "For God's sake, let's hang on to our sacred differences!" he cried out in pain at the sight of a world which lost its personality through the loss of personalities. Too many of us remember only the penalties of being a Jew. Its distinctness and inwardness being hidden from us, we hardly enjoy Judaism; we only know the *burden* it imposes upon us. Our souls are often anguished by the vastness of our martyrdom, but they are rarely illuminated by our messianic distinctiveness. This distinctiveness we are trying to cast aside for the sake of fellowship with others, but what does a Jew, who tries to be accepted by others at the expense of his distinctiveness, bring to this hoped-for fraternity? A hollow shell, a Hebraic cipher, a vacuum, a masquerading self, a washed-out personality who has nothing to give because he had destroyed his uniqueness which alone was the reason for the ignorant's fury, the coward's escape, and the wise man's reverence.

This author has some time ago compared two books on the subject of Jewish martyrdom, one in English and the other in Hebrew. The first is Hannah Arendt's *Eichmann in Jerusalem* in which a Jewish woman, who wasn't there, dared to be objective about gas chambers; and the other by Joseph Barzilai-Berger, a former leader of the Communist Party in Palestine, who was cured of his Communism in Siberia where he spent twenty-five years of his life in hard labor with a Stalinist death sentence hanging over his head. If Hanna Arendt's book tried to tell us, among other things, about dwarfs who were reduced to mud—and why shouldn't dwarfs be reduced to mud if giants were reduced to ashes?—Barzilai-Berger tells us about *giants* who rose *from* the mud and the ashes. When Joseph Zadkin and Dr. Avraham Haritt, of blessed memory, former Communist idealists who came to the conclusion that they betrayed the spiritual truth of their people and their own "Neshome" to serve the lie of a graven image—they not only came back to Judaism "with a vengeance," but they started to conceive Jewish martyrdom as a concept which invests one with dignity, with a mission of spiritual grandeur. They accepted their torments stoically and warned against complaints. "We deserve all this," Joseph Zadkin, devoured by remorse, kept on saying. "We have sins to atone for. . . No complaints. No, no complaints." Dr. Haritt, on the other hand, had only one great worry even when he expected to die soon of leukemia: namely, lest a Jewish prisoner, by his behavior, bring dishonor to the sacred name of Israel! Most of them perished, or were executed—there were as many deaths in those days in the Siberian concentration camp of Norilsk as there were in Bergen Belsen—but the element of remorse had added there a strength to the awakened "Neshome" of the Jew which transcended reason and defied all laws of behavioristic psychology and the social sciences based on it.

I always shudder when I hear Jewish spiritual leaders going out of their way to prove that Judaism is all reason. Most of them speak of a "reason" which is not a poetic but a logical reason, and that's where they are wrong! Isn't it a fact that Jewish history as a whole—let alone the Jewish "Neshome"—is one great miracle, inexplicable by reason? When a sceptical French king once asked his pious minister whether he can prove to him the existence of miracles, he answered: "Why, sure, Your Majesty—the Jews!" The minister was referring, of course, to the miracle of spiritual strength as displayed by the Jewish character and which is beyond any logical formulae and cannot be explained with what people call common sense. Jewish history is *uncommon* sense. It is the history of a partly expressed message which we carry in our blood and which craves full expression. Judaism possesses the richest spiritual oil fields in the world, but it hardly digs for the oil. At a time when the world we live in—whose two super powers possess enough atomic explosives to destroy two hundred globes the size of our planet earth—is looking all over for a new resource of spiritual strength, the separate voice of Judaism is hardly audible. And don't let anybody tell us that a separate voice is undesirable since "normalization is our aim." If the grand finale, so to speak, of the unique Jewish performance on the stage of history—to quote the eminent Hebrew writer Avraham Karive—will be marked by imitational normalcies—for what is normalcy, the way it is commonly understood, but a desire to be like the rest?—not only will all our history become meaningless, but all our Prophets, martyrs and sages down the ages will turn into sterile and pitiable Don Quixotes. . . .

The Jews cannot be just another people, as Israel cannot be just another state. We have promises to keep; we have messages to deliver; we have a story to tell; we have a way to show. Thousands of years ago we wiped the nose of a paganistically infantile humanity, stuck a prayer book under its arms and told it: "Go on, walk!" Now when this humanity, in its older days, has lost its way in the jungle of history—it is for us to help find it. That's what we expect from ourselves, and that's what the world, the soulful world that is, expects from us. That world is not misled by the word "normalcy." What's so normal about the world's greatest democracy—the U.S.A.—spending forty-five billion dollars a year for entertainment and being bored stiff? And what's so normal about Europe's oldest democracy whose most widely read newspapers were not too long ago vying with each other for the publication rights of the memoirs of two prostitutes? And I am mentioning only the free countries. We don't have to lose a word about the pathology of the totalitarian regimes. The world is, at best, subnormal; and if Judaism is to subscribe to this trend, the secret of the spiritual tigers of our people will be forever buried under the skin of the assimilationist lamb or the self-hating skunk. Judaism, in its true sense, is a call to rise above normalcy; for the Jew, the historical Jew, if he is not above it, is below it. And it all depends on ourselves. Only if we shall regard ourselves as Yehuda Halevi regarded his people—namely as the "heart" of the peoples—will Israel become the heart of the nations, for that is what it was meant to be.

But if we shall continue to regard our people only as victims of persecution who happened to be carriers of a heritage, then the maximum we can hope for is equality, and equality alone will not secure survival. Survival will be secured only if we regard ourselves both as the trustees of a heritage and as the carriers of a mission; we are not trying to convert anybody to our faith, but we must spread the word of our hope. We are called upon these days to provide the world with an idea about our deterrent against evil, for we live in a world which needs it. Not too long ago a German author was quoted in *The New York Times* as having expressed himself that "the Germans, within themselves, have no deterrent against evil". And they are not the only ones.

And that is what Judaism was meant to be from its very inception—a deterrent against evil. The Jews had barely begun to spread the word of this deterrent when they were expelled from their land. "There is still a long road ahead of us," writes Rabbi Kook, "to finish what we have begun to do. . . . We began to speak a great word among ourselves and in the ears of the entire world, and we have not yet completed it. We stand in the midst of our speech. . . . We cannot stop it, nor do we want to. . . . The truth within us is sufficiently powerful to speak up, but it is so rich and overflowing that we are not yet capable to express it in clear language. . . . In our inwardness our thoughts are very clear to us and, in the course of time, our speech, too, will be liberated from the stultifying cobwebs of exile so that we shall be able to speak again."

Rabbi Kook wrote those lines long before Auschwitz, for had he written them following the perpetration of this greatest of all crimes, he would have known only too well that words like "the stultifying cobwebs of exile" are by far too mild to express the devastating impact of the Hitler era on the Jewish soul. Let's not hesitate to talk about it. The evil in Europe was of such heinous proportions that some of the survivors survived with totally crushed souls. These souls may remain crushed forever and, what is more, they may transmit this state of inner devastation to their children and children's children unless there is an attempt, on a universal scale, to spiritually cure the wounded Jewish soul. Israel provided only the beginning of the cure, for political, social and economic remedies are not enough. They are not enough for the survivors as they are not enough for Jewry in general. If the birth of Israel is only a political, social or economic phenomenon—as the advocates of "normalization" claim (I was never quite sure as to what they mean by "Israel's *cultural* message")—the inevitable result will be that one day, Jewry, both Israel's and the Diaspora's, will be devoured by levantinization, on the one hand, and assimilation, on the other. That is why Avraham Karive was so right when he said that the decision concerning the spiritual meaning of Israel's rebirth is one of the greatest and gravest which we have faced in our long history. This decision, moreover, is bound to generate tremendous tensions, clashes and "Kultur Kampfs," but the very life of Israel, as a people and as a nation, depends on it. Any attempt to tackle this problem from the angle of the immediate or intermediate alone is morally unforgivable, historically untenable and spiritually unacceptable. It is in the very nature of Judaism to totally reject the idea of existence for existence's sake. Israel had sought an ultimate meaning for its existence when the forefathers of some of our defamers were still climbing trees and cracking chestnuts in the woods. And if this was the case millenniums ago when our father Jacob "wrestled with God",—how much more so today? Today, after Auschwitz—and we shall say "after Auschwitz" for the next thousand years, no matter how little the complacent amongst us and amongst our neighbors like to hear it—something has to be done on a grand spiritual scale so that Auschwitz becomes to us what the torments of Job became to the man of Oz. Let's open the Bible and see what it tells us about the latter days of Job: "And there were not found in the whole land maidens more beautiful than the daughters of Job. . . ." In the eyes of the God-inspired Holy Scriptures the goodness that was bestowed upon Job's latter days would have been incomplete if his daughters were *as* beautiful as other beautiful women of the land. The daughters of Job *had* to be *more* beautiful. Why? Avraham Karive gave the following inspiring answer to this question in an address to the annual conference of the Hebrew Writers' Association in Israel. And what he said in essence was this: Let's think about it, about the man himself, Job, at the end of his days, following the plagues, the disasters, the deaths that befell him in succession; following the days and the nights on the ground with ashes on his head; following the excruciating pains that wrecked his body and the terrible doubt that imprisoned his soul; following his agonized discussion with his so-called "comforters" and, finally, following his hearkening to God's voice out of the darkness. Is it at all conceivable that Job, when his health, power and possessions returned to him, became a regular, normal citizen like the other inhabitants of his city and that he would even take a daily walk to the market place where he would discuss the news and indulge a little in gossip? No, not to such a Job was the most

194

stormy, the most tragic and the most heroic book of the Bible dedicated. And not only that to *such* a Job no such book would be dedicated, but it would not be worthwhile even to mention his name. But Job did *not* become a "normal" citizen, for had he become one, this normalcy would have rendered the abnormalcy of his torments *meaningless*. The Job of the Scriptures, who was a good and decent man even before his trials, emerges from them infinitely more *refined*. He emerges with a soul that radiated a beauty which was out of the ordinary. And it was this beauty which was reflected in the bodies and souls of the daughters that were born to him at the end of his days. What this great passage in the Bible actually means is not only that Job's daughters were more beautiful than the other maidens of the land, but that their beauty was of a *different kind*—a beauty which arose from the depths of misery and from the heights of purity alike. The beauty of the daughters of Job was not only a kind of indemnity paid by the Almighty for the terrible damage inflicted upon His loyal servant, but a direct *result* of this *damage!* Job, in other words, did not seek, nor did he get, following his torments, a "normalization" of his situation. And he did not seek it, nor did he get it, because normalization and sameness are hardly the corollary to a life such as Job's. The vindication of a life such as Job's—the meaning of his life—his life's message and mission—lay in the blessing and beauty of regained and refined spiritual power that were reflected in the souls and bodies of his children. That is why "in all the land there were no women found so fair as the daughters of Job. . . ."

Survival for what?

For the sake of a day in which the ordeals of Job's people will be as vindicated as the ordeals of Job.

PART TWO

YOSSEL RAKOVER SPEAKS TO GOD

Mr. Kolitz wrote "Yossel Rakover Speaks to God" in 1946 and published it in a Jewish daily in Buenos Aires where he was visiting. A year later, the story was published in New York, by the Creative Age Press, as part of a collection of eleven short stories and parables of the years of death under the name *The Tiger Beneath the Skin*. Eight years later, Mr. Kolitz, arriving in New York after a long stay in Israel, was amazed to learn, from the local Jewish press, that a discussion was going on in Jewish literary circles as to whether "Yossel Rakover Speaks to God" was a work of fiction written by an author whose identity was unknown or, as suggested by the majority, an authentic document that was actually found in the ruins of the Warsaw ghetto. The discussion stopped, of course, when Mr. Kolitz easily identified himself as the author. Soon afterwards he found out how a story that was twice published before under his name as fiction was presented—and accepted—as an authentic document. What happened was that an old, well-meaning Jewish citizen of Buenos Aires who read the story in the High Holiday issue of the leading local Jewish daily, was misled by the realistic tone of the opening lines ("In the ruins of the ghetto of Warsaw. . .Among heaps of charred debris . . .there was found the following document. . .written by a Jew by the name of Yossel Rakover," etc.) and sincerely regarded it as a document. He was so taken by what he read that he made a few typewritten copies of the story and dispatched it to other lands describing it as an authentic document that was actually discovered in the Warsaw ghetto. The story was soon published and broadcast time and again over Radio free Berlin. The impact of

199

the story there was very great. The late Nobel Prize winner Thomas Mann described it, just before he died, as a "shattering human and religious document" while the Jesuit monthly *Stimmen Der Zeit*, long after it became known that the story was fiction, hailed it as an outcry of a "modern Job." In the U.S.A., the organization of conservative Rabbis recommended to include the story in the prayer book for the High Holidays.

The two meditations that follow the story were written during its shortlived "documentary" period by two well-known German writers.

The Publishers

YOSSEL RAKOVER'S APPEAL TO GOD *

In the ruins of the ghetto of Warsaw, among heaps of charred debris, piled up over the place that once housed the largest Jewish community in Europe, there was found, packed tightly into a small bottle, the following testament, written during the ghetto's last hours by a Jew named Yossel Rakover.

Warsaw, April 28, 1943
"I, Yossel, son of David Rakover of Tarnopol, a Hassid of the Rabbi of Ger and a descendant of the great and pious families of Rakover and Meisel, inscribe these lines as the last houses of the Warsaw ghetto go up in flames, the house I am in being one of the last not yet consumed by the fire. For several hours now an unusually heavy artillery barrage has been crashing down on us, and the walls, it seems, are about to disintegrate under the fiery impact. It will not be long before the house I am in is transformed, like almost every other house of the ghetto, into a grave for its defenders. By the dagger-sharp, unusually crimson rays of the sun that strike through the small, half-walled up window of my room through which we have been shooting at the enemy day and night, I see that it must now be late afternoon, just before sundown, and I cannot regret that this is the last sun I shall see. All of our notions and emotions have been altered. Death, swift and immediate, seems a liberator, sundering our shackles; and beasts of the field, in their freedom and gentleness, seem so lovable and dear that I feel hurt whenever I hear the evil fiends that lord it over Europe referred to as beasts. It is untrue that the tyrant who rules Europe now has something of the beast in him. Nothing of the kind! He is a typical child of modern man; mankind as a whole, even mankind's dominant religion, spawned and reared him. He is

---

* By permission of Farrar, Straus and Cudahy.

merely the frankest expression of the innermost, most deeply buried instincts of man.

"In a forest where I once hid, I encountered a dog one night, sick and hungry, his tail between his legs, and both of us, it seemed to me, immediately felt the kinship of our situations. He cuddled up to me, buried his head in my lap, and licked my hands. I do not know if I ever cried so much as that night. I threw my arms around his neck, crying like a baby. If I say that I envied the animal at that moment, it would not be remarkable. But what I felt was more than envy. It was shame. I felt ashamed before the dog to be a man, and I was glad that there are dogs in the world to put man to shame. That is how matters stand with us now. That is the spiritual level to which we have sunk. Life is a tragedy, death a savior; man a calamity, beast an ideal; the day a horror, the night a relief.

"When my wife, my children and I—six in all—hid in the forest, it was the night and the night alone that concealed us in its bosom. The day turned us over to the seekers of our souls. I remember with utmost clarity the day when the Germans raked with hails of fire the thousands of refugees on the highway from Grodno to Warsaw. As the sun rose, the airplanes rose as well, and the whole day long they murdered us, aided by the sun. In this massacre, my wife with our seven month old child in her arms, perished. Two others of my five remaining children also disappeared that day without a trace. Their names were David and Yehuda, one was four years old, the other six. They were holding hands as they were last seen running into the forest.

"At sunset, the handful of survivors continued their journey in the direction of Warsaw, and I, with my three remaining children, started out to comb the fields and the woods at the site of the massacre in search of the two lost children. The entire night we called for them. Not even echoes replied. I never saw my two children again, and later in a dream was told not to worry for they were in God's hands.

"My other three children died in the space of a single year in the Warsaw ghetto. Rachel, my daughter, ten years old, heard that it was possible to find scraps of bread in the public dump outside the ghetto walls. The ghetto was starving at the time, and the people who died of starvation lay in the streets like heaps of rotten rags. The people of the ghetto were prepared to face any death but the death of hunger. Against no death did they struggle so fiercely as against death by starvation. But it was starvation, combined with

202

humiliation,—the Nazi system that worked so well!—which made them lose the ability to fight against the life they lived.

"My daughter, Rachel, told me nothing of her plan to steal out of the ghetto, a crime punishable by death. She and a girl friend of the same age started out on the perilous journey. She left home under cover of darkness, and at sunrise she and her friend were caught outside the ghetto walls. Nazi ghetto guards, together with dozens of their Polish underlings—oh, those Polish underlings!— at once started in pursuit of these two Jewish children who had dared to venture out to hunt for crumbs in a garbage can. People witnessing the chase could not believe their eyes. It was unusual even in the ghetto. Hordes of furious madmen running amok in pursuit of a pair of starved ten-year-old children who did not endure very long in the unequal match. One of them, my child, running with her last ounces of strength, fell exhausted to the ground, upon which the Nazis put a bullet through her head. The other child saved herself, but driven out of her mind, died two weeks later.

"The fifth child, Yacob, a boy of thirteen, died on his Bar Mitzvah day of tuberculosis. The last child, my fifteen-year-old daughter, Chaya, perished during a Kinderaktion—a children's operation—that began at sunrise last Rosh Hashana and ended at sundown. That day, before sunset, hundreds of Jewish families lost their children. Whoever witnessed this deportation, as I did, witnessed not only the death, or the condemnation to death, of children, but the death, or the condemnation to death, of man. After that, man is dreadfully dead. And let him be.

"Now my time has come. And like Job, I can say of myself, nor am I the only one that can say it, that I return to the soil naked, as naked as the day of my birth.

"I am forty-three years old, and when I look back on the past I can assert confidently, as confident as a man can be of himself, that I have lived a decent life, in love with God and His law. I was once blessed with material means, but never boasted of it. My house was open to the needy. I served God enthusiastically, and my single request to Him was that He should allow me to worship Him with all my heart, and all my soul, and all my strength.

"I cannot say that my relationship to Him has remained unchanged after everything I have lived through, but I can say with absolute certainty that my belief in Him has not changed by a hair's breadth. Previously, when I was well off, the father of a large, happy family, the husband of a good, loving and beloved wife, my relation to God was as to one who granted me a favor for nothing, and I felt constantly obliged to Him for it. Now my relations to Him are as to one who owes *me* something, nay, owes me much, and since I feel so, I believe I have the right to demand it of Him. But I do not say, like Job, that God should point out my sin with His finger so that I may know why I deserve this punishment, or why *we* deserve this punishment. Far greater and saintlier men than I are now convinced that it is not a question of crime and punishment. Oh, no! Something entirely different is taking place in the world. It is, to be exact, a time when God has veiled His countenance from the world, sacrificing mankind to its wild instincts, and mankind's instincts are very wild! This however, does not mean that the pious members of my people should justify the edict, saying that God and His Judgments are right. For saying that we deserve the punishment we have received is to malign and desecrate the Holy Name of God as well as of His true children. For those that desecrate our name, desecrate the name of the Lord; God is maligned by our self-deprecation. He who curses us, curses God.

"In a situation like this, I naturally expect no miracles, nor do I ask Him, my Lord, to show me any mercy. May He treat me with the same veiled countenance with which He treated millions of His people. I am no exception, and I expect no special treatment. I will no longer attempt to save myself, nor flee anymore. I will facilitate the work of the fire by moistening my clothing with gasoline. This we are permitted by the Law. This is no suicide. I have three bottles of gasoline left after having emptied several scores over the heads of the assassins. It was one of the finent moments in my life when I did this, and I was shaken by it with joyful laughter. I never dreamed that the death of people, even of enemies—even such enemies—the scum of the earth—could cause such great pleasure. Foolish humanists may say what they choose. But vengeance was, and always will be, the last means of waging lost battles and the only spiritual comfort of the humiliated. I had never until now understood the precise meaning of the expression in the Talmud that vengeance is sacred because it is mentioned between two of God's names: 'a God of Vengeance is the Lord.' I understand it now,—oh Lord, how well I understand it!—I understand it and I rejoice in my understanding it as my heart swells in angry laughter at the thought that the followers of Jesus have always found fault in the 'Old Testament' vengefulness! Yes, they are right: the 'Old Testament,' as they call it, is replete with death sentences, as they say, but when the supreme court of our people in their free land, so the Holy Talmud tells us, pronounced *one* death sentence in *seventy* years the people would call them 'murderers!' That other 'Testament,' by everlasting contrast, is very full of love and forgiveness, as we all know, but how many of our murderers, now and always, confess faith in it? The Lord of Vengeance reared men of love, but the God of Love reared men of vengeance. I too, crave vengeance, of course I do! But my vengeance is not their vengeance and my love is not their love. I don't crave vengeance for a God who died, but for *man* who died before our very eyes, and it is not the death of the son of man—the mature grown-up man—whose blood I want to avenge, but for the *child* of man who was executed! Man cannot create a vengeance for the blood of an executed child, nor even Satan, but God can—nay, *God must!* This is the vengeance I am talking about now before I am going to meet my maker, and that is why my heart is so overjoyed at remembering that for thousands of sorrow-laden years we have been calling our father in heaven 'a God of Vengeance.' Yes, a God of Vengeance is our Lord!

"I have had only a very few opportunities to witness vengeance the way man can experience it—only a very few. When I did, however, it presented to me a sight too marvellous to behold, a sight which caused a new life to spring up in me for a while. I must recount the last incident in detail: a German tank had suddenly broken into our street, and it was bombarded with flaming bottles of gasoline. They failed to hit their target, however, and the tank continued to advance. We waited, my friends and I, till the huge tank was almost upon us. Then, through the half bricked-up window, we suddenly attacked it with our gasoline bottles. The tank burst into flames, and six burning Nazis jumped out. Oh, how they burned! They burned like the Jews they had set afire, but they shrieked much more. The dying Jews don't shriek. They welcome death as a Savior. They are sometimes afraid *not* to die. Yes, they are! I have seen with my own eyes a young Jew jumping from the roof of a collapsing house in an attempt to kill himself. The terror that seized him upon realizing that he was still alive, with his legs broken, with the Nazis drawing closer, did not drive him out of his mind, but it drove him to end his life on the spot by violently smashing his skull against the asphalt before the Germans closed in on him. That is the kind of battle we are waging here under the eyes of a humanity which was reared on 'love'! The Warsaw ghetto now perishes in battle. It goes down shooting, struggling, blazing, but no—not shrieking!

"I have three more bottles of gasoline left. They are as precious to me as wine to a drunkard. After pouring one over my clothes, I will place the paper on which I write these lines in the empty bottle and hide it among the bricks filling the window of this room. If anyone ever finds it and reads it, he will, perhaps, understand the emotions of a Jew, one of millions, who died forsaken by the ever-living God in whom he believed to the very end. I will let the two other bottles explode on the heads of the murderers when my last moment comes.

"There were twelve of us in this room at the outbreak of the rebellion. Twelve. For nine days we battled against the enemy. All eleven of my comrades have fallen, dying silently in battle, including the small boy of about five who came here only God knows how and who now lies dead near me. His face, a pure, beautiful face of a Jewish child with ear locks, wears the kind of smile that appears on children's faces when they dream peacefully. Even this child died with the same epic calm as his older comrades. It happened early this morning. Most of us were dead already. The boy scaled the heap of corpses to catch a glimpse of the outside world through the window. He stood beside me in that position for several minutes. Suddenly he fell backwards, rolling down the pile of corpses, and lay like a stone. On his small, pale forehead, between the locks of black hair, there was a spattering of blood.

"Up until yesterday morning, when the enemy launched at sunrise a concentrated barrage against this stronghold, one of the last in the ghetto, every one of us was still alive, although five were wounded. During yesterday and today, all of them fell, one after the other, one on top of the other, aiming and firing until death. Now I am left alone. I have no more ammunition, apart from the three bottles of gasoline. From the floors of the house above still come frequent shots, but they can hold out no more hope for me, for by all signs the stairway has been razed by the shell fire, and I think the house is about to collapse any moment. I write these lines lying on the floor. Around me lie my dead comrades. I look into their faces, and it seems to me that a quiet but mocking irony animates them, as if they were saying to me, 'A little patience, you foolish man, another few minutes and everything will become clear to you too.' This irony is particularly noticeable on the face of the small boy lying near my right hand as if he were asleep. His small mouth is drawn into a smile exactly as if he were about to laugh, and I, who still live and feel and think—it seems to me that he is laughing at me. He laughs, or is about to laugh, with that quiet subtle laughter so characteristic of the wise, speaking of knowledge with the ignorant who believe they know everything. Yes, he is omniscient now, this holy little boy. Everything is clear to him now. He even knows why he was born, but had to die so soon; why he died only five years after his birth. And even if he does not know why, he knows at least that it is entirely unimportant and insignificant whether or not he knows it, in the light of the revelation of that godly majesty in the better world he now inhabits, cuddled up in the arms of his murdered parents to whom he has returned. In an hour or two I will make the same discovery. Unless my face is eaten by the flames, a similar smile may rest on it after my death, for nobody to notice but God. Meanwhile, I still live, however, and before the quickly approaching end, I wish to speak to my Lord as a living man, a simple, living person who had the great but tragic honor of being a Jew.

"I am privileged—yes, privileged!—that I am a Jew, not in spite of the world's treatment of us, but precisely because of this treatment. I should be ashamed to belong to people who spawned, raised or tolerated the scum which is responsible for the deeds that are perpetrated against us.

"I am privileged to be a Jew because it is an *art* to be a Jew. It is no art to be an Englishman, an American, or a Frenchman. It may be easier, more comfortable, to be one of them, but no—not more honorable, more responsible, more meaningful. Yet, it is an honor to be a Jew!

"I believe that to be a Jew means to be a fighter, an everlasting swimmer against the criminally turbulent human currents. The Jew is a hero, a martyr, a saint. You, our enemies, say that we are bad. I believe that we are infinitely better and finer than you, but even if we were worse—I should like to see how you would look in our place!

"I am happy to belong to the unhappiest of all peoples of the world, whose precepts represent the loftiest and most beautiful of all morality and laws. These immortal precepts which we possess have now been even more sanctified and immortalized by the fact that they have been so debased and insulted by the enemies of the Lord.

"I believe that to be a Jew is an inborn trait. One is born a Jew exactly as one is born an artist. It is impossible to be released from being a Jew. That is our godly attribute that has made us a chosen people. Those who do not understand this will never understand the higher meaning of our martyrdom. If I ever doubted that God once designated us as the chosen people, I believe now that our tribulations have made us the chosen one.

"I believe in You, God of Israel, even though You have done everything to stop me from believing in You. I believe in Your laws even if I cannot excuse Your actions. My relationship to You is not the relationship of a slave to his master but rather that of a pupil to his teacher. I bow my head before Your greatness, but I will not kiss the lash with which You strike me.

"You say that we have sinned, O Lord? It must surely be true. That You are less lenient with our sins than with those of others? I know that, too. But I should like You to tell me *whether there is a sin in the world deserving of the punishment that was meted out to us?*

"You assert that You will yet repay our enemies? I am convinced of it. Repay them without mercy? I have no doubt of that either. I should like You to tell me, however, *whether there is any punishment in the world capable of compensating for the crimes that have been committed against us?*

"You say, I know, that it is no longer a question of sin and punishment, but rather a situation in which Your countenance is veiled for some reasons known only to you, and humanity is abandoned to its evil instincts. I should like to ask You, O Lord—and this question burns in me like a consuming fire—*what more, O what more must transpire before you unveil your countenance again to the world?*

"I want to say to You that now, more than in any other period of our eternal path of agony, we, we the tortured, the humiliated, the buried alive and burned alive, we the mocked, the degraded, the abandoned, we the loneliest among the lonely of the earth,— we have the right to know: *what are the limits of your patience?*

"And I should like to say something about our patience too: do not put the rope under too much strain, lest, alas, it snaps. The test to which You put us is so severe, so unbearably severe, that You should—You must—forgive those members of Your people who, in their despair, have turned away from You.

"Forgive those who have turned away from You in their misery, but also those who have turned from You in their happiness. You have transformed our life into such a hell that the cowards among us have been forced to flee it; and what is happiness but a place of refuge for cowards? Do not chastise them for it. One does not

208

strike cowards, but has mercy on them. Have mercy on *them,* rather than *us,* O Lord.

"Forgive those among Your children who have desecrated Your name, who have gone over to the service of other gods, who have become hostile to their own kith and kin. You have castigated them so severely that they no longer believe that You are their Father, that they have any Father at all!

"I tell You this because I do believe in You, because I believe in You now more strongly than ever, because now I know that You are *my* Lord, because after all You are not, You cannot possibly be, the God of those whose deeds are the most horrible manifestation of ungodliness.

"If You are not *my* Lord, then whose Lord are You? The Lord of the murderers?

"If those that hate me and murder me are so dark, so evil, what then am I if not he who reflects something of Your light, of Your goodness?

"I cannot extol You for the deeds that You tolerate. I bless You and extol You, however, for the very fact of Your existence, for Your awesome mightiness, so awesome and so mighty that even what is transpiring right now in this world doesn't cause You to redeem it or destroy it at once!

"And I don't speak of destruction as a punishment inflicted from above. The murderers themselves, I am sure, have already spelled out, by what they did to us, to Your people, the nature of their own sentence. For the conscience of man was drowned in our blood; for a world has died with the death of Israel.

"Yes, the open murderers will sooner or later be consumed by their own wickedness, by the fire of evil which they unleashed. But may you carry out a double severe sentence on those who, while not being murderers themselves, are silently condoning the murder.

"Those that condemn murder orally, but rejoice at it in their hearts. . .Those who meditate in their foul hearts: It is fitting, after all, to say that he is evil, this tyrant, but he carries out a bit of work for us for which we will always be grateful to him!

"It is written in Your Torah that a thief should be punished more severely than a brigand, in spite of the fact that the thief does not attack his victim physically, and merely attempts to take away his possessions stealthily.

"The reason for this is that a brigand, in attacking his victim in broad daylight, shows no more fear of man than of God. The thief, on the other hand, fears man, but not God. His punishment, therefore, is greater.

"I should be satisfied if you dealt with the murderers as with brigands, for their attitude towards You and towards us is one and the same.

"But those who are silent in the face of murder, those who have no fears of You, but fear what people might say (fools! they are unaware that the people will say nothing!); those who express their sympathy with the drowning man but refuse to rescue him though they can swim—punish them, I implore You, with the punishment of the thief—a doubly-severe sentence!

"Death can wait no longer. From the floors above me, the firing becomes weaker by the minute. The last defenders of this stronghold are now falling, and with them falls and perishes the great, vibrating, and God-fearing Jewish Warsaw. The sun is about to set, and I thank God that I will never see it again. Fire lights the small window, and the bit of sky that I can see is flooded with red like a waterfall of blood. In about an hour at the most I will be with the rest of my family and with the millions of other stricken members of my people in that better world where there are no more doubts.

"I die peacefully, but not complacently; persecuted, but not enslaved; embittered, but not cynical; a believer, but not a supplicant; a lover of God, but no blind amen-sayer of His.

"I have followed Him even when He repulsed me. I have obeyed His commandments even when He castigated me for it; I have loved Him and I love Him even when He has hurled me to the earth, tortured me to death, made me an object of shame and ridicule before the eyes of the whole world.

"My rabbi would frequently tell the story of a Jew who fled from the Spanish Inquisition with his wife and child, striking out in a small boat over a stormy sea until he reached a rocky island. A flash of lightning killed his wife; a storm hurled his child into the sea. Then, as lonely as a stone, naked, barefoot, lashed by the storm, the thunder, and the lightning, hands and eyes turned up to God, the Jew, setting out on his journey through the wastes of the island, addressed his maker with the following words:

"God of Israel, I have fled to this place in order to worship You without molestation, to obey Your commandments and sanctify Your name. You, however, have done everything to make me stop believing in You, to turn against You. Now, lest it seem to You that You will succeed in driving me from the path of Your righteousness, I notify You, my God and the God of my fathers, *that it will not avail You in the least.* You may insult me, You may castigate me, You may take from me all that I cherish and hold dear in the world, You may torture me unto death—I will still believe in *You,* I will love *You* no matter what You do to me.

"And these are my last words to You, my wrathful God: Nothing will avail You in the least. Nothing! You have done everything to make me renounce You, to make me lose my faith in You, to make me scream at You in Your face, but I die exactly as I have lived, singing the glory of my God.

"Eternally praised be the God of the dead, the God of love and vengeance, of truth and justice, Who will soon reveal His face to the world again and shake its foundations with His almighty voice.

Hear, O Israel, the Lord our God the Lord is One.
Into Thy hands, O Lord, I consign my soul.

MEDITATIONS ON YOSSEL RAKOVER
by
Rudolf Kramer Badoni

Yossel Rakover!

I have just read your letter which, twelve years ago, with death waiting for you to finish it, you wrote to God.

How great must have been your soul that in such hours it didn't show any signs of faltering but, instead, was able to utter words of strength and wisdom to your God. And how great must be your God who undertakes to awaken such souls in man. You belong to the people of God, a people who at all times, before anything else and no matter what happened to them, knew how to find a common language with the Lord.

You were right, Yossel Rakover. There is no greater evidence to the effect of your being the chosen people than your sufferings. But no evidence to boundless faith in spite of boundless pains is greater than yours, Yossel Rakover!

I belong to the people to whom you would have been ashamed to belong. You can say: *I would have been ashamed*. I have no choice but to say: *I am* ashamed! Why, then, do I laugh and joke and work in spite of my shame and as if I were not ashamed at all? Who are we that we unashamedly continue to complacently inhabit the earth instead of striving, in the face of unavoidable death, to live up to the graveness of the responsibility ordained by the God to all of us? Only God knows how and why He made us the way we are: Why, on one hand, people die ashamed of their being men, and, on the other hand, other people are ashamed to belong to a certain group of men, but continue to live as if they are not ashamed at all.

But I belong also to those to whom you referred to as thieves,

Yossel Rakover. I did not belong to the fearless robbers and murderers at whom you fired in the Ghetto of Warsaw and upon whom you would rather see God bestowing His mercy than upon the thieves—the thieves who, in addition to other evil, were also guilty of the inexcusable crime of fear of man. Yes, I had compassion for the drowning! I hated the robbers and I continue to hate them with all the fibers of my heart. But I admit that in spite of it, because of fear and because I desired to live, I wore their insignia and their uniform. I hated Satan but I entered into a pact with him. Something new has been happening to us, Yossel Rakover: the hater came to terms with the one whom he hated in order to save his skin. I saw trainloads of Jews about to be deported, and I shut my mouth with my hand lest I scream. I was received like a son in a Jewish family in Hungary, but I didn't use my gun when the Nazis came to take them away. I saw how the little Mr. Strauss in Geinsenheim on the Rhine was dragged to be thrown into the gutter, and ashamed, wrathful, yet cowardly silent, I passed him by. Never more, as long as I live, shall I be able to free myself of this feeling of shame. The life which I live is a stolen life now, and yet I laugh and I joke as if I were no thief!

That the robber deserves more of God's mercy than the thief, that is certainly the profoundest word of the Torah that came to your mind in the hour of your death. Jesus, whom your people called Rabbi Joshua, always preferred the outcasts to those who chose to linger in the midway between good and bad, always entertaining the treacherous hope that they will get away with everything. How right he was! I have faith in his words though I don't follow his ways. I may not fool myself with the treacherous hope that I will get away with what we and I did; I may not hope for anything but unmerited mercy, but what do I do in myself, by myself and for myself in order to deserve it? God's ways with men are as inexplicable to me in my shame as they were to you in your death throes, Yossel Rakover. We cannot follow you when you raise your voice against God, when you accuse and demand explanations. The meaning of your words can be conceived only by one who loved God as you did. That's how Clement Brentano's "slave out of the depth," shrieked to God: "Lord, oh, Lord! I can't take it any longer!—Let Your rainbow appear! . . . Lord, I demand it from You—save! . . . Can't you forgive your slave that he dares to speak to you like that?"

But what was left to you, Yossel Rakover, in your holy despair, is the same that is left to us in our burning shame, namely, to keep on trusting in Him even when all earthly hope is gone. All that is left for us to do in our despair is to raise our voices and scream, or, maybe, to try to drown our despair in an even louder cry of praise to the Lord.

There were murderers, amongst us—I am sure you know that, Yossel Rakover—who died like saints, accompanied into eternity by a forgiving God. But isn't it possible that even a wretched thief, yearning for a spark of your greatness or, at least, for the fearless soul of the murderer, would ultimately find mercy in God's eyes? This is the only hope which is left to those who under the cover of silence and under the masks of darkness succeeded to steal their lives from Satan's hand. It is *my* unmerited hope anyway.

A people of murderers and silent cowards; a people of brave soldiers, but cowardly citizens; a people longing for faith, but pitifully lacking in love. That's what we are! The few among us who withstood Satan's onslaught and died or were imprisoned, cannot possibly make up for the crime of our silence, the silence of our vast majority; on the contrary, it makes our crime only weigh heavier upon us. We are facing trial now. The court is in permanent session. We stand before it with devastated hearts, living our stolen lives. I may not speak for all my people. I don't even know whether these are peoples or individuals that count before God. I don't accuse anybody. I have no right to. The only right I have is to accuse myself. To accuse myself in order to wait and see whether the Eternal shows mercy to my soul. Woe, if these words of mine are to be construed by anybody as literature! Our men of letters have already succeeded in proving to themselves and to others that they had nothing in common with the murderers, that the murderers were "the others", "the others", always "the others"! . . . But all our words, all our big, self-acquitting words collapse like card houses before our inner gaze. So here I stand, innocent before the law of the World, but with an over-burdened conscience, with a burning shame in my heart, and, quite often, with tears in my eyes. Yes, here I stand, doing my daily work and, sometimes, even joking and laughing, and your curse, Yossel Rakover, weighs upon me as on one who was neither a murderer nor a saint! There are no deeds that I can point at and that can speak in my favor and there is nothing I can say in my defense, except, perhaps, that I hope—oh, let us all hope!—that God's mercy is more real than our weaknesses, than our plagued wisdom, than our smashed self-righteousness.

SECOND MEDITATION ON YOSSEL RAKOVER

by

Sebastian Muller

Half a year ago I read for the first time your letter to God, Yossel Rakover. Since then I read it several times all over again, and these last days I re-read it. Since I belong to the people of your murderers, I feel that I must take a stand to what you say. Rudolph Kramer Badoni did it in his own way. What he said about himself, is also true of me. It is true that we are ashamed of what has happened and, in spite of it, we live as if nothing *had* happened. I, too, didn't belong to the robbers and murderers, but to the thieves. I belonged to the thieves who hated the murderers but were too cowardly in their silence to think about anything else but their own skin. And that's how it happened that I, like many surviving thieves, am still alive. I am still alive, but there is a place in my heart which is dead, utterly and irreparably destroyed. I don't know how to call this place. Maybe it is the cell, the seed which alone enables men to say yes or no: A place which is central in me, which is all internal, and which orders the "yeses" and the "no's" to my heart, to my mind, to my hands.

I say this only for myself, though there must be many among my people who realize by now that in their hearts, too, this place is, and will continue to be, paralyzed. How else could we explain why we behaved like thieves, stealthily watching the play of the murderers? There are times when it seems to me that there is nothing I would want more than a drop of Jewish blood in my veins. Do you understand me, Yossel Rakover? I long to be your brother and a brother of your people. There are a few people, friends of mine, who know about this "complex", for it is what people conveniently refer to today as a "complex." The story may bore you, Yossel

Rakover, but I feel in me a great need to tell you how I came to this wishful thinking.

I am, as is Rudolph Kramer Badoni, a Christian, baptized as a Catholic. What does it mean? Not very much. I was neither Christian nor Catholic when the murderers were in power. But precisely because of the rule of the murderers and because of their downfall, do I hope now that I am on the right path to become a Christian. I hope to become a Christian, Yossel Rakover, and I say it to you, because I cannot become a Jew! I don't belong to your chosen people; even if I convert myself, I would have still remained a stranger among your own. I have only one possibility left to me: to become a Christian!

Jesus was flesh of Your flesh and blood of Your blood. I don't belong to those who say: the Jews crucified Jesus. Jesus had to be crucified because your God so willed. That is my belief. Listen to me, Yossel Rakover! I believe that your God is the same God we pray to: The God who created Heaven and Earth, who rules His creation, who has chosen your people from amongst all the families of the Earth and made it His own. And because I believe in this God of yours, the God of Abraham, Isaac and Moses, I also believe that your people are the chosen ones, the people of God, to whom nobody can belong but those who can claim direct descent from Abraham. That is why I believe that only you and your people can talk to God on equal footing. That is also why I believe that only You and your people can argue with Him. It is only your people that were chosen to manifest to your God the devotion of an Abraham and to sound into His ears the lamentations of a Job.

I am telling you all this, Yossel Rakover, in order to make you realize why I am obsessed with the complex of wanting a drop of your blood in my veins; it is because of my love for your God and because of my yearning for the power of your faith. For the Christians it is that "nobody comes to the father but through the son": That is *our* destiny. We don't belong to your old bond with the Almighty. We are part of the new bond, and the only hope we have for God's mercy is through the intermediacy of His son. Only because He died to atone for the sins of mankind—and He died with the courage so typical to His people which is also yours—did He enable those who don't belong to the chosen people to find a way of their own to your God.

That is, Yossel Rakover, what separates us from the bond of your people. To you God spoke directly, and thus His word remained imbedded in you forever. That's what makes your people and your blood indestructible to the last day.

My people, however, in my own days, exterminated millions of your people with all the cruelty which man is capable of. I know that your God, who became also our God through Jesus, will not leave our deeds unpunished. It may not happen today or tomorrow, but God's vengeance is bound to come. We, the people of your executioners, may be doomed to go under along with other peoples who tried to destroy you.

But you must realize, Yossel Rakover, that there is nothing I can contribute toward that final punishment. I am not even in a position to take direct revenge on your people's murderers, once identified. I am condemned to live as a German no matter how ashamed I am to call myself by this name. I could have left this country and have gone somewhere else, as your people so often did when they left behind them the lands of their tormentors and went to other lands. I could have become an American, a Canadian or something of the kind. Many of my people left Germany because of shame, because they didn't want to belong to a people of murderers. (I don't mean those who left my exposed country because of fear of a new war.) But I can't do it yet. Do you understand me? Not yet! Because I, if I want to stand up before your and my God and seek His mercy, I have to do here and now the things that must be done. I cannot pour out gasoline through the window when I see your murderers passing by in the street before my very eyes—and there are still some who pass it, boasting and bragging of being your murderers!—I don't fight them as you did in the Warsaw Ghetto. But the only thing I can do for the final downfall of the murderers of God's chosen people, is to become a Christian myself.

This may not be the holy revenge that you speak of, Yossel Rakover. Those who don't belong to your chosen people, even the thieves, can only hope and pray for mercy. And this is the only thing that I can do now for you, for your people and for my own hope of Divine Guidance. This is also the only contribution I can make toward the punishment and downfall of the murderers, no matter how long it will take before punishment strikes. But by doing so, I am also bringing nearer the day when each descendant of those who murdered you will recognize but one life and one identity: that of being a Christian, a follower of Jesus. For only He can lead to your and my God all those who are not chosen as you and your people are!

217

Forgive me, Yossel Rakover, that I have taxed your patience so much. A drop of your blood, a spark of your faith, a grain of your love of God is enough to give one strength for the day when we shall all face the same Maker.

All that is left for me to do is to become a Christian and, as such, help my people eradicate every vestige of the thoughts and deeds of your murderers, and thus embark upon the only course that is left open to us: That of Christ. Without Him, we robbers and thieves that we are, will never find our way to God—*Your* God and *our* Judge in all eternity.

"Do you remember how Yehovah speaks to men? Have you seen how men and mountains melt in His hands, how kingdoms are engulfed beneath His foot? Man shouts, weeps, begs, hides in caves, burrows into ditches—struggles to escape. But Yehovah is planted in his heart like a dagger."

Nikos Kazantzakis, Journey to Sinai

C